ESPECIALLY FOR

Jody Pigeon

FROM

Christian Stevens

DATE

12/25/2022

You have been a blessing
to my life. Glad to have
you as a brother in Christ.

Merry Christmas,
Christian

# DAILY WISDOM FOR MEN

## —— 2023 ——

### Devotional Collection

BARBOUR
PUBLISHING

# INTRODUCTION

Happy New Year! Welcome to the 2023 edition of *Daily Wisdom for Men*!

The key word for this year's *Daily Wisdom for Men* is *heart*. The word *heart* appears more than one thousand times in the Bible, usually in reference to a person's spiritual/emotional/moral/intellectual center.

The heart of a man is very important to God, simply because it is the most important part of our inner being. That is why the Bible says, "Above all else, guard your heart, for everything you do flows from it" (Proverbs 4:23 NIV) and why God commanded His people to "love the LORD your God with all your heart and with all your soul and with all your strength" (Deuteronomy 6:5 NIV).

The inspiration for this year's daily devotionals is taken from each day's scripture readings in our popular "Read thru the Bible in a Year Plan," which you can find at the end of this book. That will help you to read the daily Bible passages and then spend a few minutes reading that day's devotional writing.

God wants to grow you into a man whose heart is 100 percent committed to Him and His Word. It is the hope of the men who played a part in writing this year's *Daily Wisdom for Men* devotionals, as well as the people at Barbour Publishing, that God will use your daily Bible reading, as well as the writings in this book, to help make you a man who follows, loves, and obeys God with all his heart.

The Editors

# THE PREDECIDED

*You're not at all like the wicked, who are mere windblown dust—*
*without defense in court, unfit company for innocent people.*
PSALM 1:4–5 MSG*

· · · · · · · · · · · · · · · · · · · · · · · ·

There's potential in a new year and a sense of relief at the universal dawning of the *second chance*. Maybe this was just the place and condition King David found himself in when talking to others. He spoke words of life to people he knew were trying their best to follow God.

Decisions must have been made in advance that made it less difficult to obey God. King David must have recognized this choice in his unnamed friends. Their actions prevented them from being dust in the wind, accused men without a defense lawyer, or those easily thought of as bad company.

These were choices other people made, and the result was less than desired.

You have choices to make going into a new year. Sure, start with the kind of predecided choices that keep sin choices at a distance, but also find people who will encourage better choices. Finally, keep a strong connection to the God who does not make wrong choices. Start there, and allow the best sense of community to move you from where you are to where God wants you to be.

---

*Lord, I resolve to follow and to turn back to You as often as I need to.*
*Walk with me, and turn me around when my heart begins to wander.*

*A Read thru the Bible in a Year Plan that follows each devotion can be found at the back of this book.

## ACTIONS YOU REGRET

*King Herod was deeply disturbed when he heard this, as was everyone in Jerusalem.*
MATTHEW 2:3 NLT

. . . . . . . . . . . . . . . . . . . . . .

Herod was made a king. His heart demanded that he stay in power. When told that there was a new king born in Israel, his thoughts turned toward finding a way to eliminate the threat. He acted on a vile thought born deep in his heart and chose to murder children.

The Bible is clear, the heart that lies to you desperately seeks opportunities to identify wickedness and then to engage in that wickedness without ever understanding why (see Jeremiah 17:9).

This may be why any resolution you make this new year will be harder than you think. Your mind may agree that it's a worthy goal, but your heart may object, lie, and desperately seek a way to derail your best intentions. You've seen that strategy work in your own life before. It never ends the way you planned.

There will always be a combination of factors that leave you seeking a good solution, but when the heart and mind don't agree, then the action you take will often be an action you regret.

---

*Father, it's easy to condemn someone like Herod, who made a horrible decision. And it's just as easy to think I should receive mercy when I make a poor decision. Help my mind and my heart to agree with You so that my actions look more like Your plan.*

# A GOOD CHOICE

*Noah was a righteous man, blameless in his generation. Noah walked with God.*

GENESIS 6:9 ESV

. . . . . . . . . . . . . . . . . . . . . . . .

Noah was a righteous, blameless man who walked with God. He was a difference maker whose story began when God gave him a job and he agreed to do it. A simple yes from Noah ultimately led to the saving of all future generations. The boat this man built saved eight people who would be the new beginning for all mankind. You're probably glad Noah thought obedience was a good choice.

Disobedience comes with a cost. Sometimes when you don't follow the rules, it can lead to job loss, the absence of freedom, and strained relationships. That cost is the temporal consequence of sin.

Think about the choices you must make. The more critical thinking you do, the less likely you are to make a bad choice. You tend to make quick and bad choices when you're not informed or aware enough to make your best decision. Actions taken without proper consideration often lead to the need for forgiveness.

Noah provides an exceptional example of someone who loved God enough not to turn Him down. You can follow that example. You can *be* that example.

---

*I want to use my entire being to enhance the value of obedience, God. Help me believe, think, and act in a way that allows my life to show that following You really does bring change to life.*

# THOUGHTS CORRUPTED

*Be angry and do not sin; on your bed, reflect in your heart and be still.*
PSALM 4:4 HCSB

. . . . . . . . . . . . . . . . . . . . . .

Some of your best and worst thinking will happen just before you go to bed. You can entertain thoughts that put you in a dark place and leave you there most of the night. But you could also spend time connecting who you are with the *God of the good thought*.

Negative emotions like anger, anxiety, hatred, and fear can leave your body sleepless as your mind considers things that aren't true as well as unkind thoughts about people.

Sin throws a party when it takes what God said to avoid and uses it to corrupt your thoughts. It's like poison to your heart and soul. These thoughts can get to the place where they simply won't listen to reason, let alone submit to a God who is both orderly and wise. This thinking puts you at odds with God and then refuses His advice. *It can actually make you sick.*

Stop. Think. Pray. Be still and realize that the thoughts you avoid may lead you to thoughts that bring you closer to the awe-inspiring God.

---

*Lord, I can begin—and end—my day thinking about You, or I could go to sleep mad, wake up mad, and then stay that way most of the day. I don't need coffee as much as I need Your influence in my life. Help me get quiet and then think about You.*

# REMEMBERED AS BLESSED

*"Blessed are those who hunger and thirst for*
*righteousness, for they will be filled."*
MATTHEW 5:6 NIV

. . . . . . . . . . . . . . . . . . . . . . .

Jesus spoke the words you just read—and there were more. Jesus prayed that God would bless the poor in spirit, the sad, the meek, those who hunger and thirst for righteousness, the merciful, the pure in heart, the peacemakers, and those who are persecuted because of right choices. Have you ever wondered what these *blessed* individuals have in common? They all—*every single one*—had decisions to make.

They recognized their need for God, were sorry for their sin, chose not to be bullies, chased after God, chose mercy before justice, didn't want their hearts to be sin-stained, chose peace, and sometimes endured harassment because they followed Jesus. Yet each made choices that resulted in blessings from God—even when people thought they were foolish.

You can trade the contempt of individuals for a relationship with God. You don't have to play it safe to discover safety. God takes care of your heart, mind, and soul. Be one of the blessed. It is a choice you can make.

*God, when I think about my legacy, I want to be remembered as a*
*man You blessed. Give me the courage to dive into the best life I could*
*possibly live here on earth. That life begins and ends with Your blessing.*

## NO, THANK YOU

*Abram told the king of Sodom, "I swear to GOD, The High God, Creator of Heaven and Earth, this solemn oath, that I'll take nothing from you, not so much as a thread or a shoestring. I'm not going to have you go around saying, 'I made Abram rich.'"*
GENESIS 14:22–23 MSG

• • • • • • • • • • • • • • • • • • • • • •

Abram set out on a campaign to find and rescue his nephew, Lot. In the process, he brought back people, animals, and wealth. Families who had wept for those the enemy had taken away found a new reason to celebrate.

The king of Sodom offered to give this hero every material possession he recovered. Abram could have entered early retirement. God had other plans, and Abram had already made a choice that took trust in God and made material goods worthless until God supplied them.

That can be a very hard choice for any of us. It would have to mean that we are convinced God is good. More than that, we must believe that He's worth more than winning a sweepstakes or lottery.

Banking on God's promises brings us away from the selfishness that takes up residence in our hearts and causes us to seek fewer *things* if that means greater opportunities with God.

---

*Father, may the words "No, thank you" form when I'm offered something that doesn't come from You. May my interest in trusting You see these things for what they really are—distractions. Help me to walk with You.*

# FOUND TO BE AMAZING

*Turn, LORD, and deliver me; save me because of your unfailing love.*
PSALM 6:4 NIV

. . . . . . . . . . . . . . . . . . . . . .

David was one smart king. Truth had nudged its way deep into his heart, and he came away with a prayer that recognized God's love in an amazing display of courage. This wasn't a knee-jerk response. This was knowledge and understanding that led to wisdom.

When someone talks about the goodness of God, it's often a proclamation based on personal experience. That experience requires the head and heart to agree. It's an experience based on time spent with God, where discoveries are made. It's an investment that grows, thrives, and produces a harvest that's bigger than your most impressive dream.

David needed help, and he knew who to call. He needed deliverance, and he knew the Deliverer. The king needed love, and what he found is described as a love unfailing. Do you think that every part of your being could conspire to follow the God you can call on? Do you think you could accept His love?

This above verse isn't a pep rally. It's the outcome of a journey experienced and discovered to be amazing.

*God, I can find trouble. Sometimes trouble finds me. Help me learn enough, understand enough, and trust enough to know that You are enough. May I come boldly to You and ask for help I cannot find on my own, no matter how hard I try.*

# AN ALLEGIANCE DIVIDED

*"No one can be a slave of two masters, since either he will hate one and love the other, or be devoted to one and despise the other. You cannot be slaves of God and of money."*

MATTHEW 6:24 HCSB

. . . . . . . . . . . . . . . . . . . . . .

Can you have more than one best friend? The word *best* suggests there is no one better than that. You can have many good friends, but there is usually one that somehow "gets you" like no one else. It's easier to trust that person because he's proved himself as someone who will always be there for you.

If you call two people your best friend, it might seem like your allegiance is divided. You might change best friends over time. One might move away, circumstances might change, or the relationship becomes seasonal.

You can be undivided when every part of what makes you *you* wrestles intellectually and spiritually with the issue of who you trust most, follow hardest, and can't live without. One choice is God. The other choice is anything but God. It could be money, amusement, or friends. This list is much longer, but the truth is you can't have both God and anything else vying for the top spot in your heart.

*Father, I can never be successful doing what I want to do and what You want me to do at the same time. Help me make following You the most important decision I will ever make.*

# THE HARDEST CHOICES

*[God said to Abraham,] "Take your son, your only son—*
*yes, Isaac, whom you love so much—and go to the land*
*of Moriah. Go and sacrifice him as a burnt offering*
*on one of the mountains, which I will show you."*

GENESIS 22:2 NLT

. . . . . . . . . . . . . . . . . . . . . .

*What?* Did you really read that? Humanly speaking, God's command for Abraham to sacrifice his beloved son seems crazy. But it's also the choice God had to make with His Son, Jesus. God spared the life of Abraham's son, but He sacrificed His own Son, Jesus, as your substitute.

Consider for a moment what it would be like to hear a request from God that He had never requested before, seemed out of character with His nature, and was harder than any request He had made before.

There was a long walk to Mount Moriah, where young Isaac was to be sacrificed. Abraham had a long time to think about what God had asked, meditate on what he knew to be true about Him, and to become convinced that God had a plan, a bit unexpected but brilliant.

God was testing obedience versus excuses, willingness versus refusal, and trust versus fear. And Abraham acted on this very *hard-to-honor* request because he knew in his heart that God could be trusted. God honored His faithfulness and accepted a substitute. Father and son walked home—but never alone.

*Father, please help me trust You when Your*
*plan for me seems harder than mine.*

# MERCY

*They who know Your name [who have experience and acquaintance with Your mercy] will lean on and confidently put their trust in You, for You, Lord, have not forsaken those who seek (inquire of and for) You [on the authority of God's Word and the right of their necessity].*

PSALM 9:10 AMPC

. . . . . . . . . . . . . . . . . . . . . . .

God's mercy is found whenever you don't get something bad that you deserved. It is the withholding of a penalty. It's a bit like a child deserving a time-out but instead getting time to talk to his dad and being reminded that he's loved.

When you experience mercy, it alters your thinking, rearranges your emotional response, and deepens trust. Mercy should never embolden you to make sin your go-to response but should instead remind you about the character and goodness of the God who extends mercy as a gift.

When you seek God, there are no questions about how much you make, where you live, or what skin tone you have. God's mercy never hinges on anything except the love He has had for you since before time began.

Mercy invites trust in the life of the timid, offers a road map to the God who never abandons, and removes a deserved time-out and reminds you of God's love instead.

*Father, may Your mercy transform me. From deep inside, where I have harbored hidden habits and unwise opinions, change me as I focus on You and Your Word. Thank You for what You are teaching me.*

# THE MIRACLE MAPMAKER

*[The wicked say,] "God has forgotten,
he has hidden his face, he will never see it."*

PSALM 10:11 ESV

. . . . . . . . . . . . . . . . . . . . . . . .

Imagine what kind of internal conversation can lead someone to today's verse. He had concluded that God is forgetful, that He chooses to be blissfully ignorant, and that He does not want to pay attention to him. God's Word calls this kind of thinking *wicked*.

The struggles you face can lead you to a dark place, giving you a room where you can allow your pain to become a burden to you and a barrier to the relief you need. Your mind can turn the problem over and over again until you have entertained every real offense and hurt and then welcome things you can only assume or imagine to be true without proof. Each moment in this place peddles the idea that you're a victim, you can't overcome, and everyone wants to hurt you. This dark place is a complex layer of lies, half-truths, and deception. *Leave this room now.*

God offers a better way to think and a greater future to consider. He's the author of overcoming stories, the mapmaker for miracles, and the God who brings freedom to the fallen.

---

*God, because people hurt me, it is easy sometimes to think You will hurt me too. Help me to remember this is not who You are and that You would rather have me run to You than to desperately seek dark thinking.*

# WHAT JESUS IS DOING

*Behold, the whole city came out to meet Jesus: and when they saw him, they besought him that he would depart out of their coasts.*

MATTHEW 8:34 KJV

. . . . . . . . . . . . . . . . . . . . . .

Jesus performed a miracle, but the response was fear and hostility. A man who had been in a dark place for a long time was rescued. The people had never seen him like this. Instead of marveling at the goodness of God, the people took back any hospitality they would normally offer.

Their thinking centered on money, possessions, and normalcy. What they saw in Jesus was none of those things. It's possible they were afraid of the change He could bring to their shoreline. In their opinion, it would be best if He just left. They may have been polite or insistent, but they were clear: "It's time for You to go away."

You may not always understand what Jesus is doing, but you would do well to spend time considering the incredible things He's done so far. It's not in your best interest to walk away or try to send Him away. The truth is He'll keep seeking you out no matter how often you try to hide.

The time you spend learning who God is will be incredibly well spent.

*Father, when You do something in my life that doesn't feel normal, help me to quiet my heart and wait to see the outcome. Keep encouraging me to follow where You lead.*

# NOT GOING ANYWHERE

*[God said,] "I am with you and will watch over you wherever you go, and I will bring you back to this land. I will not leave you until I have done what I have promised you."*

GENESIS 28:15 NIV

. . . . . . . . . . . . . . . . . . . . . . .

An analyst collects data and observes things like truth and trends, input and discovery. It may not be something everyone does, but God gave thousands of applications for life that any person who considers them would have a hard time refuting.

Jacob was a young man seeking to find his own path after leaving his parents, Isaac and Rebekah. He'd lived with whatever faith his parents possessed, but he had some analyzing to do. God wanted Jacob to learn—and grow. Jacob took in the words of God when He essentially said, *"I'm with you now, and I'll be with you and watch out for you every step of life's journey. You won't always be a wanderer. There's work to do, and I'm not going anywhere."*

This promise to Jacob runs parallel to other passages that tell you something similar. Let the importance of this information bathe your soul, inform your mind, and impact your heart. He's God, He loves you, and He's not going anywhere.

*Lord, I need Your assurance that there's something better ahead. I've tried so many things on my own, and they often turn from bad to worse. Thanks for not going anywhere.*

## ONE SET OF RULES

*God's words are pure words, pure silver words refined seven times
in the fires of his word-kiln, pure on earth as well as in heaven.*
PSALM 12:6 MSG

. . . . . . . . . . . . . . . . . . . . . . .

The Bible constantly confronts our unsound thinking with the truth
about God and how He works. Then if we wonder if He really means
what He says, we can read that His words are pure and refined and that
they apply to situations on earth and carry the same authority in heaven.
This prevents us from picking and choosing what we think God wants
for us today.

This type of confrontation makes us think through what God has said
and then why we believe what we've read. If we think that God doesn't
mean what He says, then we might struggle with an encouraging verse
such as "God's Word stands firm and forever" (Isaiah 40:8 MSG).

God Himself settled the debate on whether He could possibly lie
when His Word said, "God can't break his word. And because his word
cannot change, the promise is likewise unchangeable" (Hebrews 6:18 MSG).

This unchanging God should be a reason for righteous rejoicing. He
doesn't have two sets of rules. He doesn't play favorites. His forgiveness
and power are available to all who believe Him in their hearts.

*It wouldn't make sense for me to question Your truth, Father.
Thanks for making sure I would never have to wonder what
truth looks like. I find it whenever I read Your Word.*

# NO REASONABLE EXCUSE

*[Jesus said,] "Everyone who acknowledges me publicly here on earth,
I will also acknowledge before my Father in heaven. But everyone who
denies me here on earth, I will also deny before my Father in heaven."*
MATTHEW 10:32–33 NLT

. . . . . . . . . . . . . . . . . . . . . . .

Are you ever tempted to keep your faith a private matter? There are work environments where sharing your faith is frowned upon, but there are other hours in the day when you can speak about Jesus. Even during work hours, you can still let your relationship with Jesus show up in your work ethic and decision-making.

Think about it this way: Jesus never once turned His back on His followers, even when they ran away or betrayed Him. When you make the choice to journey with Jesus, you should be willing and able to acknowledge who you serve—hesitancy is not required. Being vague isn't helpful. Denying you know Him will mean a change in thinking.

Because Jesus rescued you, changed your mind, revived your soul, and lives in your heart, there is no reasonable excuse not to say something about it. If you've been changed, then give credit where it's due.

*Jesus, You have done the most amazing thing for me and in
me. May I never act like the life I now have isn't worth a God
cheer. I didn't get here on my own, and I want Your help.
I don't want to make it seem like You're no big deal.*

# REFUSE TO JUMP

*The fool hath said in his heart, There is no God.*
PSALM 14:1 KJV

. . . . . . . . . . . . . . . . . . . . . .

It doesn't take much thinking to say, "God does not exist." Some see this as common knowledge and even feel superior when they make such a bold declaration. But God calls this easy thinking foolishness.

Why? Maybe partly because this belief refuses help only God can give. Wouldn't it be foolish to do that? Maybe it's also because some don't want to consider that they must answer to someone greater than themselves.

By definition, a fool is someone who either doesn't think or makes irresponsible choices.

Consider what it might mean to accept that God exists, that He made the world and everything in it, that He created laws for mankind to follow, and that even you have failed to follow perfectly (see Romans 3:23). Is it any wonder some people do not want to believe God exists?

Don't view God as just a judge. Sure, He hates sin, but He has always loved the people who do the sinning, which is everyone—everywhere.

Refuse to jump to a conclusion that rejects God. This impulse decision is not only unwise, but it will negatively impact your life every day that you live.

---

*Getting to know You is a lifelong pursuit, Father. It would be easy to deny that You exist, but there's proof everywhere I look. Help me keep recognizing You and follow where You lead.*

# GOD OBJECTS

*Then Jesus began to denounce the towns in which most of his miracles had been performed, because they did not repent.*
MATTHEW 11:20 NIV

• • • • • • • • • • • • • • • • • • • • • • • •

This above scripture verse speaks to an idea introduced yesterday. Foolish people proclaimed that God was fictional so they weren't responsible for their sin. When they broke God's law, their actions proclaimed, "It doesn't matter because God doesn't exist, and if He doesn't exist then I have nothing to worry about."

If you've entertained that thought, then it might be time to entertain these thoughts—God is real, even if you refuse to believe. You've broken His law, even if you don't think it applies to you.

The people in the towns where Jesus spoke were eyewitnesses to miracles. They heard His words yet gave a spiritual yawn while looking for anything else to fill their time. They accepted a little entertainment but refused to engage the core of their being into quality decision-making.

You can feel the same way, can't you? You can enjoy music about God but never really honor the One who is the object of the song. You can feel a connection to *God objects* without worshipping God. Don't let that happen to you. Don't miss out the blessing in honoring God from the heart.

*Lord, I don't want to be someone who thinks of You as a showman. I want to be someone who thinks of You as the only One worthy of my praise and adoration.*

# THE MARINADE OF BITTERNESS

*"Here comes the dreamer!" [Joseph's brothers] said. "Come on, let's kill him and throw him into one of these cisterns. We can tell our father, 'A wild animal has eaten him.' Then we'll see what becomes of his dreams!"*

GENESIS 37:19–20 NLT

. . . . . . . . . . . . . . . . . . . . . .

When you feel that you've been wronged, it can be easy to be vocal about the wrong and about the character of the person who has wronged you. It's a familiar sound, but one that instills a sense of discomfort in those who hear the story over and over again.

Joseph's brothers believed in their hearts that he had wronged them. They talked among themselves and were determined to treat him like an enemy. This infection of thought impacted every part of their lives and resulted in a conclusion that made a group of brothers conspire to commit murder and then to a cover-up that would leave them lying for years.

While no murder actually took place, the brothers made sure Joseph was sent away. They never wanted to see him again.

When you give your mind and heart a deep soaking in the marinade of bitterness, you will find that there's no part of your body, mind, or spirit that is not contaminated by the invasive spread of revenge.

*Father, letting others have so much control over my thinking that I cannot be reasonable will never really help me. But You can. Allow me to consider better thoughts.*

# COURAGEOUS PURSUIT

*I'm not trying to get my way in the world's way. I'm trying
to get your way, your Word's way. I'm staying on your trail;
I'm putting one foot in front of the other. I'm not giving up.*

PSALM 17:4–5 MSG

. . . . . . . . . . . . . . . . . . . . . .

Have you made God your personal quest? King David did. He rejected conventional adventure and accepted one that was born in his soul. David was bold in his declaration, courageous in his pursuit, and confident in his Guide.

It's easy to second-guess God because He does things differently than you do. And because you don't always understand what He's doing, it can mean the application of internal brakes, the halting of what you should do, and a hesitancy of the heart that leaves blessings delayed.

Never let conventional wisdom stand in the way of God's plans. Follow hard after a good God. Exercise spiritual mobility, and use the Bible, which is God's life GPS.

Giving up is never your best option unless it's giving up on doing things your own way. God's plan for you is simple, even when you think it's complex. He knows where you need to go and what you need to do, so it's simple—just follow Him. Or you could make things complex and second-guess or resist His guidance.

---

*Lord, remembering that You know what You're doing is
important. I don't want to take more steps using only my
own wisdom and miss the adventure You've planned for me.*

# BE ALL IN

*[Jesus said,] He who is not with Me [definitely on My side] is against Me, and he who does not [definitely] gather with Me and for My side scatters.*

MATTHEW 12:30 AMPC

• • • • • • • • • • • • • • • • • • • • • • •

*Definite* is an amazing word. It means something is settled and decided, firm and unchanging. Thought has been given to something, and a new choice is fueled by confidence. This is great when you're making a great decision but extremely harmful when the choice is less than ideal.

If you are not *all in* when it comes to following God, then you might look like an enemy from time to time. If you're not telling others about how to follow God, then you may be unintentionally pointing people in a different direction. This may be why the Bible indicates people should be all in or all out, because no one has to guess where they stand. It's when you spend time in between that people get confused about where you stand and why. They shouldn't have to guess.

You never have to wonder what God thinks, because He's given you His Word. Don't make people wonder if you're all in.

*Father, I am a man who doesn't mind if people know what I do for a living, what hobbies I enjoy, and some of the things I like most. May it never be a burden for me to share with others how important You are to me.*

# THE SKELETON IN TEN CLOSETS

*[Joseph's brothers] said to one another, "In truth we are guilty concerning [Joseph], in that we saw the distress of his soul, when he begged us and we did not listen. That is why this distress has come upon us."*

GENESIS 42:21 ESV

. . . . . . . . . . . . . . . . . . . . . . .

Years had passed since ten brothers sold their brother into slavery. There is little indication that they expressed remorse or regret for their sin. What they had done became the skeleton in ten closets. So, when personal disaster struck, they could finally admit cause and effect. They were in Egypt, and they needed food for their families. Everything that could go wrong showed up in one potent delivery.

It was easy on their bad day to conclude that what they had done to Joseph was the reason they struggled on their shopping trip. The brothers must have been thinking a lot about their past. It must have been on their minds, if not their lips, for a very long time. It must have gnawed a hole in their heart. Guilt grew into something they could not contain, and after an agonizingly long time, they finally spoke truth and admitted their sin.

This is a place where things can change, second changes begin, and burdens are removed.

*Father, waiting for years to admit I was wrong is a waste of time. When I've made the wrong choice, help me recognize my sin and admit You've always been right.*

## QUESTIONS AND PROCLAMATIONS

*Who is God except the LORD? Who but our God is a solid rock?*
PSALM 18:31 NLT

. . . . . . . . . . . . . . . . . . . . . .

There are two questions in the above verse that God wants you to answer—and your answers will show whether you will need to keep thinking or whether your mind, heart, and spirit agree on something incredibly important. It is vital that you know the real God who never changes.

If every part of you can answer "God" to both questions, then there is profound wisdom and acceptance of truth in your heart. If your mind and heart can't agree on the answer, then you still have a problem. You could rephrase these proclamations: God alone is the Lord *and* no one is stronger than God.

You have the incredible privilege of reading God's Word, thinking about what He has said, and making decisions based on what you've learned. The questions of the Bible exist because God wants you to think. He wants you to learn. The truth is that you also need to know if what you're studying is making sense and changing your heart.

*Thanks for giving me teachable moments, Father. I don't want
to skip past Your questions. I want to spend time thinking
about how what I've learned will help answer Your questions.
You are God, and there's no one and nothing stronger.*

## THE STORYTELLER

*All Jesus did that day was tell stories—a long storytelling
afternoon. His storytelling fulfilled the prophecy: I will
open my mouth and tell stories; I will bring out into
the open things hidden since the world's first day.*
MATTHEW 13:34–35 MSG

. . . . . . . . . . . . . . . . . . . . . . .

The stories Jesus shared were some of the most important we've ever heard. As we read them, we are invited to identify with the main characters and ask ourselves what impact the choices made had on the outcome of the story. The stories Jesus told weren't just interesting, they were designed to make us think. There was always a purpose behind the stories.

The passage above found Jesus taking a day to simply tell stories, but there was nothing simple about these stories for the disciples. They were with Jesus every day, and even they struggled to understand what they were supposed to learn from the story.

There was benefit in the stories because once the disciples knew what they meant, they didn't forget. The stories connected with them when facts were forgettable.

Jesus' stories are worth considering. They can give you insight into God, other people, and the way God wants you to respond to what you learn.

*God, with Your help I can learn from Your Son's stories.
I want to pay attention to what He said so I can know
how to respond with an informed heart.*

## GOD'S STRENGTH OFFSETS

*Some trust in chariots and some in horses,*
*but we trust in the name of the LORD our God.*
PSALM 20:7 NIV

• • • • • • • • • • • • • • • • • • • • • • •

You might watch movies and assume that men are willing to use brute force to advance a cause—good or bad. Conventional wisdom says you meet strength with strength—and while this is true, you cannot adequately meet opposing strength with only the strength you possess.

God's strength offsets your weak spots. You could enlist the help of as many willing people as you can find, and it still would not compare favorably to placing your trust, hope, and confidence in God alone.

The kind of decision that places trust in God requires faith—and thinking. Faith starts the process, and then thinking plays a role, because once you believe, then you can really begin to understand things that didn't make sense when you didn't believe.

It's very hard to trust both God and the strength of humans. The idea behind trusting in God is that in the difficult moments you'll face, the best answer will be the one that arrived—without any doubt—by the hand of a very good God.

---

*Father, it's not hard to think everything is up to me. You have given me things to take care of, but I can't do it alone. Thanks for using my trust to deliver Your strength. Believing the impossible is possible because You have always done what I can't.*

# CHARIOTS, HORSES, OR GOD

*[Pharaoh said,] "Come, let us deal shrewdly with them, lest they multiply, and, if war breaks out, they join our enemies and fight against us and escape from the land."*

Exodus 1:10 esv

· · · · · · · · · · · · · · · · · · · · · · ·

The Egyptian king thought in terms of strategy and dominance. He forgot that the Israelites were invited as guests. Their guest status had been revoked at some past point, and they became slave labor. The king likely found it difficult to think about what it would be like without the labor of Joseph's family (which numbered more than two million people).

God had thoughts of His own, and they were solidly in the *deliverance camp*. Moses was His choice for spokesperson. God was aware of Pharaoh's thinking. This king thought through his options and concluded that the best response was harshness. The people needed to know he was in control. *But he wasn't.*

This king put his trust in chariots, horses, and the might of men to enforce his will. God would take the weakness of a different man, a man afraid to speak, and save a nation that had endured slavery for far too long.

What are you holding on to even after knowing that it doesn't match God's plan? Why is His thinking more important on any subject?

*Lord God, You've done big things. You're doing big things. You'll continue to do big things. May I never stand in the way of Your next Big Thing.*

# FAULT FINDING

*[God said,] These people draw near Me with their mouths and honor Me with their lips, but their hearts hold off and are far away from Me.*
MATTHEW 15:8 AMPC

. . . . . . . . . . . . . . . . . . . . . . .

The evidence had been weighed, decisions were made, and the outward response looked pretty good. God had shown up in the thinking of the Jewish religious leaders, and they treated rule keeping as their primary duty.

God knew their hearts, and He knew that their response was intellectual, not the response of a grateful heart. They changed what they did without really knowing the who and why behind their adopted mask. These religious leaders did not have a change of heart. They refused to love others because they were more interested in finding fault. They assumed that just doing the right thing made them right with God. But God wanted their hearts so He could change more than behavior.

You were made to be more than a good person. You were made to get close enough to God to learn how He leads and what He will do through a man like you, one willing to surrender personal ambition to invest in a relationship with Him.

*The choice is mine, Father. I can follow You or I can make it seem like I'm following You. I will be satisfied if I can follow instead of pretending. Help my mind and heart to stay in sync and make the wise choice to really journey with You.*

# REMINDED TO REMEMBER

*He has never let you down, never looked the other way when*
*you were being kicked around. He has never wandered off*
*to do his own thing; he has been right there, listening.*
PSALM 22:24 MSG

. . . . . . . . . . . . . . . . . . . . . .

The verse above is a great example of one person who thinks, responds in faith, and is convinced that God is good. He takes the time to remind someone who may have forgotten. It's an invitation to prayer and a place of praise.

Thinking sometimes requires memory. There needs to be a willingness to follow God's footsteps leading to the place where you find yourself today. You'll likely find yourself remembering where and when you moved away from His path—as well as the times your conversations with God kept you close.

God doesn't let you down. He never pretends He doesn't know you, and He's never too busy to help. No matter what may happen, God pays attention to you.

What a great series of thoughts! They can just inspire you to pray, invite you to use your voice to speak words of praise, and infuse gratitude in your response.

Remembering can be like adrenaline to your spiritual life. God has been amazingly good—just remember.

*God, Your footprints were beside me, and Your fingerprints proved*
*You were close. I can remember that at my worst, You offered hope*
*that I'd never need to be alone. My life journey is better because*
*You kept teaching, even when I didn't know I needed to learn.*

## PROTESTING TO GOD

*Then Moses went back to the LORD and protested, "Why have you brought all this trouble on your own people, Lord? Why did you send me? Ever since I came to Pharaoh as your spokesman, he has been even more brutal to your people. And you have done nothing to rescue them!"*

EXODUS 5:22–23 NLT

. . . . . . . . . . . . . . . . . . . . . .

Does it seem shocking to read that Moses protested to God? Perhaps, but those protests didn't change God's composure. These outbursts proved that in voicing his displeasure, Moses showed that he was thinking about God's role in his circumstances.

There was a time in Moses' life when he heard God's plan, obeyed God's voice, and then failed. Hadn't Moses done his best? Perhaps he believed Pharaoh would simply agree and the happy ending he hoped for would follow. Moses felt like his obedience simply meant things were harder for the people. He didn't feel qualified to help, and his lack of success seemed to make that point clear.

God's story for His family wasn't over, but Moses needed to continue obeying. There would be celebrations that honored God's deliverance through a man who seemed to challenge God.

Bring your honest questions to God. Seek His help in finding answers. Use your mind to seek God's will in His Word for this moment.

---

*Father, I have always wondered if I could ask questions or say that the world is in a bad place and wonder if You're there. May my questions lead to greater trust in Your best plan.*

# PAY ATTENTION TO HIM

*While [Jesus] was still speaking, a bright cloud covered [the disciples], and a voice from the cloud said, "This is my Son, whom I love; with him I am well pleased. Listen to him!"*

MATTHEW 17:5 NIV

. . . . . . . . . . . . . . . . . . . . . . .

This is one of the rare moments when God Himself spoke to the disciples. They heard Jesus, the Son of God. They followed Him. But at that moment, they were sidetracked. God had allowed them to see Elijah and Moses, and they were starstruck. They wanted to build monuments to the elder statesmen of the faith. This was a miracle, and they wanted to commemorate the unbelievable moment.

God was not disrespecting His two servants, but He did seem to find fault with the disciples' thinking and actions. He shifted the spotlight back on His Son and basically said, *"Pay attention to* Him.*"*

Jesus was more important. He would change eternity. He could offer what Elijah and Moses longed for. His life would be perpetually celebrated and His name honored. *Pay attention to Him.*

He loved enough to rescue without protest. He cared enough to live the life of a human for you. He died willingly to pay the price for your sin. *Pay attention to Him.*

*Jesus, it's easy to think of a Christian leader as someone important and honorable. They should be respected, but the message they share isn't about themselves, it's about You. Help me pay attention to You.*

# THE INSTRUCTOR AND THE STUDENT

*[God] leads the humble in what is right,*
*and teaches the humble his way.*

PSALM 25:9 ESV

. . . . . . . . . . . . . . . . . . . . . .

Psalm 25 includes at least eight times when references to instructing or teaching are prominent parts of praise. It appears the ones who get the most from God's instruction are humble. They are willing to listen, consider, and meditate on what they're learning.

You've met students who take classes simply because they have to for a diploma or degree. They have little interest in the subject and just want to do well enough to pass the class and put it behind them. This kind of thinking just makes it harder when you're a student of God. His lessons are for your benefit and teach you about His character.

God can teach you best when you show yourself teachable. You can learn what He wants to do for and with people. He can make right thinking the norm. He will find joy as you discover truth.

Make learning from God something you anticipate. Make truth something you believe in with your whole heart. Make sure your instructor is God.

---

*You have given me the ability to learn, Father. I don't want to be so arrogant that I can't accept what You say. The quality of my learning is only as good as my ability to really listen to Your instructions. Tune my ears to Your words.*

# TAKING NOTE OF GOD

*The LORD brought the Israelites out of the land of Egypt.*
EXODUS 12:51 HCSB

. . . . . . . . . . . . . . . . . . . . . . .

Their spirits were weak, hope had diminished as nine plagues passed through Egypt and they were still slaves, and their thinking was erratic and prone to melancholy. Then came Passover. This would be the commemoration of the event that led to their deliverance.

Moses had stood before Pharaoh often, and there wasn't a time when there was the feeling of visiting an old friend. The meetings were contentious, and Pharaoh had been mean-spirited.

With each passing plague, the instruction was more to the point and left a greater negative impact on the country. What most don't think about is that both the Egyptians and the Israelites wrestled with uncertainty. Opinion could shift quickly on both sides, and yet God promised deliverance. The people's doubts didn't alter the promise.

By the time the people of Israel began their walk away from Egypt, they were in awe of God. The Egyptians also took note of this God who could defy Pharaoh and deliver the Israelites from slavery.

God shows up. Pay attention to what He does. Stand in awe of His power. He can bring you through whatever enslaves you.

*Paying attention to what You do is an important part of praise, God. Help me stand in awe of what You do in the midst of great opposition. May I never stand in Your way.*

# THE RULE OF 490

*Then Peter came up and said to him, "Lord, how often will my brother sin against me, and I forgive him? As many as seven times?" Jesus said to him, "I do not say to you seven times, but seventy-seven times."*

MATTHEW 18:21–22 ESV

· · · · · · · · · · · · · · · · · · · · · · ·

How many times do you forgive someone before cutting them out of your life? According to Jewish law at the time of Jesus, we should forgive someone three times. This comes from Old Testament passages in Amos and Job, where God forgave nations who oppressed Israel three times before bringing judgment against them.

When Peter doubled the number and added one, he likely thought he was being generous. But Jesus took Peter's example to the extreme. We can easily remember if we've forgiven someone three or even seven times for some repeated offense, but to keep track of whether it's been 486 times or 499 times seems ludicrous. Essentially, Jesus was telling His disciples to stop keeping track and to just keep forgiving from the heart.

God doesn't stop at forgiving us 490 or 400,000 times; He just keeps forgiving us. Because we are forgiven, we are able to forgive others like Him—which is to say, every single time someone needs forgiveness.

*Father, help me forgive like You, not counting the times I've been hurt by someone's sin, but remembering the countless times You've forgiven me.*

# MAN OF WAR

*The Lord is my Strength and my Song, and He has become my Salvation; this is my God, and I will praise Him, my father's God, and I will exalt Him. The Lord is a Man of War; the Lord is His name.*
Exodus 15:2–3 AMPC

. . . . . . . . . . . . . . . . . . . . . . .

There's a word that describes someone who is able to turn rivers to blood, control the angel of death, and destroy an army of battle-tested charioteers with the pent-up force of billions of gallons of water: *terrifying.*

When God brought the Israelites out of Egypt, His chosen people must have been both elated to have Him on their side and scared witless at the thought of being His subjects. This God, who had promised land and prosperity to their forefathers, had allowed them to become an Egyptian slave force. Then, after long years of whispered retellings of His promises, God showed up in force to set His people free.

Thousands of years later, God is still fighting to free His people from slavery. This time, from sin itself. We would do well to remember the joy—and the terror—of being called His people and praise Him from our hearts accordingly. Remember: "The Lord is a Man of War; the Lord is His name."

---

*Lord, You are more than a loving Father; You are a Warrior who fights for His people. Keep me from trying to fight battles by myself when You are eminently more equipped to fight on my behalf.*

# THE COST OF A FREE GIFT

*"And everyone who has left houses or brothers or sisters or father or mother or wife or children or fields for my sake will receive a hundred times as much and will inherit eternal life."*

MATTHEW 19:29 NIV

• • • • • • • • • • • • • • • • • • • • • •

Ready for the paradox of Christian living? Salvation is a free gift that will cost you everything.

The Bible is pretty clear about how people can earn God's grace. They can't: "For it is by grace you have been saved, through faith—and this is not from yourselves, it is the gift of God—not by works, so that no one can boast" (Ephesians 2:8–9 NIV).

Because grace cannot be earned, we describe salvation as a gift. At the same time, it is a gift that comes with a cost: "Then Jesus said to his disciples, 'Whoever wants to be my disciple must deny themselves and take up their cross and follow me' " (Matthew 16:24 NIV).

We give up everything—our lives, relationships, family connections, and claims to property—when we choose to accept God's call to follow Him. But in giving up everything, God will give us even more. We will receive far more than whatever we give up, *and* we'll inherit eternal life.

Stop counting the cost of following God, and start counting your blessings.

---

*Father, may I have a heart that is willing to give up everything, knowing that You have offered me far more than what I sacrifice.*

## ON COVETING

*"You must not covet your neighbor's house. You must not covet your neighbor's wife, male or female servant, ox or donkey, or anything else that belongs to your neighbor."*

EXODUS 20:17 NLT

. . . . . . . . . . . . . . . . . . . . . .

The tenth of the Ten Commandments uses a word we don't often hear outside of people quoting the Ten Commandments: *covet.* To covet is to want something for yourself without consideration of the original owner. It goes beyond jealousy. It's a passionate desire. In a sense, it is shifting what we should feel toward God—the generous Provider of all good things—to the things He's provided to someone else.

Following the previous four commandments—you shall not murder, commit adultery, steal, or bear false witness against your neighbor—the order to not covet commands motivation instead of a direct action. Our neighbors need never know that we covet their wife, their status, their sports cars, or their estates. The sin happens in our hearts.

When we find ourselves enamored with the blessings others have received, we lose sight of the ways we've been blessed. To combat the sin of covetousness, it's helpful to make a list of all the ways we've been blessed. Thankfulness smothers covetousness every time, and it realigns our hearts with the only One who can truly make us content: God Himself.

*Giver of all good things, help me be thankful for my blessings. May my attention remain on You so I am not distracted by my neighbor's relationships and things.*

# WIDOWS AND ORPHANS

*"You shall not mistreat any widow or fatherless child. If you do mistreat them, and they cry out to me, I will surely hear their cry, and my wrath will burn, and I will kill you with the sword, and your wives shall become widows and your children fatherless."*

EXODUS 22:22–24 ESV

. . . . . . . . . . . . . . . . . . . . . . .

There are four groups God continually mentions as being close to His heart: widows, orphans, foreigners, and the poor. These groups were most likely to be disenfranchised—denied their basic human rights—because people tend to prioritize those with power over everyone else. But justice isn't justice when it only applies to those with power.

In today's scripture verses, we learn of God's compassion and care for widows and orphans. We learn of His desire for justice through His promise to *make* more widows and orphans from those who mistreat disenfranchised folks.

Since our hearts are naturally drawn to care for our own families, God's message is one of enlightened self-interest. It is in the interest of our own families for us to help those who have no husbands or parents. In doing so, our hearts will more closely resemble God's, who has adopted us into His family and treated us with love, forgiveness, and kindness.

Today, speak up for those whose voices have been silenced by society. Doing so ensures that our own voices won't be silenced prematurely.

---

*Lord, give me a heart for those who are close to Yours.*

# WHO IS THIS?

*The entire city of Jerusalem was in an uproar*
*as he entered. "Who is this?" they asked.*
MATTHEW 21:10 NLT

. . . . . . . . . . . . . . . . . . . . . . .

As Jesus entered Jerusalem, riding on a donkey, fulfilling prophecies about the long-awaited Messiah, the Jewish religious authorities and the common folks alike asked the same question: "Who is this?"

The religious authorities asked because they saw Jesus as a threat to their dominance. If Jesus was truly the Messiah, all their authority—the respect they commanded and the lives of relative ease they enjoyed under Roman rule—would be cast aside when Israel's true King led His people. They were afraid.

The common folk heard rumors of Jesus and hoped He would overthrow the Roman authorities so they could be free from oppression. They were hopeful.

Jesus often inspires a mixture of fear and hope in people. He is the Messiah who came to rule men's hearts. His kingdom is not found on earth but in His subjects.

Who is this? This is Jesus. The real question is how we react when He comes to claim His rightful place as King of our lives. Are we afraid of losing our power like the religious authorities? Or are we hopeful that we'll finally be free from the oppression of this world?

---

*Jesus, take Your throne in my heart and in my life. Fill me with hope, and take away my fear. Teach me who You are by helping me love like You.*

# LIFE UNDER SIEGE

*Praise be to the LORD, for he showed me the wonders of his love when I was in a city under siege. In my alarm I said, "I am cut off from your sight!" Yet you heard my cry for mercy when I called to you for help.*

PSALM 31:21–22 NIV

. . . . . . . . . . . . . . . . . . . . . . .

Cities under siege don't experience constant fighting. They are simply surrounded by their enemies and waited out. Eventually, the residents within the walls run out of food and water. It would be easy to see why King David, the author of today's passage, would have felt cut off from God's sight.

We may not live in fortresses these days, but we can probably still relate to being surrounded by enemies, to being starved of our needs—if not food and water, then time and attention. Some workplaces may not be openly hostile environments, but we might be able to think of coworkers who would attack at the first sign of weakness. Maybe it feels like God has lost sight of us.

In truth, God is with us, just like He was with David. He hasn't lost sight of us, even if we've stopped looking for Him. We can start our search by recognizing His greatness through praise and trusting Him with our prayers.

God wants to show you the wonders of His love. Are you looking?

*Lord, help me see how You are working in my life, even when I'm living under siege.*

# TRICK QUESTIONS

*"Teacher, which is the most important commandment in the law of Moses?" Jesus replied, " 'You must love the LORD your God with all your heart, all your soul, and all your mind.' This is the first and greatest commandment. A second is equally important: 'Love your neighbor as yourself.' The entire law and all the demands of the prophets are based on these two commandments."*

MATTHEW 22:36–40 NLT

. . . . . . . . . . . . . . . . . . . . . .

When questions are simple, it still sometimes feels like the answers are complicated. For instance, "Why is the sky blue?" The answer is pretty complex—it involves the atmosphere and prismatic light waves—and it took scientists a long time to work out.

When the Jewish religious leaders asked Jesus which commandment was greatest, they were trying to trip Him up. It was a simple question that the Pharisees themselves had spent years debating, but Jesus didn't hesitate. As God, He had given the Law to Moses and intimately understood what it was meant to accomplish: helping people love God and others.

When we face situations that are deceptively complex, we'd be wise to ask how our actions could be most loving toward God and others. The answers don't always need to be complicated. Following through on them may not be easy, but loving from your heart is always the right answer.

*God, help me love You more, and help me give Your love to others.*

## BELIEVING GOD

*And they shall know [from personal experience] that I am the*
*Lord their God, Who brought them forth out of the land of Egypt*
*that I might dwell among them; I am the Lord their God.*
EXODUS 29:46 AMPC

• • • • • • • • • • • • • • • • • • • • • •

Things too good to be true require proof. In Exodus 6:7 (AMPC), God told the Israelites, "And I will take you to Me for a people, and I will be to you a God; and you shall know that it is I, the Lord your God, Who brings you out from under the burdens of the Egyptians."

It was great news, but. . . "Moses told this to the Israelites, but they refused to listen to Moses because of their impatience and anguish of spirit and because of their cruel bondage" (Exodus 6:9 AMPC).

The people needed some proof, so God performed miracle after miracle, bringing them out of their bondage and toward the Promised Land. Then He reiterated Himself in today's verse.

God still wants to dwell among His people. It *is* too good, but it's true nonetheless. And He is still willing to prove His intentions. Through Jesus' life, death, and resurrection, God has brought us out of our bondage to sin and leads us toward His promised land. He wants us to personally experience His goodness and trust Him even more.

---

*God, You have freed me from captivity and called me into a relationship*
*with You. Help me always believe in Your promises in my heart.*

# IN GOD WE TRUST

*Our soul waits for the LORD; he is our help and our shield.*
*For our heart is glad in him, because we trust in his holy name.*
PSALM 33:20–21 ESV

. . . . . . . . . . . . . . . . . . . . . . .

IN GOD WE TRUST is the official motto of the United States. It was adopted in 1956 and has appeared on US currency ever since. Although the phrase's inclusion still remains popular with most Americans, its truth is not self-evident.

People trust in all kinds of things for their safety: physical strength, personal firearms, a strong military. They trust their political representative (at least more than they do the other party's political representative). They trust in their bank accounts and their work ethic to take care of their needs.

The problem is that all these things will fail. Physical strength is meaningless against disease. Statistically, homes where firearms are present are more likely than those without to experience gun violence—both homicides and suicides. Political representatives are famous for being untrustworthy. And bank accounts can be wiped out in an instant by a poor economy or unexpected expenses.

Only God is fully trustworthy. He alone is our Help and our Shield. He is the source of all good things. His plans do not fail. Take a moment today and let your heart be glad in Him.

---

*Lord, help me trust in You alone, not in the things of this world or in my own strength. Be my Help and my Shield.*

# FORGETTING ABOUT GOD

*When the people saw how long it was taking Moses to come back down the mountain, they gathered around Aaron. "Come on," they said, "make us some gods who can lead us. We don't know what happened to this fellow Moses, who brought us here from the land of Egypt."*

EXODUS 32:1 NLT

. . . . . . . . . . . . . . . . . . . . . . .

How long does it take to forget about God?

For the Israelites who left Egypt, it took almost no time at all. After Moses climbed up Mount Sinai to receive God's laws, the people got tired of waiting. Instead of recognizing that it was God who had led them out of Egypt, they blamed Moses for being slow. Even while they heard the rumblings on the mountain overhead, they called on Aaron, Moses' brother, to make new gods who better fit their idea of how deities were supposed to work.

When God doesn't act like we expect Him to, or when things take longer than we think they should, we too may be tempted to forget about God. We may not make golden calves to worship, but the idea of taking things into our own hands can seem appealing.

No, forgetting about God isn't a good option. When we grow tired of waiting on Him, we need a heart change, not new gods. The answer is to increase our faith in His timing, not to pretend we're in charge.

*God, when Your timing doesn't fit my plans,*
*keep me from forgetting about You.*

# BROKENHEARTED

*When the righteous cry for help, the L*ORD* hears and
delivers them out of all their troubles. The L*ORD* is near
to the brokenhearted and saves the crushed in spirit.*

PSALM 34:17–18 ESV

• • • • • • • • • • • • • • • • • • • • • •

Affliction happens. The righteous and wicked both face it, but not everyone is broken by it. Rather, not everyone is broken *in the same way*.

When painful events happen—the death of a loved one, a serious medical diagnosis, losing a good job, the end of a relationship—those who trust in God are reminded that He is strong in their weakness. He is near to the brokenhearted and can weather our recriminations. God hears our sorrows and sits beside us in our grief. He wraps us in His love and reminds us that nothing happens apart from His plan, and even when we don't see how our pain fits into His glory, our trust does.

When those who don't trust in God experience affliction, they have no such comfort. They have only themselves, which have just been shown to be quite fragile.

When we suffer affliction, we shouldn't be surprised. But how we deal with our pain matters. Cry out to God, and He will come near. It is better to be brokenhearted and seeking God's comfort than simply broken by affliction we know will come.

*Father, You promised that I would have to endure
pain, but You also promised that You'd be there
for me when I do. Keep my heart broken for You.*

## WISE STEWARDS

*"For to everyone who has, more will be given, and he will
have more than enough. But from the one who does not
have, even what he has will be taken away from him."*
MATTHEW 25:29 HCSB

. . . . . . . . . . . . . . . . . . . . . .

On the first read-through, today's verse seems inherently unfair. Take from the poor and give to the rich? Really?

Well, no. What today's verse refers to is using our gifts wisely. Go back and read the passage from which it was taken (Matthew 25:14–30). The master of the house entrusts his servants with a portion of his riches. The wise servants use what they have to grow the riches, but the lazy servant does nothing with what he's been given. When the master returns, each servant gives an account of how he's used his gifts for the master's benefit.

God has given each of us gifts to use for His glory. To some, He's given speaking abilities or artistic talent or a magnetic personality. Others might have material wealth to provide for the needs of others. It doesn't matter what the gift is, if we aren't using it for God's glory, we might as well bury it in the ground.

In the end, we'll have to answer our Master for how we've used His gifts. Will He say well done?

*Lord, help me use my gift, talents, and abilities for Your
glory instead of burying them in my selfish ambitions.*

# A VALENTINE FOR GOD

*"For I was hungry and you gave me something to eat, I was thirsty and you gave me something to drink, I was a stranger and you invited me in, I needed clothes and you clothed me, I was sick and you looked after me, I was in prison and you came to visit me."*
MATTHEW 25:35–36 NIV

. . . . . . . . . . . . . . . . . . . . . . .

In AD 496, Pope Gelasius marked February 14 as a celebration in honor of Saint Valentine, a mysterious figure from AD 269 who may have been martyred for performing secret marriages for Christians. *Or* maybe Valentine healed the blind daughter of a judge who was antagonistic toward Christianity, eventually converting him and his household and persuading him to free the Christians he had imprisoned.

Officially speaking, even the Roman Catholic Church doesn't know much about Saint Valentine. That's why they removed Valentine's Day from the General Roman Calendar in 1969, even though he's still recognized as a saint.

With all the confusion over Valentine's life, let us be clear about the expressions of love his name brings to mind. While today may feature written expressions of love, true love expresses itself in meeting the needs of others. When we care for those in need, we're actually showing love to the Creator who made all people in His image.

On this Valentine's Day, show others God's love in practical ways, and give a valentine to God Himself.

*Lord, help me love like You, and in so doing,
show You love by caring for others.*

# CLOUD AND FIRE

*The cloud of the LORD hovered over the Tabernacle during the day,
and at night fire glowed inside the cloud so the whole family of
Israel could see it. This continued throughout all their journeys.*

EXODUS 40:38 NLT

. . . . . . . . . . . . . . . . . . . . . . .

After their exodus from Egypt, the Israelites followed God as no one
had before—as a physically manifested cloud, visible by day and lit by
an inner fire by night. There was no mistaking God's presence leading
the nation of Israel.

The cloud didn't just lead them, though; God used it to fight for
His people. Exodus 14:24–25 (NLT) says, "But just before dawn the
LORD looked down on the Egyptian army from the pillar of fire and
cloud, and he threw their forces into total confusion. He twisted their
chariot wheels, making their chariots difficult to drive. 'Let's get out of
here—away from these Israelites!' the Egyptians shouted. 'The LORD is
fighting for them against Egypt!' "

We may not have a pillar of cloud to physically guide us toward God's
promised land, but we have something even better: God's presence within
us. "Don't you realize that your body is the temple of the Holy Spirit,
who lives in you and was given to you by God?" (1 Corinthians 6:19 NLT).

Today, make it as obvious to others as it was to the Israelites that
God's presence is with you.

*Father, may I follow your lead from within as
You keep me safe as I do Your will here on earth.*

# WHISPERING SINS

*Transgression speaks to the wicked deep in his heart; there is no fear of God before his eyes. For he flatters himself in his own eyes that his iniquity cannot be found out and hated.*

PSALM 36:1–2 ESV

. . . . . . . . . . . . . . . . . . . . . .

Sin is pervasive. It seeks to infect every area of our lives. When sin whispers that we are the most important person in existence, that we deserve to be happy, and that it doesn't matter what we do because no consequence will catch up to our sneakiness, we may forget this truth: we are not our own because God has paid a hefty price to rescue us from those whispering sins.

Sin pulls us out of reality and places us into fantasy. It makes us like children who cover their eyes and think they're invisible. *No one can see me,* they think, *because I can't see anyone.*

God always sees. Nothing is hidden from Him, even what is within our hearts. When sin comes to blind us toward its effects and convince us that we should act as we please, we need to remember the truth. We live for the glory of God (not our own) and at the pleasure of God's will (still not ours).

Don't believe the whispering sins. Believe the Spirit that dwells within. Spend time with God each day so you can tell the difference between their voices.

*Loving God, thank You for forgiving me of my sins at the cross. Close my ears to sin's whispers, and open my eyes to reality.*

# REMORSE AND REPENTANCE

*When Judas, who had betrayed him, saw that Jesus was condemned,*
*he was seized with remorse and returned the thirty pieces of silver*
*to the chief priests and the elders. "I have sinned," he said, "for I*
*have betrayed innocent blood." "What is that to us?" they replied.*
*"That's your responsibility." So Judas threw the money into the*
*temple and left. Then he went away and hanged himself.*
MATTHEW 27:3–5 NIV

· · · · · · · · · · · · · · · · · · · · · · ·

Judas had a lot to be remorseful about. He sold out the sinless Son of God for thirty pieces of silver. Judas didn't need the money. If he really wanted money, he could have simply taken what the other disciples had entrusted to him and slipped away. Instead, he betrayed his master to the religious authorities, and Jesus was sentenced to death. Of course Judas felt bad!

There are two ways to react to remorse. Judas chose to punish himself. The other option was to repent—to admit he had done wrong, to apologize for his actions, to make restitution to those affected, and to live as a changed man. Between remorse and repentance, Judas took the easy way out.

When you do wrong, do you beat yourself up, or do you confess your shortcomings and try to make things right? Don't take the easy way out. Allow God to show the world just how great His grace and love are.

---

*Jesus, turn my remorse into repentance so*
*that I may enjoy a right relationship with You.*

# DESIRES OF THE HEART

*Delight thyself also in the LORD: and he*
*shall give thee the desires of thine heart.*

PSALM 37:4 KJV

. . . . . . . . . . . . . . . . . . . . . . .

It appeals to us on nearly every level: God's promise to give us the desires of our hearts. Our hearts have *so many* desires, and God has every ability to fill them! God can give us wealth and fame, security and happiness. He can make us well liked and our children well behaved. God can do it all without even scratching the surface of His power.

But that isn't what today's verse is about.

Our heart having many desires is not an opportunity for God to show His power, but evidence that our heart doesn't desire the right things. The only thing our heart should delight in is the Lord. When it does, we can have all the goodness we can handle.

Far from ensuring that we will live lives of plenty, God promises that no matter how lean our diets or how scarce our resources, we'll have enough to do His will when we delight in His providence. We'll always be happiest when doing what God has planned for us than when we're following what we *think* will make us happy.

Delight yourself in the Lord, first and foremost, and your heart will desire exactly what God wants to give you.

*God, teach me to desire You most and to be*
*happy with whatever You have planned for me.*

# GOD'S SCHEDULE

*Be still in the presence of the LORD, and wait patiently*
*for him to act. Don't worry about evil people who*
*prosper or fret about their wicked schemes.*

PSALM 37:7 NLT

. . . . . . . . . . . . . . . . . . . . . .

God's timeline differs from ours. How could it not? He brought time and existence into being. Second Peter 3:8 (NLT) says, "But you must not forget this one thing, dear friends: A day is like a thousand years to the Lord, and a thousand years is like a day."

That's all fine until we experience what we think is an urgent need. When we see other people succeeding while we toil in obscurity, it feels like God has fallen asleep at the wheel. God can be as timeless as He wants as long as it doesn't mess up our promotion schedule, right? Let's put everything into perspective.

All time, from when God spoke light into existence to now, is a blip on the line of eternity. Everything that has happened is like less than a second of someone's life span, if that second was very busy and if the person lived forever.

In light of eternity, does it matter who looks like they're prospering when their life is about to end? Real success isn't measured like that. Real success is knowing God, relaxing in His presence, and waiting for the blessings He's promised us after this life is over.

*Lord, help me live according to Your schedule*
*and wait on You to act as You see fit.*

# LEADING WITH SOBER MINDS

*"Drink no wine or strong drink, you or your sons with you,*
*when you go into the tent of meeting, lest you die. It shall*
*be a statute forever throughout your generations. You are to*
*distinguish between the holy and the common, and between the*
*unclean and the clean, and you are to teach the people of Israel*
*all the statutes that the LORD has spoken to them by Moses."*

LEVITICUS 10:9–11 ESV

• • • • • • • • • • • • • • • • • • • • • •

God led Israel, literally by cloud and fire, morally by giving them His Law, and vicariously through the priesthood He designated to provide offerings on behalf of the people. Aaron, Moses' brother, was the first high priest of Israel, and he knew how serious his job was.

In Leviticus 10, Aaron's sons—Nadab and Abihu—didn't take their jobs seriously, possibly even performing their duties while drunk. As a result, God struck them dead, and Aaron wasn't allowed to mourn them as he might have, lest he become ritually unclean. Instead, his other sons—Eleazar and Ithamar—stepped up and fulfilled their dead brothers' responsibilities.

Leaders, whether high priests or presidents or Little League coaches, are to lead with sober minds, teaching those in their care the difference between clean and unclean living. We are to uphold those things that are important to God through our example and through our words. If we don't, God may replace us with someone who will.

---

*God, may I follow You as I lead others with a sober mind.*

## FOLLOWING THE GREATER TRUTH

*As Jesus walked beside the Sea of Galilee, he saw Simon and*
*his brother Andrew casting a net into the lake, for they were*
*fishermen. "Come, follow me," Jesus said, "and I will send you*
*out to fish for people." At once they left their nets and followed him.*

MARK 1:16–18 NIV

. . . . . . . . . . . . . . . . . . . . . . . .

Seeking after truth will, by necessity, take you from lesser understanding to greater. The things you thought were the answer turned out to be just the foundation for understanding them better. Following the greater truth takes time and adaptability. At least, that's how it was with Andrew.

Andrew was John the Baptist's disciple, and he was there when the locust-eating preacher identified Jesus as the Lamb of God (see John 1:35–40). "The first thing Andrew did was to find his brother Simon and tell him, 'We have found the Messiah' (that is, the Christ)" (John 1:41 NIV).

After spending time with Jesus, Andrew was convinced. Then, when Jesus called Andrew and Simon, they dropped their livelihoods and former ways of thinking and became His disciples.

As you grow in your faith, don't be afraid to let go of previous understandings when God has shown you new ways to trust Him, new ways to think, and new jobs to do. Follow Him as well as you can, and when you know Him better, follow closer.

---

*Jesus, show me how to follow You more closely as I grow in my faith.*

# WHAT LASTS

*"O LORD, make me know my end and what is the measure of
my days; let me know how fleeting I am! Behold, you have made
my days a few handbreadths, and my lifetime is as nothing
before you. Surely all mankind stands as a mere breath!"*

PSALM 39:4–5 ESV

. . . . . . . . . . . . . . . . . . . . . .

God's understanding and experience with time, as previously mentioned,
are not like ours. Our lives are fleeting, but that doesn't mean we are
insignificant or that our actions have no permanent consequences.

It is precisely because of our brief lives that we must be especially
careful to spend our time well. When we use it to build spiritual foundations
of Christ in others, time will reveal them to stand against all afflictions.
When we use our time toward selfish ends, our accomplishments will not
last any longer than straw in a fire (see 1 Corinthians 3:10–15).

To have a lasting impact on this world, we should busy ourselves
with those things God deems most important, the things Jesus cared for
during His ministry. James 1:27 (ESV) says, "Religion that is pure and
undefiled before God the Father is this: to visit orphans and widows in
their affliction, and to keep oneself unstained from the world."

When we care for the poor, the forgotten, the voiceless, we store up
treasures that will last far beyond the span of our years.

*Lord, give me perspective so I use my time on things that matter.*

# NOTHING TO HIDE

*But on the seventh day he shall shave all his hair off his head,*
*his beard, his eyebrows, and his [body]; and he shall wash*
*his clothes and bathe his body in water, and be clean.*

LEVITICUS 14:9 AMPC

. . . . . . . . . . . . . . . . . . . . . .

Stick any large group of people together in the wilderness where personal hygiene might be difficult to maintain, and you'll likely encounter some skin diseases. The term *leprosy* in the Bible probably refers to a variety of skin diseases, many of which would have easily passed from person to person by skin contact. That's why Hebrew law dealt with its treatment so thoroughly (check out Leviticus 13).

Today's verse covers the final step of restoration after a person has been healed from a skin disease. Before being allowed to reenter society, the person must shave off all their hair, eyebrows included. In so doing, they're showing the world they have no lingering marks of the disease hiding anywhere. They have nothing to hide.

The disease of sin is more virulent than any form of leprosy described in the Old Testament. Even after we've been born again by Christ's blood, we are drawn toward sinful behavior. But each time we repent—each time we ask Jesus to help us shave the sinful growth in our lives and wash us again in His blood—we are made clean. We too have nothing to hide.

*Jesus, help me live with nothing to hide so*
*others will see Your righteousness in me.*

## TRAITORS AND SINNERS

*When the scribes of the Pharisees saw that He was eating with sinners and tax collectors, they asked His disciples, "Why does He eat with tax collectors and sinners?" When Jesus heard this, He told them, "Those who are well don't need a doctor, but the sick do need one. I didn't come to call the righteous, but sinners."*

MARK 2:16–17 HCSB

. . . . . . . . . . . . . . . . . . . . . . .

With the Romans in charge of Israel during Jesus' ministry, the Jewish people were required to pay taxes to Caesar, and the ones to collect these taxes were considered traitors to both their nation and their faith. To say that tax collectors were unliked was like saying hurricanes are windy.

What the Jews wanted was for the Messiah to show up and overthrow the Roman rulers, punish those who collaborated with their oppressors, and establish a new, harmonious kingdom on earth. They didn't expect the Messiah to show up and eat with traitors and sinners or butt heads with the religious leaders of the day.

But Jesus doesn't do what we expect. He welcomes everyone who will listen, regardless of their past allegiances. If Jesus welcomed everyone into a relationship with Him, we must do likewise.

Are there people you don't think fit in Jesus' kingdom? Ask God to renew your heart; then invite those folks to dinner. You may find out you were the sick person in need of a doctor all along.

*Lord, expand my love for everyone You love.*

## PLANTING THE SEED

*Then Jesus said to them, "If you can't understand the meaning of
this parable, how will you understand all the other parables?"*
MARK 4:13 NLT

. . . . . . . . . . . . . . . . . . . . . .

Scattering seed by hand, then plowing the ground to bury the seed, was
a common farming technique during the time of Christ. The seed is
spread over all kinds of ground, but it will only flourish in the ground
that is plowed and made ready for it. Jesus mentions this practice as an
apt comparison for those who spread God's Word to the world.

When the disciples asked Jesus to explain the parable of the sower
to them in private, Jesus commented that understanding this parable
was foundational to understanding the rest of them. Why? Because if
the seed of God's Word fell on their hardened hearts, it wouldn't flourish
into self-replicating fruitfulness.

There are many reasons why our hearts may be hardened to God's
Word: disappointment over God's timing, sinfulness in our lives, a lack of
understanding about God's reasons for His actions, a reluctance to allow
Him to break up the soil of our hearts. But if we want to understand His
Word, we must allow ourselves to be turned upside down and buried for
His sake. Only when we are planted in the plowed ground will we be
useful for His kingdom.

*Jesus, plant Your seeds in my heart and prepare my life
to be fruitful, no matter how uncomfortable it is.*

# ON VENGEANCE

*Thou shalt not avenge, nor bear any grudge against the children of thy people, but thou shalt love thy neighbour as thyself: I am the LORD.*
LEVITICUS 19:18 KJV

· · · · · · · · · · · · · · · · · · · · ·

In an honor-based culture, people view every slight as an attack to be avenged. If someone criticizes you, you beat them up. If they kill one of your family members, you burn down their village and take all their livestock. Exacting vengeance was meant to prevent future attacks on one's honor, but due to its escalating nature, it was also likely that a nation would wipe itself out over petty arguments, thus saving a rival nation the trouble of going to war.

Instead of seeking vengeance or holding grudges, God's people were to let Him do justice while they were to treat each other with love. The practical reasons for avoiding self-annihilation were obvious, but it flew in the face of the prevailing culture. In many ways, it still does.

We often want to see our enemies pay for their attacks on us, but God doesn't want us to take matters into our own hands. Romans 12:19 (ESV) says, "Beloved, never avenge yourselves, but leave it to the wrath of God, for it is written, 'Vengeance is mine, I will repay, says the Lord.'"

When someone wrongs you, pray for them. Recognize who is really in charge, and leave the vengeance to God.

*God, transform my thirst for vengeance*
*into genuine love for my neighbor.*

# GIVEN AND PURSUED

*"Consecrate yourselves, therefore, and be holy, for I am the LORD your God. Keep my statutes and do them; I am the LORD who sanctifies you."*
LEVITICUS 20:7–8 ESV

- - - - - - - - - - - - - - - - - - - - -

In today's verse, we are called to be holy, but that's impossible, right?

Holiness is God's natural state. He is perfect in His nature, as set apart from sin as light is from darkness. When God calls us to holiness, He isn't meaning that we can achieve His level of perfection, but that we are to set ourselves apart—to consecrate ourselves—and live for Him by keeping His laws. Namely, we are to love God above all things and love our neighbor as ourselves.

Before we abandon the effort as hopeless (we're just going to mess up again, so why try?), God says we aren't the only ones responsible for our holiness. Even as we consecrate ourselves, God sanctifies us for His use. We *can* reach His level of holiness because He gives it to us when we work toward honoring Him with our actions and attitudes.

Yes, holiness is an impossible standard to achieve, but that's no problem for God. Today, consecrate yourself and be holy. Look for opportunities to love God and others. Show the world God's holiness in action, not that it comes from you, but that it comes *through* you from God Himself.

---

*Lord God, set me aside to do Your will today. May others see who I belong to because You will shine through.*

# HOMETOWN MIND-SET

*Jesus left that part of the country and returned with his
disciples to Nazareth, his hometown. The next Sabbath he began
teaching in the synagogue, and many who heard him were
amazed. They asked, "Where did he get all this wisdom and the
power to perform such miracles?" Then they scoffed, "He's just
a carpenter, the son of Mary and the brother of James, Joseph,
Judas, and Simon. And his sisters live right here among us."
They were deeply offended and refused to believe in him.*

MARK 6:1–3 NLT

• • • • • • • • • • • • • • • • • • • • • •

It must have been strange for the people of Nazareth to see Jesus leading
His disciples into the synagogue. They might have seen Him in a new
light and recognized how they didn't really know Him as well as they
thought. Instead, they dismissed Jesus as "just a carpenter."

Have you ever dismissed someone as "just" this or that because you
thought you knew who they were? The people of Nazareth missed out
on opportunities for their sick to be healed and their hearts to be united
with God's because they *thought* they knew who Jesus was.

Don't give into the hometown mind-set when someone you know
starts acting in new, better ways. Get to know them for real. If nothing
else, you'll encourage them as a dynamic person who is capable of doing
better. They might even help you deepen your own relationship with God.

*Jesus, keep me from making assumptions about people.*

# PRAISE FROM THE HEART FOR THE KING

*My heart is stirred by a noble theme as I recite my verses*
*for the king; my tongue is the pen of a skillful writer.*
PSALM 45:1 NIV

. . . . . . . . . . . . . . . . . . . . . . .

Words of praise for the Lord Jesus Christ—whether spoken, sung, or written—should come from the deepest parts of our hearts. Our King Jesus, after all, left His eternal home to come to earth to live as a man, die a sacrificial death, and then be raised from the dead. And one day, He will return and then reign as King of kings and Lord of lords.

Jesus is worthy of nothing less than the very best we can give Him, and that includes the expressions of praise that bubble up from our very hearts.

What can you praise God for today? For the wonder of creation? For loving you so much that He sent His Son to die for you? For giving you His Holy Spirit so that you can live the way He wants you to live and so you can tell others about Jesus?

Just open your mind and your heart; then write down a nice, long list of things you can praise God for. Then praise Him with everything you have!

---

*Glorious Father, there are countless reasons for me to open my mouth and praise You. Fill my heart with a spirit of praise and my mouth with words that lift up Your wonderful name.*

# THE (VITAL) IMPORTANCE OF PRAYER

*After leaving them, [Jesus] went up on a mountainside to pray.*
MARK 6:46 NIV

. . . . . . . . . . . . . . . . . . . . . . .

The Bible tells many stories of great men of prayer, and none was greater than Jesus. The Gospels include several accounts of the Son of the living God praying to His Father in heaven. For example, He prayed at His baptism (Luke 3:21), before choosing His twelve disciples (Luke 6:12), before Peter's confession (Luke 9:18), at His transfiguration (Luke 9:29), and before He was arrested and crucified (John 17).

But why did Jesus, who was God in the flesh, need to pray? Didn't He have the authority to do everything He could possibly ask God to do?

Jesus was fully God and fully human. He needed to sleep, eat, and drink water—just like any of us. But to keep Himself ready to do the things He'd come to earth to do, He needed help from His Father in heaven. That means He needed to take regular time to connect from the heart with the Father.

When Jesus prayed, He set an example for each of us of the need for consistent, regular prayer. If Jesus, the Son of God, needed to pray, then we know we need to pray too!

*Father in heaven, may I never neglect taking time to connect my heart to Yours through prayer. Jesus needed to pray, so I know I need to follow His example and spend regular time with You.*

## REAPING AND SOWING

*"If you follow my decrees and are careful to obey my commands, I will send you rain in its season, and the ground will yield its crops and the trees their fruit."*
LEVITICUS 26:3–4 NIV

. . . . . . . . . . . . . . . . . . . . .

Every decision we make has consequences. We decide how we're going to respond to other people, to our circumstances, and to our God. . .and all those decisions affect our lives—and the lives of others—in some way, negatively or positively.

The apostle Paul used farming—something most ancient people understood well—as a metaphor when he wrote, "A man reaps what he sows. Whoever sows to please their flesh, from the flesh will reap destruction; whoever sows to please the Spirit, from the Spirit will reap eternal life" (Galatians 6:7–8 NIV).

In other words, our attitudes, thoughts, and actions all impact ourselves and others in some way.

At the end of Leviticus, God lists the many blessings that awaited the Israelites if they obeyed Him. But He also lists the punishments they would suffer if they disobeyed.

Today, God gives us the same choices He gave the ancient Israelites. If we choose to sow seeds of disobedience, we'll harvest destruction. But when we sow seeds of faith and obedience, we'll harvest the very best God has for us.

*Lord, thank You for Your promises of blessing when I obey You from my heart.*

## WHO IS JESUS?

*Jesus and his disciples went on to the villages around Caesarea Philippi. On the way he asked them, "Who do people say I am?" They replied, "Some say John the Baptist; others say Elijah; and still others, one of the prophets." "But what about you?" he asked. "Who do you say I am?" Peter answered, "You are the Messiah."*

MARK 8:27–29 NIV

. . . . . . . . . . . . . . . . . . . . . .

One day, Jesus asked His disciples about rumors that had been going around about Him and who He was. The twelve eagerly volunteered what they knew—that some believed He was John the Baptist, while others were saying that Elijah or one of the other prophets returned to earth in the flesh.

Jesus listened intently to the disciples' answer to His first question, and then He dropped the question He'd intended to ask them all along, the most important question in all of human history.

Who do *you* think I am?

Eleven of the disciples kept their mouths shut, maybe afraid they would answer incorrectly. But Peter, as he so often did, blurted out what the others may have been thinking: "You are the Messiah, the Son of the living God" (Matthew 16:16 NIV).

*Who do you think Jesus is?* That's the most important question you'll ever answer!

*Father in heaven, thank You for revealing to me who Jesus really is.*

# JUST SING!

*Sing praises to God, sing praises; sing praises to our King, sing praises.*
*For God is the King of all the earth; sing to him a psalm of praise.*
PSALM 47:6–7 NIV

. . . . . . . . . . . . . . . . . . . . . .

The Psalms are filled with encouragements to praise God by lifting our voices and singing. That includes the two verses above, which encourage readers to sing to Him no fewer than five times!

But the Psalms aren't the only place in the Bible that encourages believers to sing praises to God. In the New Testament, the apostle Paul enjoins Christians to "be filled with the Spirit, speaking to one another with psalms, hymns, and songs from the Spirit. Sing and make music from your heart to the Lord, always giving thanks to God the Father for everything, in the name of our Lord Jesus Christ" (Ephesians 5:18–20 NIV).

Clearly, God likes it when we sing praises to Him!

So even if you don't think you can carry a tune, sing praises to God every chance you get. Sing in the Sunday worship service, in your car on the way to work, on the golf course. . .anywhere you can draw air, just open your heart, lift your voice, and sing out praises to the Lord!

*Glorious Father, thank You for the gift of song. May I never waste an opportunity to open my mouth and sing songs of praise to You.*

# HONESTY WITH GOD

*The father instantly cried out, "I do believe,*
*but help me overcome my unbelief!"*
MARK 9:24 NLT

. . . . . . . . . . . . . . . . . . . . . . .

The words spoken in today's verse came from the mouth of a man who desperately needed Jesus to act on behalf of his demon-possessed son. He had no doubt heard of the man who had healed many sick, lame, and demon-possessed people. But still, he struggled with unbelief.

At a glance, we may wonder how a man who had heard so much about Jesus could possibly doubt Him. But maybe we shouldn't assume that he had a hard time believing Jesus could help people. Maybe we should look at his words as an admission that he wondered if Jesus could and would help *him*.

The thought of speaking to God with this kind of honesty scares many of us. There are things, after all, we wish we could hide from Him, things we don't even want to admit to ourselves. But when we come to the end of ourselves and still need God to do something great for us and within us, it's just the kind of heart-to-heart honesty He desires.

Do you sometimes find yourself doubting that God wants to do something great for *you*? If so, then confess your doubt to Him. He can handle it, and He can also open your heart and mind to what He has planned for you.

*Jesus, help me to be honest with You when I struggle in my faith.*

## LIKE A LITTLE CHILD

*People were bringing little children to Jesus for him to place his hands on them, but the disciples rebuked them. When Jesus saw this, he was indignant. He said to them, "Let the little children come to me, and do not hinder them, for the kingdom of God belongs to such as these. Truly I tell you, anyone who will not receive the kingdom of God like a little child will never enter it."*

MARK 10:13–15 NIV

. . . . . . . . . . . . . . . . . . . . . . .

Jesus was more than a little piqued when His disciples blocked people from bringing their small children to Him so He could bless them. He then used their error to teach them an important lesson about faith.

Jesus used the children as an object lesson about the kind of faith God requires from each of us. The kind of faith God honors, Jesus taught them, is a childlike faith. It's a faith that comes to Him with an open heart and an open hand, with a simple trust, and with an expectation that He wants to do good for those who come to Him.

How would you describe your faith in God today? In what ways do you think it needs to change?

*Father in heaven, help me come to You daily with childlike faith—trusting, helpless, open-hearted, and fully dependent on You for everything.*

## SET APART

*Then the LORD said to Moses, "Give the following
instructions to the people of Israel. If any of the people,
either men or women, take the special vow of a Nazirite,
setting themselves apart to the LORD in a special way."*
NUMBERS 6:1–2 NLT

. . . . . . . . . . . . . . . . . . . . . .

In the Old Testament, a Nazirite was a man or woman who took a vow to set themselves apart to God so that He could use them for a special purpose.

When a man took the Nazirite vow, he promised not to cut his hair, to avoid consuming any product made from grapes (including wine), and to avoid making physical contact with dead bodies.

Jesus has set you as a believer aside for a special purpose, and He wants others to see that purpose in you. The apostle Paul summarized that purpose when he wrote, "For you know that we dealt with each of you as a father deals with his own children, encouraging, comforting and urging you to live lives worthy of God, who calls you into his kingdom and glory" (1 Thessalonians 2:11–12 NIV).

We Christian men are called to live lives that look very different from those who live by the values of this world. For that reason, we should examine ourselves regularly and ask ourselves whether our lives show that our hearts are dedicated to Him.

*Father, thank You for setting me apart for Your service.
Help me to live a life worthy of that calling.*

# FELLOWSHIP WITH GOD

*When Moses finished setting up the tabernacle, he anointed
and consecrated it and all its furnishings. He also anointed
and consecrated the altar and all its utensils.*

NUMBERS 7:1 NIV

. . . . . . . . . . . . . . . . . . . . . . .

Numbers 7 describes the dedication ceremony of the tabernacle, including offerings to the Lord by each of the twelve tribes of Israel. The festivities went on for twelve days, and each tribe was responsible for specific offerings each day.

With the tabernacle completed and dedicated, Moses could meet with God there and speak with Him: "When Moses entered the tent of meeting to speak with the LORD, he heard the voice speaking to him from between the two cherubim above the atonement cover on the ark of the covenant law. In this way the LORD spoke to him" (Numbers 7:89 NIV).

God designed and commissioned the construction of the tabernacle for one reason: He wanted to spend time with His chosen people. It's the same for us Christians today. God sent Jesus into the world so that He could establish fellowship with us. He welcomes us to come into His presence each and every day just so we can spend time with Him and He with us. Only now we don't have to go to any man-made structure to do it. We can have heart-to-heart fellowship with our heavenly Father any time and any place.

*Father, thank You for doing what I could never do myself:
establish intimate fellowship between You and me.*

# OFFERING THANKS

*"Sacrifice thank offerings to God, fulfill your vows to the Most High, and call on me in the day of trouble; I will deliver you, and you will honor me."*

PSALM 50:14–15 NIV

. . . . . . . . . . . . . . . . . . . . . .

Luke 17:11–19 tells the wonderful, sad story of Jesus healing ten men afflicted with leprosy, a terrible skin disease.

"Jesus, Master, have pity on us!" they cried out. When they got Jesus' attention, He told them, "Go, show yourselves to the priests." Just like that, each man was healed. That's the wonderful, beautiful part of this account.

Now the sad part.

Jesus had healed ten men that day, but only one of them came back to Him to express his gratitude. He ran to Jesus, praising God as loudly as he could and threw himself at Jesus' feet (vv. 15–16). The other nine, however, just went on their way, seemingly unaware that they had just been the beneficiaries of an authentic, amazing miracle by God in the flesh Himself.

That one grateful man, now healed and cleansed of a disease that would terribly disfigure him and make him a social outcast, shows us something about the effect of true thankfulness, and it's this: it draws us closer to God.

*Father, help me never to forget to "sacrifice thank offerings" to You. Help me to be like that one grateful leper who came back to Jesus to say, "Thank You!"*

# HOW DO WE LOVE OUR NEIGHBORS AS OURSELVES?

*" 'And you must love the LORD your God with all your heart, all your soul, all your mind, and all your strength.' The second is equally important: 'Love your neighbor as yourself.' No other commandment is greater than these."*

MARK 12:30–31 NLT

• • • • • • • • • • • • • • • • • • • • • • • •

One day, a teacher of Jewish religious law asked Jesus which Old Testament law was most important. Jesus answered by directly quoting Deuteronomy 6:4–5 (NLT), which says, "Listen, O Israel! The LORD is our God, the LORD alone. And you must love the LORD your God with all your heart, all your soul, and all your strength."

But Jesus didn't stop there. He went on to explain the other most important commandment: "Love your neighbor as yourself." This second great commandment, which is found in Leviticus 19:18, is defined very simply in Romans 13:8 (NIV): "Let no debt remain outstanding, except the continuing debt to love one another, for whoever loves others has fulfilled the law."

On a practical level, loving your neighbor as yourself means treating people with kindness, patience, and hospitality, showing respect and civility to those with whom you disagree, and making it a point to help meet people's needs.

Loving your neighbor from your heart helps other people, and it puts you in position to receive God's blessings.

*Jesus, I want others to see You in me, so help me love from my heart and in my actions.*

# WHEN YOU SIN

*Wash away all my iniquity and cleanse me from my sin.*
*For I know my transgressions, and my sin is always before me.*
PSALM 51:2–3 NIV

. . . . . . . . . . . . . . . . . . . . . . . .

The eleventh and twelfth chapters of the book of 2 Samuel recount a series of shameful actions by King David—lust, adultery, and an attempted cover-up of his sins that included arranging for the death of one of his top military men.

What a mess David made—for himself, for his family, and for his kingdom.

Despite these horrendous sins, God still loved David and still had a plan for him, so He sent the prophet Nathan to confront the wayward king. David immediately acknowledged that he had sinned against God, and that led to him writing Psalm 51, which begins, "Have mercy on me, O God, according to your unfailing love; according to your great compassion blot out my transgressions" (v. 1 NIV).

David understood something the apostle John wrote centuries later: "If we confess our sins, he is faithful and just to forgive us our sins, and to cleanse us from all unrighteousness" (1 John 1:9 KJV).

God forgives repentant sinners. So when you mess up, don't try to rationalize, hide your sin, or hide from God. Instead, run to Him and confess from your heart, knowing that He promises to forgive and cleanse you.

*Lord, when I sin, don't let me hide from You. Instead, bring me close so that I can confess my sin from my heart.*

# DON'T MISS OUT ON GOD'S BEST

*But the men who had gone up with [Caleb] said, "We can't attack those people; they are stronger than we are." And they spread among the Israelites a bad report about the land they had explored.*

NUMBERS 13:31–32 NIV

. . . . . . . . . . . . . . . . . . . . . . .

The Israelites were gathered at the border of the Promised Land, and Moses sent spies from each of the twelve tribes to explore the land. After the spies returned to the Israelites, they all agreed that it was a beautiful land where they could grow their crops, make their homes, and raise their families. But ten of them looked at the challenges of taking the land—specifically the giants who lived there—and began spreading fear among the people.

All this led to a rebellion among the people, who complained to Moses—and to God—that trying to take the land would surely lead to their deaths. In the end, God, angered at His people's lack of faith, barred these unbelieving people from taking the Promised Land for another forty years (see Numbers 14).

If the people of Israel's failure to enter the Promised Land can teach us anything, it's this: God keeps His promises, and things that can keep us from receiving what He has for us are unbelieving hearts and eyes that focus on the "giants" before us instead of an even bigger God.

*Lord, may I always focus on You and not on the potential obstacles before me.*

# MOVING BEYOND FAILURE

*Peter declared, "Even if all fall away, I will not."*
MARK 14:29 NIV

. . . . . . . . . . . . . . . . . . . . . . .

If for no other reason, you have to admire the pre-Pentecost Peter for his good intentions.

After His Passover meal with His disciples and before He was arrested, Jesus told Peter and the other disciples that they would all soon abandon Him: "You will all fall away. . .for it is written: 'I will strike the shepherd, and the sheep will be scattered'" (Mark 14:27 NIV).

But Peter wouldn't hear of it.

Jesus knew Peter was speaking with good intentions, but He also knew that his failure was a part of God's plan for the coming hours. So He told Peter very pointedly that on that very night, he would deny even knowing his Lord—not once but three times!

Mark 14:66-72 gives the account of how miserably Peter failed. But Jesus didn't give up on Peter. After His resurrection, Jesus met with Peter one morning and "reinstated" him (see John 21:15–23). After Jesus returned to heaven, Peter fearlessly preached the name of Jesus.

When you fail to live up to your own good intentions, don't give up on yourself. God won't, and when you come to Him in humble confession, He'll restore you and get you back on the path He wants you to walk.

*Father, when I fail, remind me that You will*
*never abandon me or give up on me.*

## PRAY THE WAY JESUS PRAYED

*He went on a little farther and fell to the ground. He prayed that, if it were possible, the awful hour awaiting him might pass him by. "Abba, Father," he cried out, "everything is possible for you. Please take this cup of suffering away from me. Yet I want your will to be done, not mine."*

MARK 14:35–36 NLT

. . . . . . . . . . . . . . . . . . . . . . .

Jesus' prayers in the Garden of Gethsemane were the most heart-wrenching prayers in the entire Bible. He knew what kind of suffering He would be facing the very next day as He took the punishment for our sins, and the human side of Him wanted God to find another way to accomplish His purposes.

Jesus was painfully honest with the Father as He humbly stated His own desires. Yet He also stated that He was 100 percent committed to doing the Father's will and not His own.

That terrible night in the garden, Jesus set for us an example of prayer—honest prayer, humble prayer, and prayer that is fully submitted to the will of our Father in heaven.

---

*Father in heaven, there will be times in my life of faith when I come to You with a broken heart, a heart that desperately wants You to do something for me. In those times of anguished prayer, may I always remember to submit myself to Your perfect will.*

# DON'T BE LIKE KORAH

*He had hardly finished speaking the words when the ground*
*suddenly split open beneath them. The earth opened its mouth and*
*swallowed the men, along with their households and all their followers*
*who were standing with them, and everything they owned.*
NUMBERS 16:31–32 NLT

. . . . . . . . . . . . . . . . . . . . . .

Have you ever felt at least a small twinge of jealousy over how God is using another person? Maybe you felt even that if you were in someone's role, you could do the job better.

This is at least close to how Korah felt toward Moses and Aaron. As a Levite, Korah served in the tabernacle, but he wasn't a priest and he didn't have the same connection to God as priests had. So instead of just faithfully seeing to the responsibilities God had given him, Korah complained against Moses and Aaron: "They came as a group to oppose Moses and Aaron and said to them, 'You have gone too far! The whole community is holy, every one of them, and the LORD is with them. Why then do you set yourselves above the LORD's assembly?' " (Numbers 16:3 NIV).

Korah allowed his jealousy to consume his heart and, as a result, he not only lost out in serving God but was consumed by the earth at His command.

Nothing good will come from being like Korah!

*Father, help me to be content with what You have for me to*
*do and to not focus on assignments You've given others.*

# GOD LISTENS

*As for me, I call to God, and the Lord saves me. Evening,
morning and noon I cry out in distress, and he hears my voice.*
Psalm 55:16–17 niv

• • • • • • • • • • • • • • • • • • • • • • •

Have you ever considered the amazing biblical promise that God—the Creator of our world and the universe—actually listens to you? What a privilege it is that the Lord actively listens to His people when they come to Him!

Today's scripture reading, as well as other passages, assures us that God listens to His people. Here are some examples:

- "The Lord is far from the wicked, but he hears the prayer of the righteous" (Proverbs 15:29 niv).

- "For the eyes of the Lord are on the righteous and his ears are attentive to their prayer" (1 Peter 3:12 niv).

- "This is the confidence we have in approaching God: that if we ask anything according to his will, he hears us. And if we know that he hears us—whatever we ask—we know that we have what we asked of him" (1 John 5:14–15 niv).

Our God is the personification of love. He listens to the prayers of His people, simply because loving means listening. When you start believing He doesn't want to hear from you, ask yourself if you're where you need to be in your relationship with Him so that He will hear you. After all, He's still right where He's always been.

*Father, thank You for listening to me when I come to You in prayer.*

## THE PERFECT SACRIFICE

*"This is a requirement of the law that the LORD has commanded:*
*Tell the Israelites to bring you a red heifer without defect or blemish*
*and that has never been under a yoke. Give it to Eleazar the priest;*
*it is to be taken outside the camp and slaughtered in his presence."*

NUMBERS 19:2–3 NIV

. . . . . . . . . . . . . . . . . . . . . .

In Old Testament times, God required His people to sacrifice animals to "pay" for their sins. That is because "without the shedding of blood there is no forgiveness" (Hebrews 9:22 NIV). In the passage above, God told His people that Eleazar the priest was to sacrifice a flawless red heifer (a very rare specimen indeed) simply because God deserved perfection.

The Israelites had to repeat different animal sacrifices every year because the people kept sinning. But that all changed when Jesus— the sinless (flawless), perfect Lamb of God, who was tempted just like we are but never sinned (1 John 3:5)—gave up His life on a cross. The apostle Paul put it like this: "God made him who had no sin to be sin for us, so that in him we might become the righteousness of God" (2 Corinthians 5:21 NIV).

Jesus was God's perfect sacrificial Lamb—perfect in His sinlessness, perfect in His focus on His mission, perfect in His obedience, perfect in His humility. . .perfect in every way.

*Jesus, my heart is overwhelmed with joy that You, the perfect*
*Lamb of God, gave Your all so that I could be saved.*

# FEAR VERSUS FAITH

*In God, whose word I praise, in the LORD, whose word I praise—*
*in God I trust and am not afraid. What can man do to me?*
PSALM 56:10–11 NIV

. . . . . . . . . . . . . . . . . . . . . . .

David wrote Psalm 56 in a time of great fear, loneliness, and desperation. He had been on the run from Saul, who intended to kill him, and ended up in a place called Gath (see 1 Samuel 21:10–15).

While David no doubt felt the same emotions any man would when his life is in danger, he focused on his conviction that God was with him and for him (Psalm 56:9). This wasn't just David's hope or plea; it was his trust in what God had already said.

In today's world, very few men will ever face the kinds of threats David faced. But that doesn't mean they won't face situations that leave them feeling bewildered, confused, even afraid. But God is bigger than any*thing* or any*one* we could ever fear in this life. And not only that, this all-powerful, all-wise, all-loving God is unwaveringly for those of us He calls His children.

Knowing all this, what do you have to fear?

*Lord, life has a way of bringing fear into my heart at times. Help me to look past my fears and focus fully on Your greatness and Your plans for me.*

## A LOVING, FAITHFUL GOD

*I will praise you, Lord, among the nations; I will sing of*
*you among the peoples. For great is your love, reaching to*
*the heavens; your faithfulness reaches to the skies.*

PSALM 57:9–10 NIV

. . . . . . . . . . . . . . . . . . . . . .

David wrote today's psalm while hiding out in a cave from King Saul, who was intent on killing the young king-to-be. While David in his flawed humanity had reason to feel a sense of hopelessness over his situation, he still gave voice to his faith in the Lord when he wrote, "Have mercy on me, my God, have mercy on me, for in you I take refuge. I will take refuge in the shadow of your wings until the disaster has passed" (Psalm 57:1 NIV).

God called David "a man after his own heart" (see 1 Samuel 13:14, Acts 13:22), and Psalm 57 shows us why. David was far from perfect, but he believed God and clung to His promises—and His heart of love for David—and took refuge in Him, even in times when it seemed things couldn't get any worse.

Follow David's example. Take refuge in God always, especially when you are in a seemingly impossible place of difficulty. And while you're at it, open your mouth and praise His name!

*Loving Father in heaven, no matter how difficult—even*
*hopeless—my life situation may feel, I will choose to dwell in*
*Your love and speak to others of Your love and faithfulness.*

## SHARING THE "GOOD NEWS"

*But the angel said to them, "Do not be afraid. I bring you*
*good news that will cause great joy for all the people."*
LUKE 2:10 NIV

. . . . . . . . . . . . . . . . . . . . . .

One amazing night—the night Jesus our Lord made His arrival on earth—a group of shepherds were tending their sheep not far from the town of Bethlehem. All was quiet. . .until the silence and darkness were broken when "an angel of the Lord appeared to them, and the glory of the Lord shone around them" (Luke 2:9 NIV).

The men were terrified, but the angel quickly calmed their fears and announced, "I bring you good news that will cause great joy for all the people. Today in the town of David a Savior has been born to you; he is the Messiah, the Lord" (Luke 2:10–11 NIV). Then, a host of angels appeared on the scene, proclaiming, "Glory to God in the highest, and on earth peace among those with whom he is pleased!" (Luke 2:14 ESV).

The message of salvation is often called the "Good News," and it is most certainly that. It's good news because Jesus' arrival on earth brings the offer of salvation to the whole world. Always be ready when God gives you a chance to open your heart and share the news!

---

*Lord, the announcement of salvation through Jesus is*
*indeed good news. Please give me courage to speak that*
*news to those who desperately need to hear it.*

# THE SONS OF KORAH

*The earth opened its mouth and swallowed them along with Korah,*
*whose followers died when the fire devoured the 250 men. And they*
*served as a warning sign. The line of Korah, however, did not die out.*

NUMBERS 26:10–11 NIV

· · · · · · · · · · · · · · · · · · · · · · ·

Back in Numbers 16, we read of the terrible account of God's judgment on Korah, Dathan, and Abiram—men who openly rebelled against His appointed leadership. Because of these people's sin, God caused the earth to swallow them and their families. Today's scripture passage, however, tells us that many of the people of Korah did not die out—simply because they did not follow Korah in his rebellion.

Though Korah paid for his sin with his life, God was gracious to his descendants, many of whom went on to serve the Lord as composers, singers, musicians, worship leaders, and prophets. In fact, these noble men wrote most of Psalms 42–49 and most of Psalms 84–88.

The children of Korah serve as an important example to those of us who grew up with fathers—and other family members—who did not serve the Lord. The unbelief or rebellion of one generation doesn't necessarily have to continue on to the next. God does not hold the sin and rebellion against succeeding generations. In Christ, we can start anew.

*Father, thank You for not holding the sins of my*
*ancestors against me. Thank You for looking at men's*
*hearts and not at their family backgrounds.*

## THE IMPORTANCE OF FULL OBEDIENCE

*One day the LORD said to Moses, "Climb one of the mountains east of*
*the river, and look out over the land I have given the people of Israel.*
*After you have seen it, you will die like your brother, Aaron, for you*
*both rebelled against my instructions in the wilderness of Zin."*

NUMBERS 27:12–14 NLT

• • • • • • • • • • • • • • • • • • • • • •

Tragically, Moses wasn't allowed to complete his appointed mission of leading the people of Israel into the Promised Land. That's because, in a moment of frustration, he failed to obey a simple command God had given him.

The Israelites had complained that they were thirsty, so God told Moses to *speak* to a large rock, which would then miraculously send out a stream of water. But instead of speaking to the rock, Moses *struck* the rock with his shepherd's staff—twice.

God still provided the water, but He told Moses, "Because you did not trust in me enough to honor me as holy in the sight of the Israelites, you will not bring this community into the land I give them" (Numbers 20:12 NIV). So instead of entering the Promised Land with his people, Moses died. . .within eyesight of the land God had promised His people (Deuteronomy 34:5).

Obedience to God's commands should be of the utmost importance for the man of God. That's because God blesses those who follow His instructions and finish well for Him.

*Father, may my heart be committed to obeying You fully.*

## ALWAYS KEEP YOUR WORD

*Then Moses summoned the leaders of the tribes of Israel and
told them, "This is what the LORD has commanded: A man who
makes a vow to the LORD or makes a pledge under oath must
never break it. He must do exactly what he said he would do."*

NUMBERS 30:1–2 NLT

. . . . . . . . . . . . . . . . . . . . . .

Jesus once addressed the importance of keeping our word when He said, "Do not swear by your head, for you cannot make even one hair white or black. All you need to say is simply 'Yes' or 'No'; anything beyond this comes from the evil one" (Matthew 5:36–37 NIV).

The scripture passage above strongly affirms the importance of always keeping our word.

We Christian men are called to reflect God in every area of our lives, and that includes always keeping our word, just as He does: "God is not human, that he should lie, not a human being, that he should change his mind. Does he speak and then not act? Does he promise and not fulfill?" (Numbers 23:19 NIV).

Before you make a vow or promise, make sure to carefully consider in your heart whether you are fully committed to keeping it. While God forgives this and any other sin, you put yourself in a dangerous place when you don't follow through on what you have told God you will do.

*Father in heaven, may I always keep my word—to You and to others.*

# A COMMITTED HEART

*And the devil said unto him, All this power will I give thee, and the glory of them: for that is delivered unto me; and to whomsoever I will I give it. If thou therefore wilt worship me, all shall be thine.*

LUKE 4:6–7 KJV

· · · · · · · · · · · · · · · · · · · · · ·

From the time He arrived on earth, Jesus knew His ultimate mission—to live a perfectly sinless life and to die on a wooden cross to pay for our sins. Everything He did and said was with an eye toward glorifying God.

The devil also knew why Jesus came to earth, and that's why he offered three temptations, all of which he cleverly designed to derail God's plan for His Son. But each time the devil tempted Jesus—and make no mistake, these were very real temptations—He answered the devil by quoting the Bible back to him (see Matthew 4:4, 7, 10). When He did that, He showed His commitment to do what His Father in heaven had sent Him to do.

We can and should be grateful that Jesus was so focused on His mission here on earth, that He was so committed to the will of His Father that in everything His heart attitude was "Not my will, but Yours be done."

---

*Jesus, You were unshakably committed to doing the will of Your Father. Help me to remain committed to doing Your will every day.*

## HIDDEN SIN?

*"But if you fail to do this, you will be sinning against the
Lord; and you may be sure that your sin will find you out."*
NUMBERS 32:23 NIV

. . . . . . . . . . . . . . . . . . . . . . .

As the Israelites drew closer to the Promised Land, the tribes of Reuben
and Gad saw an excellent opportunity for themselves in the area south of
the Sea of Galilee, just outside the Promised Land. It was a great area to
raise their families and to farm and keep their livestock. The two tribes
wanted this land, so they approached Moses and made him an offer: if the
men of Reuben and Gad would lead the Israelites in taking the Promised
Land, they could then settle the land they desired.

It was an audacious offer, and Moses accepted it. But he also warned
them that if they didn't hold up their end of the agreement, they would
be sinning against God, and God would know it. . .and they would suffer
consequences.

There are two things we need to remember about sin, the first being
that you can never hide it from God. Moses himself wrote, "You have
set our iniquities before you, our secret sins in the light of your presence"
(Psalm 90:8 NIV). Secondly, sin—whether it's failing to keep your word,
sexual sin, or idolatry—always has consequences.

God takes all sin very seriously—and so should we.

*Lord, keep my heart soft and receptive to Your Word
so that I always remember the seriousness of sin.*

# JESUS IS YOUR REFUGE

*"Speak to the Israelites and say to them: 'When you cross the Jordan into Canaan, select some towns to be your cities of refuge, to which a person who has killed someone accidentally may flee.'"*

NUMBERS 35:10–11 NIV

. . . . . . . . . . . . . . . . . . . . . .

Before the Israelites entered the Promised Land, God instructed Moses to set aside six cities from among the forty-eight cities of the Levites as cities of refuge. The cities of refuge were established so that someone who killed another person accidentally could have a place to live in safety until the case could go to trial. The cities of refuge were Kedesh, Shechem, Hebron, Bezer, Ramoth, and Golan (Joshua 20:7–8).

These cities were a picture of the graciousness of a God who was deeply concerned for the lives of people who had unintentionally committed a crime against a fellow human being. But they were also representative of a believer finding refuge in God Himself.

Psalm 46:1 (NIV) says, "God is our refuge and strength, an ever-present help in trouble," and Hebrews 6:18 (KJV) promises, "We might have a strong consolation, who have fled for refuge to lay hold upon the hope set before us."

Jesus is our Refuge, but we do not need to flee to Him or to any physical place when we need help, for He is present with us every minute of every day.

*Jesus, thank You for being my Refuge when my heart is hurting and I have nowhere else to turn.*

# TOTAL DEPENDENCE

*My salvation and my honor depend on God; he is my*
*mighty rock, my refuge. Trust in him at all times, you people;*
*pour out your hearts to him, for God is our refuge.*
PSALM 62:7–8 NIV

. . . . . . . . . . . . . . . . . . . . . .

Ask the average American male about the origin of the saying "God helps them who help themselves," and there's a decent chance he'll answer, "The Bible!"

Wrong answer!

In scripture passage after scripture passage, God identifies Himself as a loving, gracious heavenly Father who wants to be our sole benefactor for everything we need. He wants us to come to Him with open, empty hands outstretched so that He can fill our hands—and our hearts—with everything He has for us.

God doesn't call any of us to lives of independence or to a mind-set of rugged individualism. Instead, He wants us to be completely dependent upon Him for everything, starting with our salvation and moving all the way down the list of things He wants to do and provide for us.

*Gracious heavenly Father, may I never believe that You call me to a mind-set of self-sufficiency. Rather, remind me daily that You want me to be 100 percent dependent upon You for everything I need.*

## PRECIOUS, BLESSED MEMORIES

*"But watch out! Be careful never to forget what you yourself have seen.*
*Do not let these memories escape from your mind as long as you live!*
*And be sure to pass them on to your children and grandchildren."*
DEUTERONOMY 4:9 NLT

. . . . . . . . . . . . . . . . . . . . . .

We humans tend to treasure certain types of memories, including weddings, the births of children, graduations. . .the list goes on and on. Opening up scrapbooks, viewing vacation videos, or just talking and recounting pleasant memories from the past are wonderful ways to spend an evening at home, and they can certainly strengthen family bonds.

It's good to do the same thing with your Father in heaven. In several passages of scripture (including the verse above), God encourages His people to remember the amazing things He has done for them in the past.

So take the time to remember God's goodness to you in the past. Think about the moment He saved you and made you part of His eternal family—and about how He's helped you to grow into the man of God you are today. Remember the times He helped you out of a terrible jam or gave you wisdom about a certain situation. And consider those amazing instances when it was obvious that He had moved on your behalf as a direct result of prayer.

---

*Father, help me to remember Your goodness to me so that my*
*faith in and love for You may remain strong and growing.*

# BE MERCIFUL

*"Be merciful, just as your Father is merciful."*
LUKE 6:36 NIV

. . . . . . . . . . . . . . . . . . . . .

If we're honest with ourselves, many of us would have to admit that Jesus' command in the above scripture verse isn't the easiest one to obey consistently. When we're carelessly cut off in traffic, when someone insults or belittles us, when the boss treats us unfairly, when. . .well, when these kinds of things happen to us, mercy and forgiveness aren't usually the first things that come to mind.

Mercy is a huge deal to God, so big that He sent His Son to die so that He could pour out mercy on us, so big that He commands us over and over in scripture to show mercy to others, even when they don't deserve it. . .*especially* when they don't deserve it!

The bottom line is that when we show mercy, especially when it's not deserved, we demonstrate a heart of obedience to the Lord, we do our part to be at peace with others, and we show gratitude to the God who forgives and showers us with mercy, freely and willingly, whenever we mess up.

*Father, thank You for being merciful to me. On my own,
I can't be as merciful to others as You call me to be.
Strengthen me and soften my heart so that I can obey Jesus'
call for me to be merciful, just as You are merciful.*

## THE MOST IMPORTANT COMMANDMENT

*Hear, O Israel: The Lord our God is one Lord: And
thou shalt love the Lord thy God with all thine heart,
and with all thy soul, and with all thy might.*

Deuteronomy 6:4–5 kjv

• • • • • • • • • • • • • • • • • • • • •

One day during Jesus' earthly ministry, a Jewish religious authority
asked Him a very important question: "Teacher, which is the greatest
commandment in the Law?" Jesus' response was a word-for-word quote of
today's scripture passage, and it still applies to us today: " 'Love the Lord
your God with all your heart and with all your soul and with all your mind.'
This is the first and greatest commandment" (Matthew 22:37–38 niv).

This commandment is the first and greatest for one simple reason:
if you love God with everything that is within you, obedience will be the
natural result. If you love God, you'll have no other gods beside Him. If you
love God, you won't engage in idolatry. If you love God, you'll make sure
you never misuse His name. If you love God. . .well, you get the picture.

Jesus once said to His followers, "If you love me, keep my commands"
(John 14:15 niv). Love is at the center of your relationship with God—
His love for you, which motivated Him to willingly go to the cross, and
your love for Him, which motivates you to willingly and joyfully do
everything He calls you to do.

*Lord, help me to love You with everything I am and everything I have.*

# GIVE GOD CREDIT

*You may say to yourself, "My power and the strength of my hands
have produced this wealth for me." But remember the LORD your
God, for it is he who gives you the ability to produce wealth, and so
confirms his covenant, which he swore to your ancestors, as it is today.*

DEUTERONOMY 8:17–18 NIV

. . . . . . . . . . . . . . . . . . . . . . .

While roaming in the desert, the people of Israel had every reason to rely
on God for their food, water, and safety. However, the scripture passage
above suggests that the wealth and bountiful harvests they dreamed about
had the potential to lead them to forgot about God.

You may also have a sense of your need for God in a time of struggle,
uncertainty, or fear. It's easy to pray and to depend on God when you feel
like life is beyond your control. Yet financial security and prosperity can
change your heart's priorities. Suddenly, there's an illusion that everything
you needed God to provide can come directly from your bank account.

Guard your mind from relying on your own resources and taking
the credit for the provision that only God deserves. Remember when
you've been in need and how God has been faithful to you so that you
never think too highly of yourself.

---

*Father, You have graciously provided what I need and cared
for me in seasons of struggle and uncertainty. Help me to
keep Your care and provision at the front of my mind.*

# HARDSHIPS ARE VALUABLE MEMORIES

*He defends the cause of the fatherless and the widow, and
loves the foreigner residing among you, giving them food
and clothing. And you are to love those who are foreigners,
for you yourselves were foreigners in Egypt.*

DEUTERONOMY 10:18–19 NIV

. . . . . . . . . . . . . . . . . . . . . .

The memory of the Israelites' past as slaves in Egypt was traumatic, humiliating, and painful. Who could blame them for leaving those painful memories behind?

Although the Lord took great pity on Israel's pain and suffering while they were in slavery, He also wanted the Israelites to use that pain to help them look on foreigners in their own land with compassion. When they remembered what it was like to live at the mercy of a foreign people or to depend on those who had plenty, they were far more likely to care for the most vulnerable members of their society: the widows, the fatherless, and the foreigners.

Your own pain is worth remembering and thinking about both because God desires to heal it and because He can change your heart toward others. Just as Jesus identified with humanity during His passion on the cross, you will identify with others when you remember how you felt at your most hopeless and most vulnerable moments. It may end up that you can be the answer to someone else's prayers.

---

*Lord, heal the pain of my past and give me a heart of
compassion and mercy to those who need them most.*

# WHAT BLOCKS LIFE?

*"The seeds that fell among the thorns represent those who hear
the message, but all too quickly the message is crowded out
by the cares and riches and pleasures of this life. And so they
never grow into maturity. And the seeds that fell on the good
soil represent honest, good-hearted people who hear God's
word, cling to it, and patiently produce a huge harvest."*

LUKE 8:14–15 NLT

. . . . . . . . . . . . . . . . . . . . . . . .

Jesus wanted His followers to know that they couldn't expect His message
to do any good in their lives if they didn't cling to it and prioritize it.
The simple knowledge of His message could be undermined by the
cares of this life and the distractions of wealth and pleasure. Growth and
fruitfulness, which brought benefits to themselves and to others, were
far from a guarantee.

Following Jesus is like tending a garden that requires planning,
watering, and weeding if you want to see any kind of life and growth. Just
planting seeds of scripture verses and leaving them to fend for themselves
in your heart is a sure way to be disappointed. The words of Jesus will be
most transformative and productive if you can make space for them and
cling to them. Beware of distractions and misplaced priorities.

*Jesus, help me to resist the temptations of this life that
would draw me away from abiding in You and from
nurturing the life-giving words You have given to me.*

## HAVE YOU SEEN WHAT GOD HAS DONE?

*Come and see what God has done: he is awesome in his deeds*
*toward the children of man. He turned the sea into dry land;*
*they passed through the river on foot. There did we rejoice in*
*him, who rules by his might forever, whose eyes keep watch*
*on the nations—let not the rebellious exalt themselves.*

PSALM 66:5–7 ESV

Perhaps one of the greatest challenges to living by faith is ignorance of what God has already done for others. The people of Israel were often reminded of God's past deeds and powerful deliverance so that they wouldn't turn to other gods or other sources of comfort. Monuments, feast days, stories, and the writings of scripture were a few of the ways the people kept the past actions of God on their minds.

You can read what God has done in scripture and also remember what God has done for you and for others. Once you see the mercy of God and His desire to be present for those who call out in faith, you'll meet the highs and lows of life with thoughts of God's past power. In your heart you can trust that God will be with you just as He has been with the faithful in past generations.

*Lord, help me to remember the ways You've remained close to*
*Your people and saved them from their trials and hardships.*

# OBEYING GOD ISN'T AN ACCIDENT

*When he takes the throne of his kingdom, he is to write for himself
on a scroll a copy of this law, taken from that of the Levitical
priests. It is to be with him, and he is to read it all the days of
his life so that he may learn to revere the LORD his God and
follow carefully all the words of this law and these decrees.*

DEUTERONOMY 17:18–19 NIV

. . . . . . . . . . . . . . . . . . . . . . .

How can you best prepare yourself to obey God and to live a holy life?
When Moses charted the course for the rulers of God's people after
leading them out of slavery in Egypt, he required them to have a copy
of God's teachings and laws on hand to read them often. That's because
our minds can be distracted, misdirected, and disobedient when left on
their own without a daily reminder of God's teachings.

The Passover festival also serves as a kind of acted-out reminder of
what God has done for His people. The Lord told Moses to institute
this annual festival so that they wouldn't place their trust in their own
wisdom and power.

Thankfully, you don't have to make your own copy of God's Word!
You need only take it with you each day and set aside time to renew your
heart and mind in the ways of God.

---

*Help me, Lord, to depend on You and to submit
my thoughts to Your love and guidance.*

## WHAT DO YOU CHERISH?

*If I had cherished iniquity in my heart, the Lord would not
have listened. But truly God has listened; he has attended
to the voice of my prayer. Blessed be God, because he has not
rejected my prayer or removed his steadfast love from me!*

PSALM 66:18–20 ESV

. . . . . . . . . . . . . . . . . . . . .

The Bible frequently describes the ways in which you reap what you sow.
The Psalms expand on this idea by linking God's attentiveness to your
prayers to what you cherish in your heart. If you resist God and hold on
to things He finds destructive or wrong, you can expect to find yourself
wondering why He isn't paying attention to your prayers.

However, that isn't to say that a moment of prayer that feels frustrating
or distant from God is inevitably linked with holding on to sinful desires.
The Psalms also mention plenty of desperate pleas for God to pay attention
and to hear one's prayers.

God cannot reject His own children or withdraw His love from
them, but persistence and patience may be required in prayer. Psalm 66
may be most useful as a kind of checklist for moments of difficulty in
prayer. If your mind and your heart are devoted to God, then you need
only hold fast and wait on the Lord.

*Help me, Lord, to assess my thoughts and desires so
that I can pray to You in peace and confidence.*

# SURRENDERING BRINGS FREEDOM

*"If you try to hang on to your life, you will lose it. But if you give*
*up your life for my sake, you will save it. And what do you benefit*
*if you gain the whole world but are yourself lost or destroyed?"*

Luke 9:24–25 nlt

. . . . . . . . . . . . . . . . . . . . . .

Jesus faced the choice between self-preservation and self-sacrifice for
the benefit of others. He saw the darkness of death and the pain that
He had to endure on the cross, but He still chose to surrender Himself
to God's will and to seek the blessings of others above His own benefit.
His resurrection and new life brought about the greatest gain possible
for you. When He asks you to stop hanging on to your life and to even
surrender it to God, He knows both how daunting it can seem—and
how much promise and possibility await you.

Jesus' reasoning is clear and sensible, even if it's still hard to accept.
You cannot hold on to your life. Whatever you do to protect it will
ultimately fail. True freedom is found in surrendering your life to God
and then trusting Him with your whole heart to determine what will
happen in the future. Letting go of your own life places it in the safest
place possible—entrusted to God.

---

*Jesus, help me to surrender my life to Your care as I remember*
*Your suffering and sacrifice for my benefit today.*

## SHARE YOUR ABUNDANCE

*When you beat the olives from your trees, do not go over the branches a second time. Leave what remains for the foreigner, the fatherless and the widow. When you harvest the grapes in your vineyard, do not go over the vines again. Leave what remains for the foreigner, the fatherless and the widow. Remember that you were slaves in Egypt. That is why I command you to do this.*

DEUTERONOMY 24:20–22 NIV

. . . . . . . . . . . . . . . . . . . . . .

Everything you have is a blessing from God, a sign of His willingness to meet your needs. Yet there may be moments of suffering, loss, or struggle in your life. Perhaps you've already endured times of need. Those moments of having less can help you remember that your season of abundance may be someone else's time of misfortune and offer you an opportunity to generously share what you have.

The pain of Israel's past as slaves was surely excruciating and worth forgetting, but the Lord wanted that past pain to be in their thoughts and hearts to prompt future generosity. By remembering their hunger, uncertainty, fear, and suffering, they grew in compassion for others. Rather than greedily amassing a harvest that went beyond what they needed at the moment, God wanted them to think of ways to provide for the vulnerable and poor.

*Thank You, Lord, for the ways You've provided for me.
Help me to share Your blessings generously with others.*

## CALLED TO HARVEST

*These were his instructions to them: "The harvest is great, but*
*the workers are few. So pray to the Lord who is in charge of the*
*harvest; ask him to send more workers into his fields. Now go, and*
*remember that I am sending you out as lambs among wolves."*

LUKE 10:2–3 NLT

. . . . . . . . . . . . . . . . . . . . . . .

When you compare the amount of work involved in preparing a field for planting and sowing seeds versus gathering the harvest, there is no doubt that gathering is the easier, far more certain task. The ground has been plowed, fertilized, watered, and tended for months. To benefit from the preparation and planting, a laborer only needs to show up and harvest what has already been started in the ground. But without the laborers needed to gather the crops, the hard work of fertilizing, plowing, and sowing will all go to waste.

With His death and resurrection, Jesus brought new life and unity with God to the world. You have been entrusted with this incredible message of hope, and it has already been at work in so many hearts all around you. As you celebrate the victory of Jesus' death and resurrection, ask God how you can go out into the "fields" around you to gather the harvest that has already been prepared.

*Jesus, help me to see the ways I can bring Your new life to others.*

# BEWARE THE PROSPERITY TRAP

*All these curses will come on you. They will pursue you and overtake you
until you are destroyed, because you did not obey the LORD your God
and observe the commands and decrees he gave you. They will be a sign
and a wonder to you and your descendants forever. Because you did not
serve the LORD your God joyfully and gladly in the time of prosperity.*

DEUTERONOMY 28:45–47 NIV

· · · · · · · · · · · · · · · · · · · · · ·

God had called the people of Israel to be a sign to all nations of the power
and glory of the Lord. If they abandoned that sacred mission to live in
obedience to and fellowship with God, their future would darken. The
greatest threat to their future was, in fact, their prosperity, which could
cause them to forget their need for God.

You or someone you know may be praying for God's provision right
now, and while such prayers are encouraged and modeled throughout
the Bible, there is a dark side. As you depend on God for your provision,
comfort and prosperity can result in depending on your own resources
and wisdom. You can lose sight of your need for God and depend on
your own wisdom or follow your own priorities. Wealth isn't necessarily
a blessing unless you continue to joyfully serve God.

---

*Lord, help me to joyfully serve You in faith and hope
without being distracted by what I have.*

# WHAT DO YOU EXPECT FROM GOD?

*"You fathers—if your children ask for a fish, do you give them
a snake instead? Or if they ask for an egg, do you give them
a scorpion? Of course not! So if you sinful people know how
to give good gifts to your children, how much more will your
heavenly Father give the Holy Spirit to those who ask him."*

LUKE 11:11–13 NLT

. . . . . . . . . . . . . . . . . . . . . . .

Jesus wants His followers to consider what they're imagining when
they pray to God. Imagining an angry God or an uncaring judge could
undermine their faith. Jesus chose the most compassionate and caring
image possible: a father who cares for his children, listens to their requests,
and provides what they need.

What do you imagine God is like when you pray? It's possible that
your past relationships or past experiences in prayer have clouded that
image of God's loving care for you. Jesus is asking you to take His words to
heart when you pray and to trust that God can meet your needs even today.

Take note that Jesus mentioned the children were asking for a
reasonable need, such as fish or an egg, and so the type of request can also
matter when praying. Live by faith and trust that God is a good Father,
but don't lose touch with your "daily bread" needs.

*Thank You, Jesus, for revealing the love of the
Father so that I can pray in confidence.*

# HEARING GOD'S WORD
# LEADS TO OBEDIENCE

*Assemble the people—men, women and children, and the*
*foreigners residing in your towns—so they can listen and*
*learn to fear the LORD your God and follow carefully all the*
*words of this law. Their children, who do not know this law,*
*must hear it and learn to fear the LORD your God as long as*
*you live in the land you are crossing the Jordan to possess."*

DEUTERONOMY 31:12–13 NIV

. . . . . . . . . . . . . . . . . . . . . . .

The people of Israel were in real danger of forgetting about the Lord and the commands passed on to them. The only way to remain faithful to God for generations to come was to set aside time for all the people, especially children and foreigners, to listen to God's law, to remember His mercy, and to consider the consequences of ignoring it.

Your moments reflecting on scripture are a vital part of God's work in your life. Through the scriptures you read, you'll learn about your weaknesses, about God's power, and about how He can deliver you from temptations and struggles. Obedience won't come automatically through simply hearing God's Word, but without His guidance in your life, you'll soon find yourself drifting off course. Like a wise man building a house on the rock, hearing and doing God's Word leads to life and spiritual security.

*Help me to slow down and ponder Your Word today,*
*Lord, so that I can remain faithful to You.*

# YOUR OBEDIENCE BLESSES OTHERS

*O God, you know my folly; the wrongs I have done are not*
*hidden from you. Let not those who hope in you be put to*
*shame through me, O Lord GOD of hosts; let not those who seek*
*you be brought to dishonor through me, O God of Israel.*

PSALM 69:5–6 ESV

. . . . . . . . . . . . . . . . . . . . . .

The choices you make today can either harm or benefit those who place their hope in God. Just as your failures or self-serving decisions may make it easier for some to fall away from God, your obedience and faithfulness will inspire others to draw near to Him. Psalm 69 brings to mind the image of the body of Christ, where each person is joined to the others and bears a responsibility for the benefit of others.

The Lord is well aware of your follies and wrongs, and yet there remains an offer of grace and mercy for you. God has not cast you away but has sent Jesus to restore you. God's honor and glory are preserved through grace and mercy, through the offer to give you a chance to live by faith the life Jesus offered those whose hearts are committed to Him.

*Lord, help me to see the ways my actions can benefit others so*
*that I can live my life to bless them and to draw glory and honor*
*to You. Give me a heart of obedience and commitment to You.*

# HOW CAN GOD'S LOVE CHANGE YOU?

*"What is the price of five sparrows—two copper coins? Yet
God does not forget a single one of them. And the very hairs
on your head are all numbered. So don't be afraid; you are
more valuable to God than a whole flock of sparrows."*

LUKE 12:6–7 NLT

. . . . . . . . . . . . . . . . . . . . . . .

At the foundation of all God's creation is the loving care of a Maker
who delights in every creature on earth. Even the most common birds,
hardly worth noticing to humans, are kept in God's loving care. If you
can hold in your heart an image of the care of God for the most ordinary,
unspectacular birds, then consider how deeply He cares for you and the
people around you.

If every bird is held in God's loving gaze, then He surely loves every
person as well. How would you pray differently today if you could fathom
even a small part of God's love for you? And beyond changing your
prayers, you can also uncover a greater depth of love and compassion for
the people around you as creations God also loves. If you are able to receive
God's love today, then surely you can also share that love with everyone
else in your circles who may not realize how deeply He cares for them.

*Jesus, help me to remember Your Father's love for me. May I
share that abundant love with those around me today.*

# FAITHFULNESS DOESN'T GUARANTEE EASY LIVING

*You know my reproach, and my shame and my dishonor; my foes are all known to you. Reproaches have broken my heart, so that I am in despair. I looked for pity, but there was none, and for comforters, but I found none. They gave me poison for food, and for my thirst they gave me sour wine to drink.*

PSALM 69:19–21 ESV

. . . . . . . . . . . . . . . . . . . . . . .

Psalm 69 documents a heartbreaking list of mentally and physically oppressive forms of adversity. While it may be tempting to suggest that the writer of this psalm believed God had forgotten him, God had not forgotten this afflicted person or the specific details of his suffering. How could God's knowledge of our suffering help us if God isn't doing anything about it?

The psalmists aren't shy about documenting the suffering of God's faithful people, which means there's no simple connection between circumstances and blessing. Sometimes the righteous enjoy prosperity, and sometimes the wicked thrive while God's people wilt. Yet God always remains with the faithful, and He will most assuredly make things right one day.

The problem for us is in the *waiting* for God to make things right, which may happen tomorrow or far away in the future. There's no definite timeline for God to act. However, He has promised to be with us in the midst of our suffering that we will one day enjoy the restoration, peace, and justice our hearts desire.

*Lord, help me to wait patiently for Your justice and restoration.*

---

# HAVE YOU GIVEN GOD CREDIT?

*"Go, consecrate the people. Tell them, 'Consecrate yourselves in
preparation for tomorrow; for this is what the LORD, the God
of Israel, says: There are devoted things among you, Israel. You
cannot stand against your enemies until you remove them.' "*

JOSHUA 7:13 NIV

. . . . . . . . . . . . . . . . . . . . . . .

The people of Israel were banned from plundering the city of Jericho
because the battle had been won by the Lord. They primarily benefited
from God's victory, and they were told to recognize the Lord as the victor
rather than enjoying the plunder—as if they had won the battle on their
own. After wandering in the wilderness, it surely was tempting to pick
up a few small valuables from the ruins of Jericho. Yet if they hoped to
live by faith in God's protection and provision, then they had to live by
faith in God, obeying His commands and relying on His deliverance.

Whatever you're facing today, you have an opportunity to rely more
perfectly on God's provision and power. If your heart is consumed with
looking for ways to provide for yourself, you're going to miss the comfort
and direction God wants to provide. Rather than looking through the
ruins for what you can get for yourself, give thanks for God's provision in
your life, and look ahead to the ways He can carry you in the days ahead.

---

*Thank You, Lord, for protecting and providing for Your people.
Help me to look to You alone for protection and provision.*

# ARE YOU PREPARED TO WAIT FOR GOD?

*May all who seek you rejoice and be glad in you! May*
*those who love your salvation say evermore, "God is great!"*
*But I am poor and needy; hasten to me, O God! You are*
*my help and my deliverer; O LORD, do not delay!*

PSALM 70:4–5 ESV

. . . . . . . . . . . . . . . . . . . . . . .

God's love and provision for His people don't mean we won't have to endure seasons of uncertainty, darkness, and waiting. Patience and uncertainty are both vitally important parts of the life of faith. Although the hopes of the writer of the scripture passage above for God's speedy response are a very normal and natural response even today, God's timetable isn't always going to line up with our own. In fact, it rarely will.

An earnest, honest prayer that pleads with God may be the best prayer you can offer during difficult circumstances. Many of the psalms make urgent requests of God or ask tough questions.

Waiting patiently can test your faith, and there's a lot you may not know about what's going to happen next. Yet you can rest assured of God's love for you and of the fact that such waiting is a normal part of the life of faith.

*Lord, help me cling to You as I wait for*
*Your response to my most urgent needs.*

# COMPASSION IS MORE IMPORTANT TO GOD

*But the Lord replied, "You hypocrites! Each of you works on the Sabbath day! Don't you untie your ox or your donkey from its stall on the Sabbath and lead it out for water? This dear woman, a daughter of Abraham, has been held in bondage by Satan for eighteen years. Isn't it right that she be released, even on the Sabbath?"*

LUKE 13:15–16 NLT

. . . . . . . . . . . . . . . . . . . . . . .

The religious teachers during Jesus' earthly ministry were ready to condemn the Sabbath healing of a woman afflicted by years of suffering. Jesus quickly pointed out what matters more to God: compassion for others rather than strict observance of religious laws.

Jesus offers you a chance to consider what kind of God you serve. Do you see Him as compassionate and dialed in to your suffering and struggles, or do you see Him as strict and uncaring? The kind of God you picture will determine what you value.

Jesus also offers you a chance to review how you look at others. Do you seek ways to disqualify others, or do you seek ways to show compassion? If you want to find an out that relieves you of caring for someone, you can always find something. Choose compassion, the kind of compassion that comes from a heart of love for God and for others.

*Jesus, help me to see others with the same compassion and mercy You show to me.*

# MEMORY OVERCOMES DOUBT

*But I will hope continually and will praise you yet more
and more. My mouth will tell of your righteous acts, of your
deeds of salvation all the day, for their number is past my
knowledge. With the mighty deeds of the Lord GOD I will
come; I will remind them of your righteousness, yours alone.*

PSALM 71:14–16 ESV

. . . . . . . . . . . . . . . . . . . . . . . .

During difficult times, it can be easy to doubt God's care or power to
provide for you. You may know of the prosperity gospel, which goes so far
as to say that hardship means God is withholding blessing from you on
purpose. Yet the writer of Psalm 71 shows himself willing to go against
the doubt of his time and the seeming hopelessness of his circumstances.
He knows that God hasn't abandoned him and that he can even resolve
to remind others of His past actions.

When facing doubts and fearful circumstances, God's people can
find hope in His past provision and care. By recounting what the Lord
has done in the past, we can see how He supported us and others when
we were besieged by doubts and adversity. What you remember about
God will influence what you believe God can do in the future.

*Father, help me to remember Your past care and provision so that I
can meet the darkest moments of life with a heart of hope and faith.*

## DO YOU BELIEVE GOD SEES YOU?

*"Instead, take the lowest place at the foot of the table. Then
when your host sees you, he will come and say, 'Friend, we
have a better place for you!' Then you will be honored in front
of all the other guests. For those who exalt themselves will be
humbled, and those who humble themselves will be exalted."*

LUKE 14:10–11 NLT

. . . . . . . . . . . . . . . . . . . . . .

Jesus is looking for people who aren't seeking greatness but who are willing
to serve others with a humble heart. Exalting yourself is a sure way to
become alienated from God. The moment you think you're worthy of a
higher place, you can't serve others and cannot submit to God's direction.
By seeking your own advancement, you'll become consumed with how
others can support your greatness. You can even turn spiritual practices
into a kind of manipulation of God.

Taking the lower seat means that you'll need to watch others push
themselves to the front. You need to have faith that God will notice you
for the right things and at the right time. You'll likely have to be content
with obscurity while others pile up accolades. Yet when God recognizes
your humility and service to others, no one can take away your position.
You won't have to battle insecurity because you are assured in your heart
to receive a position from God.

*Jesus, help me to trust that You see me and that my
faith and hope in You will one day be rewarded.*

# WHAT HOLDS YOU BACK FROM JESUS?

*"But don't begin until you count the cost. For who would begin construction of a building without first calculating the cost to see if there is enough money to finish it? Otherwise, you might complete only the foundation before running out of money, and then everyone would laugh at you."*

LUKE 14:28–29 NLT

. . . . . . . . . . . . . . . . . . . . . . .

Throughout the Gospels, people had to choose between their attachments to work, comfort, or an inheritance *or* the opportunity to follow Jesus. The choice you face today may appear different from that of Jesus' disciples, who lived in a very different time—when many were farmers, fishermen, or laborers. Yet you face the same challenge: to count the cost of following Jesus and discerning what you're attached to when considering the cost of following Him.

Rather than jumping in to follow Jesus with energy and enthusiasm that will wane over time, Jesus urges you to count the cost with sober patience. Consider that devoting your life to God's purposes will require you to make sacrifices, to measure success in different ways from others, and to miss out on the pleasure and ease that others enjoy. Yet there is a promise of life and peace with Jesus if you're willing to count the cost and follow Him wholeheartedly.

*Jesus, help me to see what gets in the way of following You so that my heart can remain fully committed to You and Your way.*

# PRAYERS FOR RULERS ARE PRAYERS FOR OTHERS

*Give the king your justice, O God, and your righteousness to the royal son! May he judge your people with righteousness, and your poor with justice! Let the mountains bear prosperity for the people, and the hills, in righteousness! May he defend the cause of the poor of the people, give deliverance to the children of the needy, and crush the oppressor!*

PSALM 72:1–4 ESV

. . . . . . . . . . . . . . . . . . . . . .

The writer of Psalm 72 recognized that a just and righteous ruler would bring benefit to everyone in the land, especially the most vulnerable. In fact, he states that the mark of a good ruler is protection of the poor and vulnerable children—those most in need of a champion to look out for them. A ruler committed to doing what's right and caring for the people who can't defend themselves will also lead people toward prosperity and peace.

Beyond your own peace and prosperity, your prayers for those in government will bring benefits to the most vulnerable today. The decisions from the lowest to the highest levels of government will have the greatest impact on those who have the fewest resources on hand. Government fails the majority of its people when laws and court rulings favor the wealthiest and most powerful, and that is why your prayers for just rulers matter so much. The peace and well-being of many hang in the balance.

---

*Lord, grant my government leaders both the wisdom and righteousness to serve all people with fairness and equality.*

# PAST OBEDIENCE DOESN'T GUARANTEE FAITHFULNESS

*"Now that the Lord your God has given them rest as he promised,*
*return to your homes in the land that Moses the servant of the*
*Lord gave you on the other side of the Jordan. But be very careful*
*to keep the commandment and the law that Moses the servant*
*of the Lord gave you: to love the Lord your God, to walk in*
*obedience to him, to keep his commands, to hold fast to him and*
*to serve him with all your heart and with all your soul."*

JOSHUA 22:4–5 NIV

· · · · · · · · · · · · · · · · · · · · · · ·

The Israelite tribes on the eastern side of the Jordan River had put their lives and the security of their families on the line by crossing to the western shore with the other tribes. Yet, as they returned home, they were still reminded to obey God's commands, to follow the law, and to love the Lord.

While past events can serve as inspiration or assurance for the future, each day you can choose between obeying God's commands and receiving God's love, or seeking your comfort and direction somewhere else. Even after you've been recognized for your faith and selflessness, a few selfish choices can send you off course. Your obedience matters a great deal today, and if you have started to veer off course, remember to return to God as quickly as possible.

*Lord, help me to return to Your love and mercy*
*so that I can obey Your commands.*

## WHAT ARE YOU HOLDING ON TO?

*"Be very strong; be careful to obey all that is written in the Book of the Law of Moses, without turning aside to the right or to the left. Do not associate with these nations that remain among you; do not invoke the names of their gods or swear by them. You must not serve them or bow down to them. But you are to hold fast to the LORD your God, as you have until now."*

JOSHUA 23:6–8 NIV

. . . . . . . . . . . . . . . . . . . . . .

When life is thrown into turmoil or uncertainty, you'll need to hold on to something for support and stability. The question is whether you will choose to hold on to the right thing when life feels out of control or all appears lost. The little decisions and choices you make each day have a way of adding up and showing their true value under such circumstances.

Just as the people of Israel faced the temptation to rely on the gods of neighboring peoples, you may be tempted to place your trust in your wealth, influence, planning, or accomplishments to carry you through the challenges of life. Joshua reminds you that compromise will be disastrous and will fail to deliver the security you desire. The alternative is to cling to the Lord, depending on Him daily for your provision, comfort, and stability. This habit of living by faith daily will help you remain faithful, even when all appears lost.

*Help me, Lord, to live with a consistent heart commitment to You, placing my full faith and trust in You alone.*

# FINDING CONTENTMENT
# IN SERVING GOD

*"When a servant comes in from plowing or taking care of sheep, does his master say, 'Come in and eat with me'? No, he says, 'Prepare my meal, put on your apron, and serve me while I eat. Then you can eat later.' And does the master thank the servant for doing what he was told to do? Of course not."*

LUKE 17:7–9 NLT

. . . . . . . . . . . . . . . . . . . . . .

While teaching His disciples about faith, sin, and obedience, Jesus summed up His discourse with a simple example of a servant knowing his place in the household. A servant takes care of his assigned work, ensures that his master has been cared for, and then addresses his own needs. By the same token, Jesus wants His disciples to see themselves realistically, not placing their own desires and needs over the work God has called them to do.

You may seek to increase your faith in God today, and perhaps the best way to do that is to see yourself first and foremost as His servant. Ask God what He has called you to do, and then diligently work at it. While doing God's work, you'll find the provision you need, and you'll also find contentment. Rather than giving in to your desires to increase your place in life, you can find contentment and peace in your place as God's servant under God's care.

*Jesus, help me to see myself as Your humble servant.*

## RECEIVING GOD'S MERCY

*I was brutish and ignorant; I was like a beast toward you.*
*Nevertheless, I am continually with you; you hold my right hand.*
*You guide me with your counsel, and afterward you will receive*
*me to glory. Whom have I in heaven but you? And there is nothing*
*on earth that I desire besides you. My flesh and my heart may fail,*
*but God is the strength of my heart and my portion forever.*
PSALM 73:22–26 ESV

· · · · · · · · · · · · · · · · · · · · · ·

The writer of Psalm 73 recognized his sin before God, and that helped him to better appreciate the Lord's mercy and kindness. He saw that God had remained with him, forgiving his sins and restoring him. God's presence wasn't diminished by his failures, and receiving that kind of mercy increased his dependence on God and his gratitude.

No matter how far you have fallen, or how hopeless you feel, or how distant from God you may feel, today's psalm reminds you that God's goal and desire for you is restoration. Even when you feel fearful and discouraged, God will provide the encouragement and stability you need—if you will only place your trust in His never-ending presence and unfailing mercy. Begin today by assessing the state of your heart before God, who can restore you no matter how brutish or ignorant you have been.

*Thank You, Lord, for Your mercy and forgiveness.*
*May I lean on You throughout today to support me.*

# GOD DOESN'T WAIT
# FOR PERFECT PEOPLE

*"Pardon me, my lord," Gideon replied, "but if the LORD is
with us, why has all this happened to us? Where are all his
wonders that our ancestors told us about when they said, 'Did
not the LORD bring us up out of Egypt?' But now the LORD
has abandoned us and given us into the hand of Midian." The
LORD turned to him and said, "Go in the strength you have and
save Israel out of Midian's hand. Am I not sending you?"*

JUDGES 6:13–14 NIV

. . . . . . . . . . . . . . . . . . . . . . .

Gideon was hardly the perfect example of living by faith. In fact, he
made a direct accusation against God, claiming that He had not saved
the people of Israel from their enemies as in times past. Although their
own sins were the cause of their calamity, the Lord didn't hold his line
of questioning against him. Rather, He sent this imperfect man to
accomplish His mission.

You may have a strong sense of your own inadequacy, or you may
be openly questioning God's wisdom right now. Yet God can meet you
in your honesty and struggles. If you remain open to doing God's will,
you don't have to be a model of living by faith. You need only obey what
God asks you to do. Much like Gideon, God can send you in the limited
strength you have and still accomplish things beyond your imagination.

*Help me, Lord, to have a humble, hopeful heart before You.*

# WHAT YOU GAIN IS BETTER THAN WHAT YOU LOSE

*Peter said, "We've left our homes to follow you." "Yes," Jesus replied, "and I assure you that everyone who has given up house or wife or brothers or parents or children, for the sake of the Kingdom of God, will be repaid many times over in this life, and will have eternal life in the world to come."*

LUKE 18:28–30 NLT

. . . . . . . . . . . . . . . . . . . . . .

In counting the cost of following Jesus, His disciples could have focused only on what they stood to lose in terms of income, reputation, and proximity to their family. Losing one of those things would be difficult, but they risked losing all three at the same time. Yet they had faith that what they gained with Jesus could be much better.

Jesus assures you today that what you give up for His sake will pale in comparison to the community and new life you'll find among God's people and in the presence of the Lord. You stand to gain a peace today that no one can take away from you and a security for eternal life that is assured by the Holy Spirit. It's true that you will lose things others who resist Jesus' call will maintain, but when all is said and done, you will find yourself with greater peace and security.

*Jesus, help me to look to You in faith and trust as I count the cost of following You today.*

# DON'T DEPEND ON OTHERS FOR YOUR FAITH

*No sooner had Gideon died than the Israelites again prostituted themselves to the Baals. They set up Baal-Berith as their god and did not remember the LORD their God, who had rescued them from the hands of all their enemies on every side. They also failed to show any loyalty to the family of Jerub-Baal (that is, Gideon) in spite of all the good things he had done for them.*

JUDGES 8:33–35 NIV

. . . . . . . . . . . . . . . . . . . . . .

The people of Israel depended heavily on the faith and leadership of Gideon to carry them through the hardships they faced. But when Gideon passed away, it seemed like their faith died as well.

It's impossible to support your faith through someone else. There must be a personal commitment in your heart to God that goes beyond what the crowd or a leader does.

Each choice you make today is an opportunity to take ownership of your faith and to decide where your allegiance remains. A supportive leader or Christian community can be extremely helpful in providing direction and encouragement, but you also need to decide whether you're going to trust in God with all your heart, mind, soul, and strength. No one else can make that commitment for you, and the more you rely on others, the more likely you'll give up when adversity hits or your relationships change.

*Lord, help me to rest fully in You, entrusting myself to Your care today and doing Your will.*

# MAKE YOUR NEEDS KNOWN TO GOD

*Have regard for the covenant, for the dark places of the land are
full of the habitations of violence. Let not the downtrodden turn
back in shame; let the poor and needy praise your name. Arise,
O God, defend your cause; remember how the foolish scoff at you
all the day! Do not forget the clamor of your foes, the uproar
of those who rise against you, which goes up continually!*

PSALM 74:20–23 ESV

. . . . . . . . . . . . . . . . . . . . .

The people of Israel knew that there would be conflict and evil. There
were people living in poverty and others dealing with injustice and
mistreatment. Yet God expected them to make their plight known.
While those opposed to God sent up an uproar of rebellion, the poor
and exploited were expected to lift up their voices for God's intervention
and justice. In fact, there's an expectation that God will remember His
covenant and act on behalf of those suffering the most.

God welcomes your intercessions today, and you can expect His care
and concern for your well-being and the well-being of your neighbors who
are in need. There is no surprise on God's part that some people are living
in rebellion and hostility. Even as you witness injustice and exploitation
around you, find your hope in God, trusting that He will remember His
people and work toward the good of all people.

*Lord, I ask for Your intervention for those who are
suffering so they can experience relief and justice.*

## DON'T BARGAIN, TRUST

*Jephthah made a vow to the LORD. He said, "If you give*
*me victory over the Ammonites, I will give to the LORD*
*whatever comes out of my house to meet me when I return*
*in triumph. I will sacrifice it as a burnt offering."*

JUDGES 11:30–31 NLT

. . . . . . . . . . . . . . . . . . . . . .

Jephthah's vow has been described as "rash" or "tragic." And why not? This judge of Israel asked God for victory in battle, promising that afterward he would sacrifice whatever stepped out of his house. Was he expecting a goat or chicken? It was, in fact, his only child.

The story warns against foolish promises. But there was a deeper issue for Jephthah, one that we as Christian men today do well to consider: when God has called and empowered a person for service, that's enough. No embellishment is necessary or desirable.

Jephthah had dealt wisely with the king of Ammon, denying his demand for Israelite land. "You keep whatever your god Chemosh gives you," he said, "and we will keep whatever the LORD our God gives us" (Judges 11:24 NLT). When the Ammonite king ignored the message, "the Spirit of the LORD came upon Jephthah" (v. 29 NLT). Heading to battle in this power, though, Jephthah seemed to hesitate, making the foolish vow in today's scripture.

Let's not make a similar mistake. With God's promises and presence, we need nothing more. Our trust honors Him more than any promised sacrifice ever could.

---

*Lord, I trust You. That's enough.*

## WANTED: HUMILITY

*Jesus said to his disciples, "Beware of the teachers of the law. They like to walk around in flowing robes and love to be greeted with respect in the marketplaces and have the most important seats in the synagogues and the places of honor at banquets. They devour widows' houses and for a show make lengthy prayers. These men will be punished most severely."*
LUKE 20:45–47 NIV

. . . . . . . . . . . . . . . . . . . . . .

No wonder the Jewish religious leaders hated Jesus. How would you like to be on the receiving end of the words above? As people who thought they were so important, so far beyond everyone else, Jesus' assessment must have cut to the quick. He had nailed their attitudes, actions, and aftereffects. They really couldn't argue, so they simply fumed and plotted.

It's easy to judge these men, but let's beware of the pride in our own hearts. "Do not think of yourself more highly than you ought," Paul wrote (Romans 12:3 NIV). Both James and Peter quoted Proverbs 3:34: "God opposes the proud but shows favor to the humble" (James 4:6, 1 Peter 5:5 NIV). We must consciously counter our pride, since our hearts are "deceitful above all things" (Jeremiah 17:9 NIV).

As Christians, we walk a tightrope—we're a "new creature" (2 Corinthians 5:17 KJV) still subject to the attack of both Satan and our own selfishness. A little humility will go a long way—all the way through eternity.

*Lord, help me recognize my pride and choose humility instead.*

# SAMSON'S MISTAKE

*When she pressed him daily with her words, and urged him,*
*so that his soul was vexed unto death; that he told her all his*
*heart, and said unto her, There hath not come a razor upon mine*
*head; for I have been a Nazarite unto God from my mother's*
*womb: if I be shaven, then my strength will go from me.*

JUDGES 16:16–17 KJV

. . . . . . . . . . . . . . . . . . . . .

What can we say about Samson? Though he gained a mention in the "Faith Hall of Fame" (Hebrews 11:32), what a messy life he led. The vengeance and violence seemed to be part of his calling as judge (or deliverer) of Israel. But a taste for unsavory women—an unnamed prostitute and Delilah, who may have been from the enemy Philistines—really tars his name.

Today's scripture encapsulates Samson's downfall. Hoping to earn twenty-eight pounds of silver offered by Philistine leaders, Delilah nagged Samson to divulge the secret of his superhuman strength. Then she lulled him to sleep, shaved his hair, and derailed his career as protector of Israel.

The man who had been so blessed by God seemed to let that blessing go to his head. Rather than using his gifts for godly things, he too often chose the illicit. Samson apparently thought his God-given strength allowed him to do whatever he pleased.

He was wrong. May we never make Samson's mistake.

*Lord God, You have blessed me in so many ways. May I always*
*respond with a heart of gratitude and obedience.*

# ALWAYS WATCHING, ALWAYS PRAYING

*"Be always on the watch, and pray that you may be*
*able to escape all that is about to happen, and that you*
*may be able to stand before the Son of Man."*

LUKE 21:36 NIV

• • • • • • • • • • • • • • • • • • • • • • •

Jesus' words must have stunned His followers. Just days after His "triumphal entry" into Jerusalem, as the disciples enthused over the beauty of the temple, Jesus declared, "The time will come when not one stone will be left on another; every one of them will be thrown down" (Luke 21:6 NIV).

Understandably, the disciples wanted to know when that would happen. What followed was Jesus' discourse that interwove both near- and long-term prophecies, of the destruction of Jerusalem and of the end of time. An explanation would require books, not a single devotional—but Jesus' concluding instruction, captured in today's scripture, is our focus now.

Today is the National Day of Prayer in the United States, a perfect time to refresh our commitment to "be always on the watch, and pray." It's one thing to read about prayer, to think about prayer, or to say, "I need to pray." It's another thing—the vital thing—*to pray*. As soon as you finish this entry, use the prayer starter below as an entryway into God's presence. He welcomes you to His "throne of grace" (Hebrews 4:16 NIV), so don't hesitate to meet Him there.

---

*Lord God, thank You for hearing my prayers. Today, I need to discuss. . .*

# TOO DISTRESSED TO PRAY

*I think of God, and I moan, overwhelmed with longing for his help. You don't let me sleep. I am too distressed even to pray!*

PSALM 77:3–4 NLT

. . . . . . . . . . . . . . . . . . . . . . .

Have you ever been so upset, depressed, angry, or overwhelmed that you couldn't even pray? If so, you're in good company.

Even Bible writers struggled like that, as Psalm 77 proves. Asaph, a Levite assigned by King David to lead music when the ark of the covenant was moved to Jerusalem (1 Chronicles 15), came to prominence in a time of joy. How different his outlook when he penned today's psalm.

"I cry out to God; yes, I shout," Asaph began. "Oh, that God would listen to me! When I was in deep trouble, I searched for the Lord. All night long I prayed, with hands lifted toward heaven, but my soul was not comforted" (Psalm 77:1–2 NLT). And then Asaph wrote the words of today's scripture, recording his moaning, longing, and sleeplessness. He found it impossible even to pray.

Happily for Asaph—and instructively for us—he discovered a way out of his morass. By verse 11 (NLT), this talented musician had decided to "recall all you have done, O LORD; I remember your wonderful deeds of long ago." And that proved to be enough. Today, let's follow Asaph's example, praying as he did:

*"You are the God of great wonders! You demonstrate your awesome power among the nations" (Psalm 77:14 NLT).*

# OVERCONFIDENCE

*"I have prayed for you, Simon, that your faith may not fail. And*
*when you have turned back, strengthen your brothers." But he*
*replied, "Lord, I am ready to go with you to prison and to death."*
LUKE 22:32–33 NIV

. . . . . . . . . . . . . . . . . . . . . .

The ups and downs of Simon Peter's life should give every man hope.
Jesus loved this impetuous apostle and stuck with him through some bad
(sometimes incredibly bad) moments. And through it all, Peter matured
into a tremendous leader, a man who helped introduce billions of people
to his Lord. Think about it: Where might you be today apart from Peter's
Pentecost sermon that kick-started the church (Acts 2)?

It's easy to judge Peter for his boastful statement above, since we
know what happened next. Jesus said, "I tell you, Peter, before the rooster
crows today, you will deny three times that you know me" (Luke 22:34
NIV). Jesus was exactly right, validating and necessitating His words
"when you have turned back."

Peter's later compatriot, Paul, warned about overconfidence in the
Christian life. After describing the failures of the ancient Israelites, Paul
said, "These things happened to them as examples and were written down
as warnings for us. . . . So, if you think you are standing firm, be careful
that you don't fall!" (1 Corinthians 10:11–12 NIV).

Peter is probably nodding in agreement, saying, "Don't ever think
you can live the Christian life in your own power."

*Lord, please strengthen me by Your Spirit.*

## SELFLESSNESS

*And Naomi said unto her two daughters in law, Go, return
each to her mother's house: the LORD deal kindly with
you, as ye have dealt with the dead, and with me.*
RUTH 1:8 KJV

. . . . . . . . . . . . . . . . . . . . . . .

The Old Testament character Ruth is rightly honored for her commitment
to her mother-in-law, Naomi. But, as today's scripture shows, Naomi
deserves high marks for her own selflessness.

Perhaps you're familiar with the backstory: to escape a famine in
Judah, Naomi, her husband, and their two sons move to pagan Moab,
where the boys marry local girls. Then, in rapid succession, all three men
of the family die. Naomi decides to return to her homeland and urges
her widowed daughters-in-law to go back to their own Moabite families.
Orpah tearfully agrees; Ruth tells Naomi *no*, insisting, "Thy people shall
be my people, and thy God my God" (Ruth 1:16 KJV).

Like a diamond displayed on black velvet, the younger woman's
goodness shines against Naomi's attempt to guide Ruth back to her own
people. We can all be grateful that Naomi failed in her efforts, since Ruth
ultimately married a Jewish man, had a child, and became an ancestor
of Jesus Christ. But Naomi's heart of selflessness is worth noting and
emulating.

In what ways can we deny our own desires (and even rights) for
the benefit of others? When we do, we're not only following Naomi's
example—we're acting like Jesus.

*Father in heaven, help me to deny myself
and take up my cross for others.*

## REMEMBER NOT TO FORGET

*For he issued his laws to Jacob; he gave his instructions to Israel.*
*He commanded our ancestors to teach them to their children, so*
*the next generation might know them—even the children not*
*yet born—and they in turn will teach their own children.*

PSALM 78:5–6 NLT

. . . . . . . . . . . . . . . . . . . . . .

By verse count, Psalm 78 is the second longest in the Bible, its 72 verses following only Psalm 119's 176.

Psalm 78 recaps Israel's history, both good and bad. It references the plagues on Egypt, the Exodus, the parting of the sea, the pillar of cloud and fire, the miraculous food and water in the wilderness. But those reminders of God's power and presence are shadowed by the Israelites' murmuring, disbelief, and outright disobedience. Sometimes, their bad behavior made God "furious," and "the fire of his wrath burned" (v. 21 NLT).

This history lesson, according to the author, Asaph, was to inform coming generations of God's awesome goodness, "so each generation should set its hope anew on God, not forgetting his glorious miracles and obeying his commands. Then they will not be like their ancestors— stubborn, rebellious, and unfaithful, refusing to give their hearts to God" (vv. 7–8 NLT).

Here is both a great goal and a practical guide to achieving it. Why not share this psalm with a younger person. . .or at least study it yourself? Remember not to forget your powerful, loving God.

*Father, remind me never to forget You and Your wonderful deeds.*

## DEEPLY DISAPPOINTED? PRAY

*Deeply hurt, Hannah prayed to the LORD and wept with many tears. Making a vow, she pleaded, "LORD of Hosts, if You will take notice of Your servant's affliction, remember and not forget me, and give Your servant a son, I will give him to the LORD all the days of his life, and his hair will never be cut."*

1 SAMUEL 1:10–11 HCSB

. . . . . . . . . . . . . . . . . . . . . .

Here's a reminder to Christian men: never overlook the example of biblical *women*.

Hannah's pain was twofold, not entirely applicable to guys today. As a woman of childbearing age, she couldn't conceive. And as part of a polygamous marriage, she was mocked by her husband's fertile second wife. Hannah's response provides the lesson for us.

Yes, she cried and, in her sorrow, couldn't eat. These were natural emotional reactions. But then she consciously chose to pray, a prayer recorded in the book named for her miracle answer.

Life throws many disappointments, trials, and tragedies at us. We will undoubtedly have immediate emotional reactions—but then, like Hannah, let's pray. We should pray even in the hardest moments. . . *especially* in those moments. Prayer is where we meet God and He can respond to our needs.

Hannah ultimately received exactly what her heart desired. We may or may not, depending on God's perfect judgment. But far better to pray, spending time in His presence, than stewing and plotting our own solutions.

---

*Lord of Hosts, please take notice of Your servant's afflictions. Remember me.*

# NO MATTER HOW IMPRESSIVE YOU ARE. . .

*"I baptize with water," John replied, "but among you stands*
*one you do not know. He is the one who comes after me,*
*the straps of whose sandals I am not worthy to untie."*

JOHN 1:26–27 NIV

. . . . . . . . . . . . . . . . . . . . . . .

Do you remember how Jesus viewed His relative and forerunner John? The Lord said, "Among those born of women there has not risen anyone greater than John the Baptist" (Matthew 11:11 NIV). Yet in today's scripture, see how John judged himself: the pinnacle of "those born of women" said he wasn't worthy of untying Jesus' shoes.

That's the attitude God wants in His children. "Humility is the fear of the LORD," Proverbs 22:4 says; "its wages are riches and honor and life." "With humility comes wisdom," Proverbs 11:2 adds, and "humility comes before honor" (Proverbs 18:12). "Do nothing out of selfish ambition or vain conceit," the apostle Paul taught. "Rather, in humility value others above yourselves" (Philippians 2:3, all quotations NIV). Encapsulating all, famed Bible teacher Oswald Chambers said, "Humility is the one stamp of a saint."

No matter how impressive you are, someone is always more so. And even if you happen to be this generation's John the Baptist, you're still unworthy of loosening Jesus' sandals. That's just fine. Remember, if we don't come to Jesus as little children, we don't get into His kingdom (Matthew 18:3).

*Lord Jesus, my life is all about You. May I always*
*view myself with appropriate humility.*

# BE CAREFUL WHERE YOU LOOK

*But the LORD killed seventy men from Beth-shemesh*
*because they looked into the Ark of the LORD.*
1 SAMUEL 6:19 NLT

. . . . . . . . . . . . . . . . . . . . . .

Though biblical accuracy isn't a hallmark of the 1981 Hollywood blockbuster *Raiders of the Lost Ark*, the film got one thing right: the ark of the covenant was not to be trifled with.

A man named Uzzah was killed when he tried to steady the ark, being transported—inappropriately—on an oxcart rather than on poles carried by priests (1 Chronicles 13:1–11). And, in today's scripture, dozens died for looking inside the ark, recently returned by Philistines who'd captured it in battle.

God had very strict rules for the ark, which was the specific point on earth where He manifested Himself. He once told Moses and Aaron that the Kohathites, a Levite clan tasked with moving the ark and its related accessories, "must never enter the sanctuary to look at the sacred objects, even for a moment, or they will die" (Numbers 4:20 NLT).

Though that was long ago and far away, the ark's story might cause us to ask ourselves, "What are some places I should be careful not to look?" One obvious answer, in our culture, is pornography. Or how about the occult (Deuteronomy 18:10–13)? Or perhaps at another man's wife (Exodus 20:17)? Remember the trouble Adam and Eve found when they pursued what God forbade.

*Lord, help me to avoid what You forbid and be content with what I have.*

## DO ALL THINGS WELL

*"Everyone brings out the choice wine first and then
the cheaper wine after the guests have had too much
to drink; but you have saved the best till now."*

JOHN 2:10 NIV

. . . . . . . . . . . . . . . . . . . . . .

Today's scripture was spoken by a very relieved master of ceremonies. Overseeing a wedding banquet, he had somehow run out of wine. Happily for him, Jesus was there, and at His mother's request performed His first miracle: six twenty- to thirty-gallon waterpots were suddenly brimful of excellent wine. The bemused banquet master raved to the groom, "Everyone brings out the choice wine first and then the cheaper wine after the guests have had too much to drink; but you have saved the best till now."

As followers of Jesus, shouldn't we also do everything to the highest level possible? Whether we're performing a task at work, serving at church, or—dare we say it—posting on social media, we Christians should be known for our top-quality, beneficial, respectful performances. As the apostle Paul so succinctly put it, "Whether you eat or drink or whatever you do, do it all for the glory of God" (1 Corinthians 10:31 NIV).

Earlier, Paul had written, "No one should seek their own good, but the good of others" (1 Corinthians 10:24 NIV). When we work hard and carefully, we serve the good of others—and honor our Lord who does "all things well" (Mark 7:37 KJV).

*Father, help me devote my best efforts to Your glory.*

# BELIEVE AND ENJOY, FOREVER

*For God so loved the world, that he gave his only begotten Son, that whosoever believeth in him should not perish, but have everlasting life.*

JOHN 3:16 KJV

· · · · · · · · · · · · · · · · · · · · · · ·

In the Chestnut Grove Cemetery in Ashtabula, Ohio, a small grave marker carries an interesting inscription:

SPENCER E. PIERCE
1922–∞

We can hope that infinity symbol represents Christian faith on Mr. Pierce's behalf. As believers, we have staked our eternal hope on Jesus' famous words to Nicodemus, captured in John's Gospel and reproduced above. By believing in the Lord's teaching, death, resurrection, and ascension, we gain a life that never ends, a place in God's presence where we'll enjoy "pleasures for evermore" (Psalm 16:11 KJV).

This reality should strengthen us for life on this earth, where the pleasures are not lasting—where we may, in fact, face some extremely difficult and disappointing things. Our human existence, as we currently know it, is not infinite, and we can actually be grateful for that. Who would want to live forever in a broken, sinful world that grows darker by the day?

But a day is coming when Jesus, the spiritual light of this world (John 8:12), will be the "light"—in every sense of the term—of a renewed, sinless world (Revelation 21:22–23). That day will be perfect, and it will be infinite. And as a believer in Jesus, you will be a part of it.

*Lord Jesus, come quickly.*

# HONOR YOUR MOTHER
# (AND ALL WOMEN)

*When a Samaritan woman came to draw water, Jesus
said to her, "Will you give me a drink?"... The Samaritan
woman said to him, "You are a Jew and I am a Samaritan
woman. How can you ask me for a drink?"*

JOHN 4:7, 9 NIV

. . . . . . . . . . . . . . . . . . . . . . . .

On this Mother's Day, many men will enjoy the physical presence of their
moms. Some will have to content themselves with a phone call. Many
guys possess only memories of their mothers, while others grieve some
emotional rupture that hinders their current relationship.

Days like this can be complicated, but Jesus provides an example
that any man—whatever his status with Mom—can follow.

On His way through Samaria, "enemy territory" in the view of His
fellow Jews, Jesus stopped to rest at a well in Sychar. It was noon, the heat
of the day. When a disreputable Samaritan woman, likely choosing this
time to avoid other people, came to draw water, Jesus spoke. Shocked at
His attention, she soon found herself captivated by His wisdom and love.
"Could this be the Messiah?" she asked her neighbors (John 4:29 NIV).

Jesus treated women with complete respect. He welcomed them into
His circle of disciples and showed special compassion to foreign women,
the sick, and widows. We should too.

Let's honor our own mothers by treating *every* woman with respect.

*Lord God, help me to honor every woman You bring into my life.*

# THINK BEFORE YOU SPEAK

*Now the Israelites were in distress that day, because Saul had
bound the people under an oath, saying, "Cursed be anyone
who eats food before evening comes, before I have avenged
myself on my enemies!" So none of the troops tasted food.*

1 Samuel 14:24 niv

. . . . . . . . . . . . . . . . . . . . . . .

Just imagine the trouble we'd avoid if we all took the advice of today's
devotional title. Individually, culturally, worldwide—how helpful to
recognize the truth of Proverbs 13:3 (niv): "Those who guard their lips
preserve their lives, but those who speak rashly will come to ruin."

King Saul spoke rashly when he pronounced a curse on any soldier
who ate before nightfall. Israel's troops could have enjoyed the refreshment
of plentiful honey they found in the woods, "yet no one put his hand to
his mouth, because they feared the oath" (1 Samuel 14:26 niv). Jonathan,
the king's son who'd been out successfully fighting Philistines when Saul
issued his foolish order, *did* eat some honey, and his "eyes brightened"
(v. 29 niv). He recognized that the soldiers would have been more effective
with food in their stomachs.

Saul's order resulted in a death penalty on Jonathan, and the mass
disobedience of the rest of the army to save the young man's life. How
unnecessary it all was.

Today, let's commit ourselves to James's wisdom: "Everyone should
be quick to listen, slow to speak and slow to become angry" (1:19 niv).

*Lord, may my thoughts be many and my words few.*

## COMPLAINING IN PRAYER?

*How long, Yahweh? Will You be angry forever? Will Your jealousy
keep burning like fire? Pour out Your wrath on the nations that don't
acknowledge You, on the kingdoms that don't call on Your name.*

PSALM 79:5–6 HCSB

. . . . . . . . . . . . . . . . . . . . . . .

We could complain that complaining is so easy, but that doesn't seem
right. Scripture clearly denounces our human tendency to murmur and
grumble: "Jesus answered them, 'Stop complaining among yourselves' "
(John 6:43 HCSB); "Nor should we complain" (1 Corinthians 10:10 HCSB);
"Be hospitable to one another without complaining" (1 Peter 4:9 HCSB).

And yet. . .

Today's passage is one of many in the Psalms that contains a complaint
(or series of complaints) addressed directly to God. Psalm 142:2 (HCSB)
even says, "I pour out my complaint before Him." How can we resolve
this tension?

Clearly, our world and the human beings in it are broken. Bad things
have happened, are happening, and will continue to happen. We will
struggle with the unfairness of life, whether it personally affects us or
other people. And sometimes, like the writers of the Psalms, we'll find
ourselves venting even to God. He doesn't like humanity's sinful, hurtful
ways any more than we do.

Just don't stop at the complaint. Like the writer of Psalm 79, ask God
to fix the problem. Then praise Him in advance for His ultimate response:

*"We. . .will thank You forever; we will declare Your praise
to generation after generation" (Psalm 79:13).*

# PRAY SPECIFICALLY

*One man was there who had been an invalid for thirty-eight*
*years. When Jesus saw him lying there and knew that he had*
*already been there a long time, he said to him, "Do you want*
*to be healed?" The sick man answered him, "Sir, I have no one*
*to put me into the pool when the water is stirred up."*

JOHN 5:5–7 ESV

At the Pool of Bethesda in Jerusalem, blind, lame, and paralyzed people waited. Occasionally, the waters would stir. Word on the street was that an angel was causing the movement, and the first person into the pool would be healed.

Jesus, in Jerusalem for "one of the Jewish festivals" (John 5:1 NIV), saw a particular man who had been disabled nearly four decades. The Lord asked a simple question: "Do you want to be healed?" Notice the man's answer: not an immediate "Yes!" but a roundabout "Sir, I have no one to put me into the pool when the water is stirred up."

Compare this man's reply with a blind man Jesus met in Jericho. The Lord asked the begging Bartimaeus, "What do you want me to do for you?" His answer was as specific as Jesus' query: "Rabbi, I want to see" (Mark 10:51 NIV).

Both men received a miraculous healing. But how much better is Bartimaeus's example? Be specific in your prayers, then thank God for His specific answers.

*Father, help me to pray clearly and with a heart*
*of expectancy for Your particular answers.*

## KNOW WHERE TO FIND HELP

*Turn us again to yourself, O God. Make your face shine*
*down upon us. Only then will we be saved.*
PSALM 80:3 NLT

. . . . . . . . . . . . . . . . . . . . . . .

When your car's in a ditch, you don't dial a plumber. If your cell phone gets cracked, you don't rush to the hospital. Should your tax return be selected for audit, you don't call a devotional writer. (Definitely not a devotional writer!) Particular crises require particular helpers, those with the specific skills and abilities to get you out of trouble.

Often, our problems aren't physical but spiritual. We have sinned. We know we're lost. We need forgiveness, guidance, and hope. If we seek help from anyone or anything but God, we'll be disappointed—eternally so.

The psalm writer Asaph recognized this truth, begging God to "show [Israel] your mighty power. Come to rescue us!" (Psalm 80:2 NLT). God's people were being harassed by other nations (v. 6), but the larger issue was spiritual: the people had strayed from their Shepherd, who was angry even with their prayers (v. 4). Asaph implored God to turn the Israelites' hearts back to Him. "Only then will we be saved," he wrote—three times (vv. 3, 7, and 19 NLT).

When you find yourself in spiritual need, go straight to God. He may use a friend or pastor or Christian book to help you through—but He is the ultimate source of salvation.

*Lord, You are my Hope and Salvation. May I never look to anyone else.*

# FIRM IN THE FACE OF TROUBLE

*You son of a perverse, rebellious woman, do not I know
that you have chosen the son of Jesse to your own shame
and to the shame of your mother who bore you?*

1 SAMUEL 20:30 AMPC

. . . . . . . . . . . . . . . . . . . . . . . .

Today's scripture contains a father's words to his son. We can only imagine the hurt King Saul's insulting accusation caused Jonathan.

At issue was the deep friendship the royal heir had with the up-and-coming hero, conqueror of Goliath. The account of that contest is in 1 Samuel 17; the next chapter begins, "When David had finished speaking to Saul, the soul of Jonathan was knit with the soul of David, and Jonathan loved him as his own life" (18:1 AMPC).

Three verses later, Jonathan seemed to recognize that he would not succeed to Saul's throne, and he gave David his royal robe. Their friendship was sealed by a vow of protection made before "the Lord, the God of Israel" (20:12 AMPC).

Jonathan's devotion was tested by Saul's angry response—which included, as David had also experienced, the king hurling a spear at him (20:33). But Jonathan, whose name is synonymous with true friendship, could stay firm in the face of trouble because of his prior, intentional commitments.

Today, we will face opposition and insults for our friendship with Jesus. Have we made a firm, intentional decision to stand with Him regardless of anyone's reaction?

*Lord, I want to stand with You, no matter
what. Give me a heart of courage.*

# GIFTS OR GIVER?

*"You've come looking for me not because you saw God in my actions
but because I fed you, filled your stomachs—and for free."*
JOHN 6:26 MSG

· · · · · · · · · · · · · · · · · · · · · · ·

The Lord is so generous that we can sometimes take His gifts for granted. Of course, that's not a fault of His—it's a bad tendency of our selfish human nature.

Jesus' comment in today's scripture comes the day after His miraculous feeding of five thousand men (plus accompanying women and children) with a young boy's lunch. Five loaves and two fish were only "a drop in the bucket for a crowd like this," according to Andrew's words in the Message Bible (John 6:9). But Jesus, who created the entire universe from nothing (Colossians 1:15–17), has no trouble turning one little lunch into a massive meal.

Though He could also impose the proper response—gratitude, worship, praise, service—He doesn't. That's entirely on us. As followers of Jesus, let's commit today to be like that crowd only in its recognition of Jesus as Provider of all good things. But let's be sure we go further, seeing God in all His actions.

May we never fall into the trap of pursuing Jesus only for what we might receive. There will be plenty of blessings if our heart's priority is to honor Him.

*Lord, I thank You for all You give me. Please forgive me for those
times when I look more to the gifts than to You as giver.*

# WHAT GOD WANTS

*Oh, that my people would listen to me,*
*that Israel would walk in my ways!*
PSALM 81:13 ESV

. . . . . . . . . . . . . . . . . . . . . . .

The way God deals with people changes over time. But because He is perfect and eternal, His desire for fellowship with mankind remains the same. It behooves us to endeavor to please God and enjoy His blessing.

As Christians, we know God at a more intimate level than did the ancient Israelites. They were His chosen nation and experienced many benefits from that status—but the work of Jesus Christ was still future and the Holy Spirit did not yet make His home in human hearts. So the Israelites often failed, sometimes spectacularly, as God cried out for them simply to do what He said.

That was God's desire then; it's still His passion now. We who know God the Father through God the Son, who entertain God the Spirit in our deepest inner being, should be even more committed to listening to Him and walking in His ways. Not to be saved—that's purely a work of grace, through our faith in Jesus Christ. But because we are thankful, because we recognize how merciful God has been, because we want to honor our Lord, and because, in the long run, it's by far the best thing for us.

We know God's desires by the Word He's given us. Listen to it, and walk in His ways.

*Lord, guide me in Your ways. I want to please You.*

# HEED THE WARNINGS

*"Praise be to the LORD. . .who has sent you today to meet me. May
you be blessed for your good judgment and for keeping me from
bloodshed this day and from avenging myself with my own hands."*

1 SAMUEL 25:32–33 NIV

. . . . . . . . . . . . . . . . . . . . . . .

We've all known fools. Hopefully, we've never let them drive us to our
own folly.

Israel's anointed but not-yet-crowned king, David, nearly succumbed
to fury over an obnoxious man named Nabal—whose name means "Fool."
The famed conqueror of Goliath, now running from a paranoid King Saul,
had treated the wealthy Nabal respectfully, never harassing his flocks or
shepherds as he and his men hid in the wilderness. During the festive
shearing time, David humbly requested food for his soldiers.

Nabal's response—"Who is this David? . . . Why should I?" (1 Samuel
25:10–11 NIV)—set the young warrior raging. He told his four hundred
men to strap on their swords (v. 13).

When Nabal's beautiful and wise wife, Abigail, perceived the coming
storm, she quickly loaded donkeys with food and hurried to meet David,
who was bent on killing Nabal and every one of his men. Her kind
demeanor and gracious words defused the situation, leading David to
speak the words of today's scripture.

David saw God's hand in sending Abigail to stop his sinful plans.
God will send people into our lives for the same purpose. Will we heed
their warnings?

*Father, thanks for looking out for me. I need it!*

# LISTEN TO JESUS

*The officers answered, Never man spake like this man.*
*Then answered them the Pharisees, Are ye also deceived?*
*Have any of the rulers or of the Pharisees believed on him?*
JOHN 7:46–48 KJV

. . . . . . . . . . . . . . . . . . . . . .

Jesus' appearance at the Feast of Tabernacles highlights the diverging opinions about Him. As He taught in the temple, people both murmured and marveled. Some said He was demon possessed (John 7:20), while others believed, asking, "When Christ cometh, will he do more miracles than these?" (v. 31 KJV).

The chief priests and Pharisees, leaders who felt threatened by Jesus, decided to send men to arrest Him. When the officers returned empty-handed, saying, "Never man spake like this man," the leadership was incensed. "Are you also deceived?" they mocked. "Have any of the rulers or of the Pharisees believed on him?"

In reality, the officers were the wise ones. Having heard Jesus directly, they made their own judgment based on His words. It didn't matter to them what the "intelligent class" thought.

Today, many oppose and mock Jesus. Others claim His name while contradicting His teaching. As Christians, we must listen to *Him*, ordering our lives by scripture, regardless of anyone else's view. Let's even double-check our favorite teachers, as the "noble" Bereans did with the apostle Paul: "they received the word with all readiness of mind, and searched the scriptures daily, whether those things were so" (Acts 17:11 KJV).

*Lord, help me tune out this world's opinions to focus entirely on You.*

## SING GOD'S PRAISES

*How lovely is your dwelling place, O LORD of Heaven's Armies.*
*I long, yes, I faint with longing to enter the courts of the LORD.*
*With my whole being, body and soul, I will shout joyfully to the*
*living God. Even the sparrow finds a home, and the swallow*
*builds her nest and raises her young at a place near your altar,*
*O LORD of Heaven's Armies, my King and my God! What joy for*
*those who can live in your house, always singing your praises.*

PSALM 84:1–4 NLT

. . . . . . . . . . . . . . . . . . . . . .

Psalm 84, by some unnamed descendants of Korah, celebrates the physical place of worship. God's house, the courts, and the altar where He was honored and praised brought joy and longing to the psalm writers' hearts. They even envied the little birds that could build their nests in the nooks and crannies of the temple.

For Christians today, Psalm 84 doesn't really point us to our church buildings. Since the day of Pentecost recorded in Acts 2, followers of Jesus are actually God's temple. As the apostle Paul wrote, "Don't you realize that all of you together are the temple of God and that the Spirit of God lives in you?" (1 Corinthians 3:16 NLT).

What could be a greater cause for joy? The God of the entire universe has chosen to make His home in *you*. That's a perfect reason to always sing His praises.

*Lord God, You are awesome. Thank You for living in me.*

# IMPORTANT TO GOD

*Then David sang this lament over Saul and his son Jonathan.*
2 Samuel 1:17 msg

. . . . . . . . . . . . . . . . . . . . . .

When King Saul and his son Jonathan died in battle, many things changed for David. His anointing to be king would now be fulfilled. He could stop running from the paranoid Saul. And he would no longer enjoy his beloved Jonathan—the kind of friend by which all future companions would be measured.

It's not surprising the poetic David would honor Jonathan in song. Less expected are his words of praise for Jonathan's dad. David sang, "Saul's sword was fearless—once out of the scabbard, nothing could stop it. . . . Women of Israel, weep for Saul" (2 Samuel 1:22, 24 msg).

How could David honor a man who had often sought his life? By recognizing God's stamp on Saul. When he learned that a foreigner in Israel's army had finished off the wounded leader, David responded, "Do you mean to say. . .that you weren't afraid to up and kill God's anointed king?" (2 Samuel 1:14 msg). He repeated "God's anointed king" in justifying the soldier's execution (v. 16 msg).

Every person we meet is stamped by God, made in His image (Genesis 1:27). Whether friend, enemy, or something in between, let's view them as David did Saul. . .as important to God. It may not change their attitude toward us, but it will diminish the tension in our souls.

*Lord, I know I'm important to You. Help me to see others the same way.*

## SAY WHAT YOU KNOW

*"Whether he is a sinner or not, I don't know.*
*One thing I do know. I was blind but now I see!"*

JOHN 9:25 NIV

. . . . . . . . . . . . . . . . . . . . . . .

When John's Gospel describes a lame man's healing at the Pool of Bethesda, it notes he'd suffered for thirty-eight years (chapter 5). But in John 9, where Jesus heals a blind man, no length of affliction is given. Perhaps twenty to thirty years—the person healed was a "man blind from birth" (v. 1 NIV), whose parents were both still alive (vv. 18–23).

Read the whole story in John 9—it's comical in places. Jesus applied spit-mud to the man's eyes, telling him to wash in the Pool of Siloam. When he returned seeing, people who'd known him only as a blind beggar debated his identity. "Others said, 'He only looks like him.' But he himself insisted, 'I am the man' " (v. 9 NIV).

Then the Jesus-hating Pharisees got involved, declaring the Healer was a sinner. But this beneficiary of Jesus' touch showed some real spunk: "Whether he is a sinner or not, I don't know. One thing I do know. I was blind but now I see!" (v. 25 NIV).

Our own experience with Jesus will go against this world's grain. But like that formerly blind man, we know Him to be good and true and powerful. Let's say what we know, sharing His truth with a world that desperately needs it.

---

*Lord Jesus, give me the courage to honor You publicly.*

## "I WILL"

*I will listen to what God the LORD says; he promises peace to his people, his faithful servants—but let them not turn to folly.*

PSALM 85:8 NIV

. . . . . . . . . . . . . . . . . . . . . . . .

These two little words—*I will*—can lead us down vastly different paths.

Consider the boastful claims of the king of Babylon, in which some see the origins of Satan's fall:

> *"I will ascend to the heavens; I will raise my throne above the stars of God; I will sit enthroned on the mount of assembly, on the utmost heights of Mount Zaphon. I will ascend above the tops of the clouds; I will make myself like the Most High."* (Isaiah 14:13–14 NIV)

Now contrast those "I wills" with the "I will" of today's scripture. "I will listen to what God the LORD says." This commitment sets us on the path to righteousness and eternal life. But it's only a start.

After the listening comes the doing. As the New Testament writer James succinctly put it, "Do not merely listen to the word, and so deceive yourselves. Do what it says" (1:22 NIV).

If we hear God's Word *and* do it, we'll avoid the "turning to folly" that Psalm 85:8 warns about. Today, may we commit our hearts and minds to the narrow path that leads to life.

*Father in heaven, I will listen to what You say—and do it.*

# UNDESERVING

*Then went king David in, and sat before the LORD,
and he said, Who am I, O Lord GOD? and what is
my house, that thou hast brought me hitherto?*

2 SAMUEL 7:18 KJV

. . . . . . . . . . . . . . . . . . . . . . .

David has undeniable importance in the biblical record. His name appears nearly 900 times in the King James Version, second only to Jesus' 942. David was good-looking, musically talented, and physically courageous, a leader of men and hero to women. He reunited a nation fractured by King Saul's folly, guiding Israel to military victories and a golden age under the leadership of his handpicked successor, Solomon.

This all began when David was just an overlooked kid brother tending his family's sheep (1 Samuel 16).

The same God who provided the physical and intellectual gifts also chose David to be king of Israel. And this man, who made many mistakes in his forty-year rule, was wise enough to see God's hand in all his success. "Who am I, O Lord GOD," he wondered, "that thou hast brought me hitherto?"

David recognized that all his abilities and achievements came from God's generosity. He was personally undeserving. But in the often-paradoxical way in which God works, that acknowledgment is what opens the door to even greater blessing. "Humble yourselves therefore under the mighty hand of God," the apostle Peter wrote, "that he may exalt you in due time" (1 Peter 5:6 KJV).

---

*Lord God, I don't deserve Your blessings.
But I appreciate them, and I welcome more.*

# WILL TO FOLLOW

*Thomas, who was called the Twin, said to his fellow disciples,*
*Let us go too, that we may die [be killed] along with Him.*
JOHN 11:16 AMPC

. . . . . . . . . . . . . . . . . . . . . . .

In the United States, this final Monday of May is Memorial Day, a time to remember military personnel who died performing their duty.

The Christian life is likened to soldiering (Philippians 2:25; 2 Timothy 2:3–4; Philemon 2), and many Jesus followers have been killed for their faith. In today's scripture, one of Jesus' disciples volunteered for potentially fatal duty as the Lord planned to visit a place where Jewish leaders had recently wanted to stone Him.

Thomas's mind-set isn't entirely clear. Perhaps he was boldly eager to give his life on Jesus' behalf. More likely, the man who comes down through history as "Doubting Thomas" was being sardonic, dreading the outcome of Jesus' return to Judea.

Emotions, like temptations, just happen—we can't control them. We can, however, overcome them by consciously performing our duty. All the disciples apparently followed Jesus to Judea, where they saw Him raise Lazarus from the dead (John 11:43–44). Then, due to the threat of violence, they all retired to a village in the desert (John 11:54).

Today, let's commit ourselves to doing the right thing, whatever fearsome possibilities come to mind. Jesus will always accompany and empower us. And even if we're killed for Him, we simply end up in His presence.

*Lord, give me the will and courage to follow You anywhere.*

# HONEST QUESTIONS

*Some of them said, "Could not he who opened the eyes*
*of the blind man have kept this man from dying?"*
JOHN 11:37 NIV

. . . . . . . . . . . . . . . . . . . . . . .

Jesus enjoyed a special friendship with three siblings in the town of Bethany, near Jerusalem. The Lord "loved" Martha, Mary, and Lazarus (John 11:5). When Lazarus became seriously ill, the sisters quickly called on Jesus—who waited two full days before leaving His place "across the Jordan" (John 10:40 NIV). His delay and the journey meant He didn't reach Bethany until Lazarus had been four days in a tomb.

When He arrived, Jesus found "many Jews had come to Martha and Mary to comfort them in the loss of their brother" (John 11:19 NIV). The Lord spoke personally with both sisters then wept publicly upon approaching the grave (John 11:35). And some of the people who'd come to support the women began wondering: "Could not he who opened the eyes of the blind man have kept this man from dying?" (John 11:37 NIV).

Unlike the troublemaking queries Jewish leaders often posed to Jesus, this was an honest question. And the Lord's miraculous raising of Lazarus answered it. John 11:45 says many came to believe in Jesus.

God can handle our honest questions—He's heard them from psalmists, prophets, and plenty of other people through time. You can feel free to ask Him anything. Just be ready to accept and believe in whatever answer He sends.

---

*Lord, I have questions. Please help me to accept Your perfect answers.*

# LOOK BELOW THE SURFACE

*The king said to the woman, "Don't keep from me the answer to what*
*I am going to ask you." "Let my lord the king speak," the woman*
*said. The king asked, "Isn't the hand of Joab with you in all this?"*

2 SAMUEL 14:18–19 NIV

• • • • • • • • • • • • • • • • • • • • • • • •

The story of Absalom's conspiracy against his father, David, is full of intrigue. Perhaps we can draw a spiritual application from the political machinations.

Exceptionally good-looking, Absalom was equally selfish. He killed the half brother who violated Absalom's full sister, then ran to another country for refuge. David longed for Absalom but maintained his banishment—so the king's military commander found someone to spin a story paralleling David's own situation. He quickly recognized the subterfuge and responded with the words above.

David allowed the return of Absalom, who then began to flatter his countrymen in an attempt to usurp the throne. Soon, a messenger told David, "The hearts of the people of Israel are with Absalom" (2 Samuel 15:13 NIV). Absalom's rebellion against God's anointed king was ultimately doomed, and his followers would have been wise to look below the surface to the young man's dark purposes.

As Christians, we shouldn't be immediately suspicious of people. But we should recognize that people and situations aren't always as they first appear. Perhaps that's why Jesus once told His disciples to be "as shrewd as snakes and as innocent as doves" (Matthew 10:16 NIV).

*Lord, give me discernment in this world of falsehood.*

# ISAIAH SAW JESUS

*Isaiah was referring to Jesus when he said this, because
he saw the future and spoke of the Messiah's glory.*
JOHN 12:41 NLT

· · · · · · · · · · · · · · · · · · · · · ·

Did you know Isaiah speaks in greater detail about Jesus than any other Old Testament prophet? What's more, Matthew, Mark, Luke, John, Philip, Peter, Paul, and Jesus Himself quote from Isaiah's prophecies scores of times—far more than all the other prophets put together.

Before Isaiah began to proclaim God's Word, he experienced two miracles. First, he experienced firsthand the awfulness of his guilt. Then, he experienced the astounding miracle of the Lord's cleansing (Isaiah 6:1–6). This new prophet of the Lord knew what it meant to deserve destruction. Therefore, his heart was ready to accept the Lord's forgiveness and remarkable commission to serve Him for the rest of his life.

In a later vision, Isaiah saw the Lord Jesus laboring to carry a bloodstained Roman cross up the hill to Calvary (Isaiah 52:13–53:12). What an awful picture! Isaiah was equally shocked to realize that he was the one who went astray, yet Jesus was crushed; he was the one who sinned, yet the Messiah was put to death.

Throughout history people have asked, "Who killed Jesus?" Fingers point at the Roman guards, at the Jewish leaders, at the fickle crowds. Isaiah knew the real answer: He died because of us.

---

*Lord, I know I was a sinner. You saved me. Thank You for both miracles.*

# WASHING FEET TODAY

*"Now that I, your Lord and Teacher, have washed your feet,
you also should wash one another's feet. I have set you an
example that you should do as I have done for you."*

JOHN 13:14–15 NIV

. . . . . . . . . . . . . . . . . . . . . . .

The night before His crucifixion, Jesus Christ wastes no time communicating what's foremost on His heart. To begin to show the disciples the full extent of His love, He washes their feet. This starts well, but then Peter makes a fuss. He disagrees not once but twice. If only he had listened to and obeyed the Lord Jesus without complaint.

To obey what Jesus says in today's key verses, Anglicans, Catholics, Lutherans, Mennonites, Methodists, Presbyterians, and other liturgical denominations practice foot washing on Maundy Thursday, the day before Good Friday. Other denominations practice foot washing as a church ordinance.

Foot washing was practiced long before Jesus, including by Abraham and his servants (2000 BC) and during the days of David (1000 BC). It also was widely practiced in the early churches planted by Paul and others. Then again, it wasn't universally practiced around the world and down through the ages.

Why don't more Christians practice foot washing? It's said to be humbling for the washer and humiliating for the washee ("My feet really aren't dirty, and what if they smell?"). Perhaps, like all the first disciples, with the lone exception of Peter, we should do it unquestioningly.

*Lord, humble me to do what You would have me do.*

## HOW TO "LOVE EACH OTHER"

*"So now I am giving you a new commandment: Love each other."*
JOHN 13:34 NLT

• • • • • • • • • • • • • • • • • • • • • •

It's still the night before His crucifixion. Jesus has washed the disciples' feet. Then He gives them a new commandment: "Love each other" (John 13:34 NLT).

Imagine Jesus pausing to let those three words sink in. Of course, the more they sink in, the more His disciples must have wrinkled their foreheads. *"Love each other." That's it?*

You can almost hear Thomas muttering under his breath: "But Jesus, what's new about that? Moses gave us the command to 'Love your neighbor as yourself' about fourteen hundred years ago. You can't get much *older* than that."

Thomas would have a good point. That is, if Jesus meant only, "Love each other as you love yourselves." But Jesus isn't finished.

He goes on to say: "Just as I have loved you, you should love each other" (John 13:34 NLT). In eleven words, Jesus radically changes what it means to love others. It's no longer enough to love others as you love yourself. Instead, Jesus calls His disciples to love each other as much as He loves them.

Then He adds: "Your love for one another will prove to the world that you are my disciples" (John 13:35 NLT). What could be better? What could be better, indeed!

---

*Lord, the full extent of Your love astounds me. How can I love like You? That's right: by Your love flowing out of me.*

# DON'T REMAIN TROUBLED

*"Let not your hearts be troubled."*

JOHN 14:1 ESV

. . . . . . . . . . . . . . . . . . . . . .

After Judas leaves the upper room, Jesus says He is about to be crucified. Then He declares today's key verse. You may be thinking, *How could Jesus say that?*

Let's consider what Jesus is *not* saying.

Just a few paragraphs earlier, John 13:21 (ESV) says, "Jesus was troubled in his spirit" because one of His disciples was going to betray Him. So, Jesus is *not* saying terrible things will never happen.

A chapter earlier, in John 12:27 (ESV), Jesus says, "Now is my soul troubled. And what shall I say? 'Father, save me from this hour'? But for this purpose I have come to this hour." So, Jesus is *not* saying you will never sacrifice or suffer according to God's eternal purposes.

Another chapter earlier, John 11:33 (ESV) says, "When Jesus saw her [Mary] weeping, and the Jews who had come with her also weeping, he was deeply moved in his spirit and greatly troubled." So, Jesus is *not* saying you won't ever feel deep sorrow and grief.

Instead, Jesus doesn't want you to remain troubled. How is that possible? In the second half of John 14:1 (ESV), He quickly goes on to say, "Believe in God; believe also in me."

Don't give in to fear. Don't freeze, fight, or flee. Instead, immediately focus on the Lord.

---

*Lord, You know how often my heart is troubled.*
*May I always turn to You right away.*

# WHO INSPIRED THE GOSPELS AND ACTS?

*"These things I have spoken to you while I am still with you."*
JOHN 14:25 ESV

. . . . . . . . . . . . . . . . . . . . . . .

It's easy to imagine Jesus teaching for scores of hours during the course of His public ministry. It's a bit tougher figuring out how the disciples remembered what He had said. That's why it's so good to remember what Jesus says immediately after today's key verse.

In John 14:26 (ESV), Jesus says, "But the Helper, the Holy Spirit, whom the Father will send in my name, he will teach you all things and bring to your remembrance all that I have said to you." In other words, the Holy Spirit directly inspired what they remembered, taught, preached, and wrote in *the four Gospels*. This includes their many quotations from the Old Testament, of course.

In John 15:26–27 (ESV), Jesus goes on to say, "But when the Helper comes, whom I will send to you from the Father, the Spirit of truth, who proceeds from the Father, he will bear witness about me. And you also will bear witness, because you have been with me from the beginning." In other words, the Holy Spirit directly inspired the apostles' words and deeds.

Of course, it's one thing for a writer to say he feels *inspired*. That's "a lightning bug." It's quite another thing for the Holy Spirit to divinely inspire a biblical author. That's "lightning"!

---

*Lord, speak to me through Your divinely inspired Word, the Bible.*

# WHO INSPIRED THE EPISTLES AND REVELATION?

*"I still have many things to say to you, but you cannot bear them now."*
JOHN 16:12 ESV

. . . . . . . . . . . . . . . . . . . . . . .

Who told Paul, James, Peter, John, and Jude how to write the twenty-one Epistles and the Revelation to John? Jesus Himself said He wanted to tell them so much more than they could bear right before His arrest, beatings, and crucifixion. That's why what Jesus says immediately after today's key verse is so good.

In John 16:13 (ESV), Jesus says, "When the Spirit of truth comes, he will guide you into all the truth, for he will not speak on his own authority, but whatever he hears he will speak, and he will declare to you the things that are to come."

In John 16:14–15 (ESV), Jesus goes on to say, "He [the Spirit] will glorify me, for he will take what is mine and declare it to you. All that the Father has is mine; therefore I said that he will take what is mine and declare it to you."

In other words, just as Jesus, God's Son, said what the Father told Him to say, so the Holy Spirit would say what the Father and Son told Him to say. The three members of the Trinity are always perfectly in sync. That's why it isn't hard to trust what you read in the New Testament.

*Lord, You said it. I gladly believe it with my whole heart!*

## MAKING YOURSELF KING

*Now Adonijah, whose mother was Haggith, put himself*
*forward and said, "I will be king." So he got chariots and*
*horses ready, with fifty men to run ahead of him.*
1 KINGS 1:5 NIV

. . . . . . . . . . . . . . . . . . . . . . . .

Poor King David. When he got older, his rebellious and proud son Absalom said, "I will be king," and usurped the throne for mere days. Then, when King David was very old, his next son born after Absalom said the same thing in today's key verse. His plot lasted only a day or two. As soon as King David heard of it, he installed Bathsheba's son Solomon as king and seated him on the royal throne. What a day of rejoicing. . .except for those party to Adonijah's plot!

Like Absalom, and like Adonijah, who doesn't want to be king? Some want to be king of their own lives. Some others want to be a prince or king at their church or workplace. Still others want to be a leader in their community, city, county, or state. And it doesn't stop there.

To declare himself to be king, however, means a man has rejected the Lord God as his Maker, Lord, and King (1 Samuel 8:7, 10:19, and 12:12). Such a self-determined, egotistical, and proud man actually doesn't care what God thinks. May that never be true of you.

*Lord, You set up one and put down another.*
*It's all in Your hands. That includes me.*

# "TAKE COURAGE AND BE A MAN"

*"I am going where everyone on earth must*
*someday go. Take courage and be a man."*
1 KINGS 2:2 NLT

. . . . . . . . . . . . . . . . . . . . . .

If only. If only Solomon would have heeded his dying father's counsel to "take courage and be a man." After all, it takes enduring courage to be a man who will continually "observe the requirements of the LORD your God, and follow all his ways" (1 Kings 2:3 NLT).

What requirements? "Keep the decrees, commands, regulations, and laws written in the Law of Moses." That seems clear enough, but why? "So that you will be successful in all you do and wherever you go" (1 Kings 2:3 NLT).

What more could David want? A son who does the same! "If you do this, then the LORD will keep the promise he made to me. He told me, 'If your descendants live as they should and follow me faithfully with all their heart and soul, one of them will always sit on the throne of Israel'" (1 Kings 2:4 NLT). Again, if only.

Most men vicariously import the "courage" of their favorite sports stars and superheroes.

Today God calls you to be different: "Take courage and be a man," in both word and deed.

*Lord, I sometimes feel like a fake, a false representation*
*of a godly man. Push me out of my comfort zone so I can*
*take courage and be a man before week's end.*

## FEELING INSPIRED VERSUS DIVINE INSPIRATION

*God gave Solomon very great wisdom and understanding, and knowledge as vast as the sands of the seashore. . . . He composed some 3,000 proverbs and wrote 1,005 songs. He could speak with authority about all kinds of plants, from the great cedar of Lebanon to the tiny hyssop that grows from cracks in a wall. He could also speak about animals, birds, small creatures, and fish. And kings from every nation sent their ambassadors to listen to the wisdom of Solomon.*

1 KINGS 4:29, 32–34 NLT

. . . . . . . . . . . . . . . . . . . . . . .

Solomon was the world's wisest man. Not only that, but the Lord promised: "I will give you a wise and understanding heart such as no one else has had or ever will have!" (1 Kings 3:12 NLT). What an amazing promise. Not only was Solomon wise, but he wrote down thousands of pithy statements and composed more than a thousand songs.

Then again, let's not forget Monday's parting lesson: It's one thing for a writer to say he feels inspired. That's "a lightning bug." It's quite another thing for the Holy Spirit to divinely inspire a biblical author. That's "lightning"!

Accordingly, less than one in four of Solomon's proverbs made it into the Bible—but what practical and divine wisdom they offer. More surprisingly, only one of Solomon's songs made it into God's Word, but what a passionate and inspired musical.

*Lord, thank You for divinely inspiring scripture. What a treasure!*

## GOD'S PROMISES USUALLY COME WITH CONDITIONS

*The word of the LORD came to Solomon: "As for this temple
you are building, if you follow my decrees, observe my laws
and keep all my commands and obey them, I will fulfill
through you the promise I gave to David your father."*

I KINGS 6:11–12 NIV

. . . . . . . . . . . . . . . . . . . . . . .

On Thursday we considered King David's dying charge to Solomon:
Take courage. Be a man. Obey everything written in the Law of Moses.
Then you will be successful in all you do. And then God will keep His
conditional promise to make us the first in a dynasty of good, godly kings.

In today's key verses, God reiterates: Obey everything written in the
Law. Then I will keep My conditional promise to establish a Davidic dynasty.

If only.

True, by 1 Kings 8, Solomon dedicates the glorious temple to bring
great wonder, honor, and praise to the Lord's name. In the years after
that, however, Solomon deliberately wanders away from God and breaks
the first half of the Ten Commandments.

Don't picture Solomon on top of the world at the end of his life. By
1 Kings 11, his kingdom has lost control of several territories. His vast wealth
is greatly reduced. And his once brilliant reputation is tarnished beyond repair.

If only, indeed.

Solomon allowed his heart to be pulled away from God, so he died
a foolish, idolatrous old man. May that never be said of you.

*Lord, please put a hedge of protection
around me for the rest of my days.*

# UNLIKE PILATE, EMBRACE GOD'S TRUTH

*Then Pilate turned Jesus over to them to be crucified.*

JOHN 19:16 NLT

. . . . . . . . . . . . . . . . . . . . . . .

Besides Jesus, no other man is spoken of more often in millions of churches around the world every Sunday than Pontius Pilate. After all, Pilate is mentioned by name in the Apostles' Creed. But why all the attention?

History portrays Pilate as a rash, capricious, and ultimately ineffective Roman provincial governor. At his greatest hour of testing, Pilate failed miserably by condemning the world's only innocent man—God's Son, Jesus Christ—to death by crucifixion.

Each of the Gospel writers records this trial at length. Ironically, they almost make it sound as if Pilate is on trial, not Jesus. And for good reason. If Pilate committed one more blunder, he knew Caesar might throw him forcefully out of office, disgraced. Yet when the pressure was on, Pilate listened to everyone—except the one person telling him the truth!

Despite his better judgment and the urgent warning of his wife (Matthew 27:19), Pilate rejected the Lordship of Jesus and bowed to the political will of the chief priests.

In a futile attempt to save his own neck, Pilate washed his hands of the truth and effectively signed his own death warrant.

*Lord, may I never make Pilate's fatal mistakes. Instead, may I repeatedly and frequently embrace Your truth with my whole heart.*

# SOLOMON AT HIS BEST

*Then Solomon said, "The Lord has said that he would
dwell in a dark cloud; I have indeed built a magnificent
temple for you, a place for you to dwell forever."*
1 Kings 8:12–13 niv

. . . . . . . . . . . . . . . . . . . . . . . .

This is the day King Solomon publicly dedicates the golden temple to
the praise of the Lord's glorious name. Three fast facts stand out.

First, everyone shows up: Elders from throughout the land. Every
priest and Levite. The nation as a whole. And then, the Lord Himself
shows up and fills the temple (1 Kings 8:1–13).

Second, Solomon blesses the people by reminding them that the
Lord God has kept His promises to his father, David. That is, Solomon
is firmly established as Israel's king and has finished building a gorgeous
temple for God's honor and praise (1 Kings 8:14–21).

Third, Solomon kneels down, lifts his arms toward heaven, and
offers a magnificent and wise prayer of dedication (1 Kings 8:22–54).
This rich prayer echoes many key themes from the books of Moses. It's
truly inspired by God and His Word.

Sometimes after your best day serving God publicly, you can linger
on its memories too long and begin falling away. Instead, give all the glory
to God and "make it your ambition to lead a quiet life" (1 Thessalonians
4:11 niv).

---

*Lord, sometimes You bless one of Your men with
public success. Instead, may I lead a quiet life.*

# GOD IS GOOD ALL THE TIME

*The LORD is upright; he is my rock,*
*and there is no unrighteousness in him.*

PSALM 92:15 ESV

. . . . . . . . . . . . . . . . . . . . . . .

No other question is more important than "Who is God?"

Get this one right—and experience who He is each day—and you'll enjoy life to the full! You can see this in Deuteronomy 7:12–13, Psalm 16:2, John 10:2, and James 1:17. You also can see this today.

One Bible college professor said, "I am convinced that the answers to every problem and issue of life for both time and eternity are resolved through a correct understanding of God." What hope! Another said, "When I don't take time to reflect on the God I serve, He becomes too small to help me; so I decide to handle the anxiety myself and blame God for it later." Yikes!

A. W. Tozer said it best: "The man who comes to a right belief about God is relieved of ten thousand temporal problems, for he sees at once that these have to do with matters which at the most cannot concern him for very long." Again, what hope!

So, what does it take to come to a right belief about God? First, continue reading the *2023 Daily Wisdom for Men* for the rest of this year. Second, memorize today's key verse. Third, review it for the rest of this week.

---

*Lord, how good that I can trust Your righteousness*
*and goodness with my whole heart, always.*

# LIKE THOMAS, WORSHIP THE LORD JESUS

*"My Lord and my God!" Thomas exclaimed.*

JOHN 20:28 NLT

. . . . . . . . . . . . . . . . . . . . . . .

Meet the original doubting Thomas. The Twin, as he was called by his friends, definitely wasn't afraid to speak his mind. And he was no wimp either.

Just a short time after some of the Jewish leaders threatened to arrest Jesus and picked up stones to kill Him, Jesus urged His disciples to go back to Jerusalem with Him. The apostles all were shaking in their boots—except Thomas, who said to them, "Let's go, too—and die with Jesus" (John 11:16 NLT).

A few days later, while Jesus was presenting some difficult new truths to His disciples, it was Thomas again who spoke up and said, "We have no idea where you are going, so how can we know the way?" (John 14:5 NLT).

So it doesn't come as a complete surprise when, after Jesus' resurrection, it's Thomas who finds it so hard to believe—until he sees Jesus with his own eyes. Suddenly, Thomas's doubts crumble and he says, "My Lord and my God!" (John 20:28 NLT).

Scripture and tradition indicate Thomas never again wavered in his faith and trust. With Peter and the other apostles, the Twin proclaimed Jesus as his Lord and his God until his dying day.

---

*Lord, I worship You. May I do so always*
*until my dying day. And then, glory!*

# UNLIKE REHOBOAM, LISTEN TO WISE MEN

*But Rehoboam rejected the advice of the older men and*
*instead asked the opinion of the young men who had*
*grown up with him and were now his advisers.*

1 KINGS 12:8 NLT

. . . . . . . . . . . . . . . . . . . . . . .

King Solomon's wisdom was a gift from God. Genetics had nothing to do with it, as his son Rehoboam soon found out after his father's death. Rehoboam's first official act as king? Rejecting wise counsel!

Older is not always better. Young people are not necessarily more foolish. Yet Rehoboam listened to foolish counsel—mostly out of pride and selfishness.

It's not enough to attempt to avoid foolish counsel if you don't know what it is.

What does foolish counsel look like?

How does wise advice sound?

Rehoboam could have asked these questions before he made a decision that cost him the greater portion of his kingdom. And he could have found the answers in the many wise proverbs his father had penned for him many years before.

Like his idolatrous, foolish father in old age, Rehoboam had no heart for the Lord God. And without the fear of God, there is no beginning to wisdom. All that's left is a mushy mind heeding foolish counsel and reaping terrible consequences.

*Lord, may I listen only to those who encourage me to heed Your Word.*

# LET'S NOT FORGET ASCENSION DAY

*And when he [Jesus] had said these things, as they were looking
on, he was lifted up, and a cloud took him out of their sight.*

ACTS 1:9 ESV

. . . . . . . . . . . . . . . . . . . . . .

Did you know the Church at large celebrates Ascension Day? This has been true from ancient times across the Roman Empire and beyond. Ascension Day now is typically celebrated thirty-nine days (on Thursday), forty days (Friday), or forty-two days (Sunday) after Easter. Yes, this diversity of dates can be a bit confusing. Then again, the answer isn't to ignore or forget Ascension Day as millions did recently. Just the opposite!

*Descension Day.* This is much better known as Christmas, the day God's Son, Jesus Christ, entered human history as true God (eternally) and now true man (forever from that point). Like Ascension Day, Christmas is celebrated on three different dates, varying by nation and denomination. The important thing is to celebrate this wonderful day every year!

*Ascension Day.* Yes, perhaps it could use a better name. It's the day God's Son, Jesus Christ, ascended from earth back to heaven, where He now sits at the right hand of the throne of God the Father, ever interceding for you. As a result, you receive many good gifts from heaven (Matthew 7:11, Luke 11:13, Ephesians 4:8–10, and James 1:17). Like Christmas, this should be greatly celebrated!

---

*Lord, thank You for Descension Day and for Ascension
Day. What great days for rejoicing!*

## LET US KNEEL BEFORE THE LORD

*Come, let us bow down in worship, let us kneel before
the Lord our Maker; for he is our God and we are
the people of his pasture, the flock under his care.*

Psalm 95:6–7 niv

• • • • • • • • • • • • • • • • • • • • • • •

Many traditions still kneel before God during Sunday worship. Will that be true at your church? If yes, great! If no, are you willing to "kneel before the Lord our Maker" at home this weekend?

True, we can sit or stand before God, but kneeling expresses deeper humility and reverence before our Maker. This has been true since the days of Abraham, Isaac, Jacob, and Joseph, since the days of Moses and Joshua, since the days of the psalmists, and since the days of Elijah, Isaiah, and other prophets.

This also will be true at the end of history, when everywhere everyone who has ever lived will stop everything, pay attention, and immediately and universally bow the knee before the Lord God their Maker (prophesied in Isaiah 45:23, reiterated in Romans 14:11, and directly applied to the Lord Jesus in Philippians 2:10).

Before that climactic day, may you kneel and worship the Lord many, many times!

---

*Lord, at the climax of history, I don't want to kneel before
You for the first, fifth, or fifteenth time. That's why I'm going
to bow the knee before You right here, right now.*

# UNLIKE AHAB, WORSHIP THE TRUE GOD!

*And as though it were not enough to follow the sinful example of Jeroboam, [Ahab] married Jezebel, the daughter of King Ethbaal of the Sidonians, and he began to bow down in worship of Baal.*

1 KINGS 16:31 NLT

. . . . . . . . . . . . . . . . . . . . . . . .

What picture comes to mind when Bible readers visualize Ahab? A pathetic, sullen, washed-out man? Yet God's Word says he was more evil than any of the other kings before him.

Then visualize Ahab's wife, Jezebel, and the picture comes into flaming color. Like a villainess from a Disney fairy tale or worse, it's easy to imagine her evil sneer.

Ahab already had defied God by worshipping idols. With the help of his pagan wife, however, his personal rebellion became a national religion. Besides playing pretend with the golden calves, Ahab endorsed Israel's official worship of Baal and the Asherah pole that Jezebel brought with her.

The Lord took the trouble to reveal Himself to Ahab over and over again. Through a predicted drought and prophesied rains, through a flash of fire from heaven, and through a miraculous military victory, the Lord sought to convince Ahab that He alone was the true Lord God, Maker of heaven and earth.

In the end, however, refusing to say yes to God eventually becomes the same as always saying no.

*Lord, thank You that Ahab wasn't my father!*
*May I never repeat his wicked choices.*

# UNLIKE ELIJAH, DON'T RUN AWAY

*There he came to a cave, where he spent the night. But the*
*LORD said to him, "What are you doing here, Elijah?"*
1 KINGS 19:9 NLT

· · · · · · · · · · · · · · · · · · · · · · ·

Moses has his place in American cinema with *The Ten Commandments* and *The Prince of Egypt*. It's about time someone commissioned a new epic about one of the Old Testament's other truly great heroes.

Elijah ranks right up there with Moses as one of the most dramatic prophets of the Lord. At Elijah's word, kings trembled, the rains stopped, a jug of oil never ran dry, a boy was raised from the dead, fire fell from the sky, revival broke out, and hundreds of idolatrous prophets were executed.

Yet James 5:17 (NLT) says that "Elijah was as human as we are."

After hearing wicked Queen Jezebel's murderous threats, how does Elijah respond?

True to life, scripture says he panics. After several days on the run, Elijah collapses—exhausted, lonely, frightened, and feeling utterly defeated. In his desperation, he foolishly begs the Lord to take his life.

Instead, the Lord renews Elijah—with a double portion of food, drink, rest. And then he sends him out again with a new commission and with the assurance that many others also were on his side.

*Lord, in that terrible moment when I'm tempted to run*
*away, turn me around and push me to run back to You.*

# THE NORMAL CHRISTIAN LIFE

*And they [the first Christians] devoted themselves to the apostles'
teaching and the fellowship, to the breaking of bread and the prayers.
. . . And day by day, attending the temple together and breaking
bread in their homes, they received their food with glad and generous
hearts, praising God and having favor with all the people. And the
Lord added to their number day by day those who were being saved.*

ACTS 2:42, 46–47 ESV

. . . . . . . . . . . . . . . . . . . . . . .

The first key verse above is frequently cited to say the normal Christian
life consists of four things. Those four things are (1) apostolic teaching,
(2) fellowship together as brothers and sisters in Christ, (3) the breaking
of bread (also called the Lord's Supper, Communion, and the Eucharist),
and (4) prayer.

The other two key verses above say the normal Christian life consists
of five more things. Those five more "day by day" things are (5) gladness,
(6) generosity, (7) praising God, (8) having favor with all the people, and
(9) adding new Christians to their number "day by day."

Few churches, let alone individual men, consistently incorporate all
nine things into their lives. That's okay. There's no need for guilt or shame.
Just the opposite. Select one thing you would like to add to your life for
a few weeks. If it adds (5) gladness, all the better!

---

*Lord, You know what I'd like to add to my life. May it also add gladness!*

# TRUST THE SPIRIT TO SPEAK THROUGH YOU

*And when they [religious leaders] had set them [Peter and John] in the midst, they inquired, "By what power or by what name did you do this?"*

ACTS 4:7 ESV

. . . . . . . . . . . . . . . . . . . . . .

The distinguished Jewish council in Jerusalem had gathered en masse to try, convict, and punish two of Jesus Christ's leading apostles. Their carefully selected leading question, however, backfired. Instead of allowing them to judge Peter and John, the Holy Spirit turned the tables. To get the best sense of what's happening, you may want to read Acts 4:9–12 aloud once or twice.

After that dramatic and inspired response, what happened next? "Now when they saw the boldness of Peter and John, and perceived that they were uneducated, common men, they were astonished. And they recognized that they had been with Jesus. But seeing the man who was healed standing beside them, they had nothing to say in opposition" (Acts 4:13–14 ESV).

Talk about turning the tables! All they could do was command Peter and John to quit talking about Jesus. Of course, that backfired badly as you'll hear rather dramatically by reading Acts 4:19–22 aloud once or twice.

Never stop talking about God the Father, God the Son, and God the Holy Spirit. May they empower what you do and say these first days of summer.

*Lord, yes, please empower me to speak about You with supernatural boldness.*

# UNLIKE ANANIAS AND SAPPHIRA, FEAR GOD

*"The property was yours to sell or not sell, as you wished. And after selling it, the money was also yours to give away. How could you do a thing like this? You weren't lying to us but to God!"*

ACTS 5:4 NLT

. . . . . . . . . . . . . . . . . . . . . .

Ananias and his wife, Sapphira, were under no obligation to give anything to the Jerusalem church. Though the early believers shared freely, no one was pressured to give up ownership of personal property or to tithe a certain amount of each sale. Still, because of greed or vanity, Ananias and Sapphira choose to falsify the size of their gift. That premeditated sin brought severe judgment upon their heads.

Ananias and Sapphira were not judged for their lack of generosity. Instead, they were judged for trying to deceive God. They presented their gift as something very different than what it actually was.

You and I may be inclined to overlook a lie, judging its severity by the perceived damage that's been done. But every lie is in reality a bold statement of unbelief against the omniscient Lord God.

Someone well may try to fool other believers, but who in his right mind would try to deceive the all-seeing and all-knowing Lord?

Unlike Ananias and his wife, let's make a point of telling the truth to God and others.

*Lord, I wince to think how many lies I've told.*
*Please forgive me. Make me an honest man.*

# LIKE ELISHA, EXPERIENCE GOD'S POWER

*He struck the water with Elijah's cloak and cried*
*out, "Where is the LORD, the God of Elijah?"*
*Then the river divided, and Elisha went across.*

2 KINGS 2:14 NLT

. . . . . . . . . . . . . . . . . . . . . . .

God has no grandchildren, and you cannot inherit the personal experience of God's power from a friend. After Elijah was swept to glory in the fiery chariot, it was time for Elisha to move beyond all he had learned from his teacher and trust himself to the Lord alone.

The big question to be answered: Would Elisha continue dwelling on the past glory days of Elijah, or would he be used and blessed by God in a daily powerful way?

Elisha continued the ministry of Elijah by declaring to Israel that the Lord was God. Through miraculous signs and miracles, he continued to prove that the Lord was infinitely greater than Baal or any other god around. Yet Elisha's power was not a leftover of Elijah's, but his own experience of God's work through him.

Elisha did more than just succeed Elijah in ministry. Though they preached the same message, God showed His power through these two men in different ways. Among other things, God poured out even more miracles through Elisha than he did through Elijah.

---

*Lord, I've never had an Elijah in my life. Still, I want to*
*experience Your power at work in and through me, please!*

# "NOTHING THERE AT ALL. . .EXCEPT"

*The wife of a man from the company of the prophets cried out*
*to Elisha, "Your servant my husband is dead, and you know*
*that he revered the LORD. But now his creditor is coming to*
*take my two boys as his slaves." Elisha replied to her, "How*
*can I help you? Tell me, what do you have in your house?"*

2 KINGS 4:1–2 NIV

. . . . . . . . . . . . . . . . . . . . . . . .

Why do wise men buy term life insurance? Typically, to provide for and protect their wives and children in the case of their untimely deaths.

Tragically, for more than five thousand years—including up to the present time especially in sub-Saharan Africa and South Asia—if a debtor dies, the creditor forces the debtor's children and/or wife to work as slaves until the debt is repaid. This accounts for nearly half of today's modern slaves.

No wonder the deceased prophet's wife was in such duress. In answer to Elisha's question, she replied, "Your servant has nothing there at all." Then she added, "except a small jar of olive oil" (2 Kings 4:2 NIV).

From that small jar, a wonderful miracle occurred, a great quantity of olive oil was sold, the debt was fully repaid, and the widow and her two boys had plenty of money left to continually meet their needs.

*Lord, please provide for and protect my family. In wisdom,*
*Help me to trust You, my Provider, with my whole heart.*

# UNLIKE GEHAZI, DON'T TAKE RICHES

*"Yes," Gehazi said, "but my master has sent me to tell you that two young prophets from the hill country of Ephraim have just arrived. He would like 75 pounds of silver and two sets of clothing to give to them."*

2 KINGS 5:22 NLT

. . . . . . . . . . . . . . . . . . . . . . .

As Elisha's servant, Gehazi had witnessed the power of God often. Still, when tempted by the chance to fill his own pockets, the glitter of gold shone brighter to Gehazi than did God's glory.

Elisha refused any gift that would distract Naaman from knowing that the Lord alone was God. While God's Word provides for the Lord's servants to receive gifts and support (Deuteronomy 18:1–8 and 1 Timothy 5:17–18), Elisha knew that now was not the time to take money, especially for miracles. No one but God must get the glory for making Naaman healthy.

Gehazi had no such insight into God's purposes for bringing the commander of the enemy's armies to the prophet of Israel for healing. Even Elisha's words didn't deter Gehazi from going after something for himself. Greed led to deception as he raced after Naaman and asked for the money his master earlier refused. That greed led straight to disaster.

While Naaman returned home with a healthy body and a committed heart, Gehazi returned home bearing Naaman's leprosy on his flesh.

---

*Lord, may I never take Your money into my own hands.*

## "DAY OF GOOD NEWS"

*They said to one another, "We are not doing right. This
day is a day of good news. If we are silent and wait until
the morning light, punishment will overtake us. Now
therefore come; let us go and tell the king's household."*

2 KINGS 7:9 ESV

· · · · · · · · · · · · · · · · · · · · · ·

Today's key verse is the fifth time the Bible says someone is *not doing
right*. This is the sixth time God's Word uses the wonderful phrase *good
news*. The implication is clear: the right and best thing is to tell good news!

Today's key verse is the second time scripture uses the word *silent*.
And it's the second to last time it uses the phrase *morning light*. The
implication is clear: tell good news now, without delay. Why? Because
everyone from gatekeepers to the king needs and wants to hear good news!

Toss the idea that the vast majority of people don't want to hear the
Good News of Jesus Christ. Many do! And what is that Good News? First,
who Jesus is: eternally true God, who came to earth two thousand years
ago, lived a perfect life, taught for scores of hours, performed hundreds
of miracles, and fed thousands of people.

Second, what Jesus did: died for you and your sins, was buried, rose
again the third day, and appeared to His followers for nearly six weeks
(1 Corinthians 15:1–7).

*Lord, You are the Good News. May I talk about You again soon!*

# "DON'T LET ANYONE. . .TELL ABOUT IT"

*Jehu said, "If you commanders wish to make me king,
then don't let anyone. . .tell about it in Jezreel."*

2 KINGS 9:15 HCSB

• • • • • • • • • • • • • • • • • • • • • • •

Like any good or great book of literature, the Bible is full of secrets. Even Jesus knew untold numbers of secrets, said only what God the Father told Him to say, and then often said them only to His closest disciples.

What's more, Jesus found it hard to keep His foreign respite location a secret (Mark 7:24) and found it even harder to convince private miracle recipients not to say anything about it publicly (Matthew 8:4, 9:30, 17:9; Mark 1:44, 8:26; and Luke 5:14).

Some secrets should be kept secret.

Other things shouldn't be kept secret. For instance. . .

Don't keep it secret that you read this devotional, the Bible, and other Christian books.

Don't keep it secret that you believe in Jesus Christ and His Good News of salvation.

Don't keep it secret that you pray to the Lord God, Maker of heaven and earth, who hears and answers the prayers of His children.

Don't keep it secret that you are a Christian and actively meet with God's people.

---

*Lord, why do I walk around pretending I know national secrets? I'm ready to talk about my faith in You.*

# LIKE STEPHEN, BE BOLD FOR JESUS

*He fell to his knees, shouting, "Lord, don't charge*
*them with this sin!" And with that, he died.*

ACTS 7:60 NLT

• • • • • • • • • • • • • • • • • • • • • • •

When you think of martyrs, who comes to mind? Stephen was an outstanding individual who was wholeheartedly committed to the Lord. Scripture tells us he was well respected, full of the Holy Spirit and wisdom, full of faith, and full of God's grace and power (Acts 6:3, 5, 8).

In life and in death, Stephen imitated his Lord and Savior. Like Jesus and the twelve apostles, Stephen performed amazing miracles and signs among the people (Acts 6:8) and was arrested for preaching about Jesus. Like Jesus and the apostles, Stephen was tried by the Jewish high council in Jerusalem.

While his accusers shook their fists in rage, Stephen saw a glorious vision of Jesus. Then, like Jesus, Stephen was dragged outside the city of Jerusalem to be killed. Before collapsing, Stephen echoed two of the most famous prayers the Lord had cried out from the cross (Luke 23:34, 46).

Today Stephen is remembered as the first Christian *martyr*. But first and foremost, he was a true *Christian*. He consciously determined to trust the Lord Jesus and obey Him no matter what. The Lord now calls you and me to follow in his footsteps.

---

*Lord, no matter what, I want to be wholeheartedly*
*committed to You always.*

# UNLIKE SIMON, DON'T SEEK MIRACULOUS POWERS

*"Pray to the Lord for me," Simon exclaimed, "that these terrible things you've said won't happen to me!"*
ACTS 8:24 NLT

. . . . . . . . . . . . . . . . . . . . . .

Do you know the difference between a miracle and a magic trick? Can you discern between the Holy Spirit's activity and the special effects of those who use His name while conjuring up remarkable displays of power?

Simon the sorcerer knew all about power. In Samaria, he was billed as "the Great One—the Power of God" (Acts 8:10 NLT)—until Philip came preaching the Good News about Jesus Christ. Through Philip's prayers, the sick were healed, the demon-possessed were released from bondage, and hearts were transformed. Simon was so impressed that he made a profession of faith and followed Philip and Peter around. Yet was Simon a sincere believer? Or was he jealous and looking for a way to steal back the show from the visiting Christians?

The truth came out when Simon watched the Holy Spirit given to the Samaritan believers. He was amazed and thought to himself, *I must get that power!* So he offered cash to Peter, who sternly rebuked Simon for his evil thoughts and bitter heart.

Unlike Simon, let's honor the Holy Spirit for who He is—not try to manipulate Him for our own glory.

---

*Lord, I want to be a sincere believer through and through, now and always.*

# LIKE ANANIAS, TRUST GOD'S SAVING POWER

*So Ananias went and found Saul. He laid his hands on*
*him and said, "Brother Saul, the Lord Jesus, who appeared*
*to you on the road, has sent me so that you might regain*
*your sight and be filled with the Holy Spirit."*

ACTS 9:17 NLT

. . . . . . . . . . . . . . . . . . . . . . .

What's your first reaction when you hear about a notorious sinner who claims to have been converted? Ananias wasn't sure he had heard the Lord right. Go and visit Saul the persecutor? The Lord knew about this man, right? Hadn't Saul viciously attacked the Christians in Jerusalem and come to destroy the believers in Damascus?

Ananias's questions were normal. But the Lord told Ananias to do what He had said. Why? Because He already had dealt with Saul and chose him to proclaim God's message throughout the world—and to endure much suffering as a result.

Ananias proved he believed the Lord by going to Straight Street. When he found Saul, Ananias placed his hands on him and called Saul his "brother." As a result of his obedience, Ananias witnessed the power of God filling Saul with His Holy Spirit and freeing him from his blindness.

Immediately afterward, other Christians feared that Saul was an impostor. They hadn't received a vision from Jesus confirming Saul's conversion. But soon they heard his bold testimony that Jesus "is indeed the Son of God!" (Acts 9:20 NLT).

*Lord, fill me with Your Holy Spirit too.*

## REDIRECT YOUR THINKING

*The Israelites secretly did what was not right
against the LORD their God.*
2 KINGS 17:9 HCSB

. . . . . . . . . . . . . . . . . . . . . . .

God was offended. The people were breaking His law, and it seemed they thought He wouldn't notice. Most weren't sinning openly but rather behind closed doors. They had set aside the seriousness of their relationship with God and did what they wanted.

The biggest problem with using your mind to entertain the idea of breaking God's law is that the more you think about sinning, the more likely you will be to sin. Maybe that's why God gives you so many good things to consider. It's why He gave you His Word. It's why you always have an invitation to pray.

You have only so many minutes in life, so ask yourself if it makes sense to waste any of your time entertaining ideas that keep you from the purpose for which God created you.

It's sort of like a well-balanced diet. You stay away from an all–cotton candy diet because it will never lead to good health. And you don't have a healthy spiritual life if you refuse quality spiritual food. God notices your walkaway choice—even when no one else suspects. Shift your thinking strategies, and allow truth to change your heart and mind.

*Redirect my thinking, Father. I don't want to get sidetracked
in my walk with You, but sometimes it's too easy to do. The
things You ask me to think always lead to Your best for me.*

# THE LEGACY

*There was a believer in Joppa named Tabitha*
*(which in Greek is Dorcas). She was always doing*
*kind things for others and helping the poor.*
ACTS 9:36 NLT

. . . . . . . . . . . . . . . . . . . . . . .

This full story is just eight verses long, and it ends with Tabitha rising from the dead. That's a miracle and worthy of celebration, but this story started in the mind, heart, and soul with the phrase *There was a believer*. These words should lead you to remember that there's a meeting between all the things that make you who you are, and that meeting results in a decision to believe. That belief is in the God who has a purpose for every part of your life.

The evidence of God's work shows up in Tabitha's life. She was kind and compassionate. These aren't natural tendencies. That would be left to rudeness and selfishness. You never need much encouragement to try these last two.

Tabitha's story is one of many that feature little-known characters in the biblical narrative who are defined by their love for God. The thoughts you think aren't just important to your actions, they lead to the choices that will be what people remember about you.

---

*God, at the end of my life, I want people to recall more*
*than what I did for a living when they think about me. I*
*want to be a thoughtful believer who's kind and helpful*
*because those are two things that look a lot like You.*

# THE ARTISTIC CREATOR

*You water the mountains from your heavenly reservoirs; earth
is supplied with plenty of water. You make grass grow for
the livestock, hay for the animals that plow the ground.*
PSALM 104:13–14 MSG

. . . . . . . . . . . . . . . . . . . . . . . .

You can look at any beautiful spot in the world and enjoy scenes that
amaze and astound. They inspire you. You're not sure you want to leave.
You take in the mountains, canyons, raging water, and serene meadows.
In those moments, do you gravitate toward the thought that there must
be an artistic Creator behind every backdrop?

Creation itself is a reason to think. Don't stop at just appreciating
what you see. Think about the God who created water and then held it
in natural channels that will take it from the clouds to the ground, from
the ground to creeks and rivers, and from there to the ocean and then
back to the clouds.

Think about the care God has for people. He's created a means to
feed them and make sure they have something to drink. Think about the
fact that He made these things for you. Think about the fact that none
of this was a challenge for God.

---

*Thank You for every mountaintop, waterfall, and forest. Father,
help me remember that these are Your gifts and point out one more
way You have supplied what I could never provide for myself.*

## CELEBRATE INDEPENDENCE

*[The people] did not listen, and Manasseh led them*
*astray to do more evil than the nations had done whom*
*the LORD destroyed before the people of Israel.*
2 KINGS 21:9 ESV

. . . . . . . . . . . . . . . . . . . . . . .

It's possible to think that freedom means doing anything you want without restrictions. If that's how you think of freedom, you may be thinking too small. Manasseh was a king who thought freedom meant keeping himself at arm's length from God. He persuaded others to follow his lead. This thinking would allow children to eat candy at every meal. It would mean students could give wrong answers without any penalty on their score. It would mean people could get a job, never show up, and still be paid.

Freedom is best found knowing what your purpose is. When you make that discovery, you're free to do everything that helps you accomplish what God made you to do. One freedom moves you to what's important while the other typically leads to chaos and distress.

Celebrate independence from those things that stunt your spiritual growth. Be grateful that your freedom can keep you from making mistakes and from continuing to make those mistakes.

There's freedom in Christ. But if you believe He has a plan for your life, then that freedom means you're released to do what you were created to do.

---

*I want to be free, God. I don't want to be irresponsible.*
*Help me discover the freedom that comes when I*
*choose to follow You with my whole heart.*

# AVOID SPIRITUAL SOLITUDE

*The church in Jerusalem. . .sent Barnabas to Antioch to check
on things. As soon as he arrived, he saw that God was behind
and in it all. He threw himself in with them, got behind them,
urging them to stay with it the rest of their lives. He was a good
man that way, enthusiastic and confident in the Holy Spirit's
ways. The community grew large and strong in the Master.*
ACTS 11:22–24 MSG

• • • • • • • • • • • • • • • • • • • • • • • •

Barnabas was known as the "Son of Encouragement." The three verses above provide a clear reason why. He could read a room. He used his intellect, emotions, and the Spirit God gave him to do what he could to honor Jesus and encourage others to do the same.

This man was Paul's ministry partner, and he saw that God was at work in Antioch. He got involved by running the race with those who were on pace to win.

You might be willing to keep your faith low key, but today's passage gives you a glimpse of what can happen when you choose to take what you know and walk with others on God's path. The very nature of God urges you to stop living in spiritual solitude and start sharing the journey with those going the same way.

---

*Help me find people to encourage, Father. Help me
understand that I sometimes need encouragement too.
Trying to do both by myself just isn't going to work.*

## SEARCH. SEEK. REMEMBER.

*Search for the LORD and for his strength; continually*
*seek him. Remember the wonders he has performed,*
*his miracles, and the rulings he has given.*

PSALM 105:4–5 NLT

. . . . . . . . . . . . . . . . . . . . . . .

When you move away from where you were born and raised, you may experience a longing to go home at various times in your life. You can yearn for a place, circumstance, or family and friends. That yearning you feel in those moments is a picture of the search described in Psalm 105. Yearn for the God who develops everyday miracles for you and those around you. He keeps everything together and moving forward.

Music can take you back to a place you remember, an aroma can transport your mind to a place with people you can't talk to anymore, and this collective yearning can help you understand the desire to be with God one day.

The combination of elements that make you who you are can work together to make you yearn for a place you've never been, trust a God you've never seen, and look forward to a future you've yet to experience. This happens when you search, seek, and remember God with your whole heart.

*One day I will get to meet You, God. Until then, help me remember*
*all the things You've done. Not just things You've done for me*
*but for those around me as well. I want to marvel at the stories*
*of Your mercy and be inspired by Your gifts of kindness.*

# RESPONSE REQUIRED

*[Paul said,] "Brothers, sons of Abraham's race, and those among you who fear God, the message of this salvation has been sent to us."*
ACTS 13:26 HCSB

. . . . . . . . . . . . . . . . . . . . . . .

A message requires someone who sends and someone who receives. The message requires thought, planning, and purpose. The message has to be accepted and understood. The best-case scenario is when the message is internalized and allowed to initiate changes in the one who receives it.

Take a soldier, for example. When they receive the message that their orders have changed, it means that someone has analyzed what is needed and then formulated a plan to give the soldier a specific role in the change. The soldier needs to receive and accept the change and then move in the direction of their new assignment. When they don't, they exist in a state of rebellion.

Christianity is a message that requires a heart response because it must be accepted by faith. It's a mind response because learning will be required. It's a spiritual response because God gave you a spirit that works with His Spirit to bring about new life. It's a choice that demands an ongoing response.

God has sent a message that is rooted in love. He waits for men to communicate it—and people to accept it.

*You've shared a message that has changed my life,
Father. Thanks for helping me enough to receive it and
then learn more about the plan You have for me.*

# A JEALOUS CONTRADICTION

*The next Sabbath almost the whole city gathered to hear the word of the Lord. But when the Jews saw the crowds, they were filled with jealousy and began to contradict what was spoken by Paul, reviling him.*

ACTS 13:44–45 ESV

. . . . . . . . . . . . . . . . . . . . . . . .

People attended a conference for the curious. They came from throughout the region to satisfy their interest in the message about Jesus. They wanted to hear more. There were those with no faith, those with some faith, and still others living in open hostility to the message. It was the hostile among the crowd who made comments that sought to discredit the truth Paul shared. They contradicted the message and ridiculed the one delivering it.

There have always been people who seek to derail God's message. They have thought about the message and entertain the notion that there are flaws. They tend to think of the message in terms of human logic or through the lens of their own past. They consider the message based on old information instead of new thinking and a new heart.

You might have faced a similar struggle when you first heard about Jesus. It's not hard to believe that some of the message is hard to accept when you think it contradicts what you were taught, what you have believed, and what you considered truth.

---

*Your message can challenge what I think, God. Give me the courage to accept with my whole heart what You have called truth.*

# HOW HE THINKS

*These tribes were unfaithful to the God of their ancestors.*
*They worshiped the gods of the nations that God had destroyed.*
1 CHRONICLES 5:25 NLT

. . . . . . . . . . . . . . . . . . . . . . .

The scripture verse above provides another cautionary tale about the struggle involved when people reject God's message. Men can turn away from what God says based on a lack of understanding, but they can also reject what they read because they simply don't want to believe it. For example, God says not to lie, but a man who knows he has lied might want to dismiss His message on the subject because acknowledging it leaves him knowing he is guilty of the sin of lying.

In this verse, it was whole tribes of people who were found to be unfaithful to God. That's bad enough, but they followed up their unfaithfulness with the worship of gods who had been vanquished by God. It's like they were telling God, "You beat them, but I worship them anyway."

It's easy to read that stark contrast and conclude that the people were clouded in their judgment, delusional in their thinking—or were poster children for foolishness.

It remains true that the way you think and the way God thinks are different. He already knows how You think and what's in your heart. He invites you to learn how He thinks.

---

*Father, I don't want to be counted among the unfaithful. Help*
*me adjust my thinking to Yours. Help me trust You enough to*
*take what I'm learning and trust You with my whole heart.*

# DESPERATELY SEEKING WIGGLE ROOM

*Remember this! He led his people out singing for joy; his chosen people marched, singing their hearts out! He made them a gift of the country they entered, helped them seize the wealth of the nations so they could do everything he told them—could follow his instructions to the letter.*

PSALM 105:43–45 MSG

. . . . . . . . . . . . . . . . . . . . . . .

Today's psalm recounts some of the key moments of the Israelites' exodus from Egypt. This passage may give a clue as to why the freedom the people received might have led them to a new type of bondage.

They left Egypt singing. They marched side by side as overcomers. God promised a land they could call their own. He gave them instructions on how to live this new, free life. The intent was that these people would have no reason to disobey. Yet they didn't do what the Lord had told them to do. They did not follow God's instructions. These people looked for wiggle room and enjoyed walking the edge of what God had said was acceptable. They often crossed that line. This response left them waiting in the wilderness for four decades.

God has given you instructions to follow. Take what you learn and follow His instructions. He has given you everything you need to obey. When you do, you'll discover joy as you receive God's gifts.

*Lord, my way has failed and continues to fail.*
*Show Your way and help me to walk in Your steps.*

# A MESSAGE ACCEPTED

*After some time had passed, Paul said to Barnabas, "Let's go back and visit the brothers in every town where we have preached the message of the Lord and see how they're doing."*
ACTS 15:36 HCSB

. . . . . . . . . . . . . . . . . . . . . .

Like a doctor checking up on patients, the apostle Paul wanted to return to some of the places he had visited on his mission trips. A spiritual checkup was in order. He hadn't made the trip sooner, likely because the people needed time for the message of the Lord to seep into their hearts and souls. The people had received the seed of God's message. The trip would allow Paul's team to see how those seeds had grown.

This would be yet another example of how thinking impacted decision-making. You see, thinking alone never really gets to the heart of the message God shared, because humans can always rationalize their personal choices while dismissing God's importance. However, if thinking moved the heart to respond with the faith needed to accept the message, then change within the spirit will be the outcome.

You need to know you're not alone in your faith and that growth is the outcome as you learn how to live your life of faith.

*It's a big decision to follow You, Father. Help me be willing to share my heart, mind, and spirit and allow You to use what words You can use to encourage others to keep thinking about You.*

# GOD MEMORIES

*They exchanged their glorious God for an image of a bull,*
*which eats grass. They forgot the God who saved them.*
PSALM 106:20–21 NIV

. . . . . . . . . . . . . . . . . . . . . .

One of the important key words in the Bible is *remembering*, which means being aware of something important you were shown or taught in the past. You had thought about something that somehow connected you to the story—but time and inattention can take that from you. It did for the people described in Psalm 106.

God had rescued them. He had been their glorious Savior. The response of the people, however, was not to remember the value of rescue but to insist it was not the only way. They paid some respects to God and then brought in the image of a bull and decided it was worthy of worship.

It's common to forget. Perhaps that is why the instructions for God's people were to make conversation about the Lord and what He had done for them in the past.

God offered Jesus as the great exchange—the perfection of His Son for the imperfection of mankind. The last thing He wanted was for you to exchange the perfection of His Son for old choices and divided allegiances. But if that happens, admit your poor choice and accept His forgiveness.

---

*I don't know why I can be so fickle, God. I can be honored to*
*be called a follower one minute, and the next I act like Peter*
*and deny I know You. Help me stop making that choice.*

# INQUIRING MINDS

*David inquired of God.*
1 CHRONICLES 14:10 ESV

. . . . . . . . . . . . . . . . . . . . . . .

There's more to the passage than "David inquired." It was a mix of strategy and military action. It was a desire to win. Yeah, there's more to the story, yet four words make this story more than an impulse decision. *David inquired of God.*

This king had fought and won wars, but he had also written psalms, hymns, and spiritual songs. He had a close relationship with God, and leaving Him out of this story made no sense to David. Instead of guessing, *David inquired.* Instead of assuming, *David inquired.* Instead of ignoring, *David inquired.*

It's easy to leave someone out of a decision, especially when you think that person would disagree with what you want to do. You like to find people who agree with you, even when you think you might be wrong. So find a spirit in tune with God, a heart that wants His best, and a mind willing to change if that's what God wants—and *inquire.*

Bring God into your plans, and allow Him to veto what He knows is a waste of your time and energy. Give Him every chance possible to answer your inquiry.

---

*Father, when I pray, I'm inquiring—or at least I hope I am.
When I just talk to You about my day and the people who need
Your help, I'm not doing enough to gain wisdom. Help me ask
for Your answers to questions that seem too hard for me.*

# REASONED. EXPLAINED. PROVED.

*Paul went into the synagogue, and on three Sabbath days he
reasoned with them from the Scriptures, explaining and proving
that the Messiah had to suffer and rise from the dead.*

ACTS 17:2–3 NIV

. . . . . . . . . . . . . . . . . . . . . . .

The apostle Paul spent most of his time sharing God's message with
people. He didn't apologize or diminish the message in any way. He
shared it with skeptics, and he confronted those hostile to the words he
spoke. Paul didn't back down.

The apostle did three things to help his audience have the best chance
at understanding the message. You won't read the words *condescending*,
*belittling*, or *harassing* in today's scripture verse. Paul used a better approach.

*Reasoned*—He appealed to people's ability to think through issues
and consider the validity of the message.

*Explained*—He knew there were concepts the audience wouldn't
understand, so he used words and examples that simplified the complex.

*Proved*—Paul dealt in facts, not fairy tales. He could prove the
message by what actually happened.

Paul could have said something you've probably heard before: "God
said it, I believe it, and that's good enough for me." While this is a fine
personal proclamation, it rarely meets people where they really are. They'll
need someone patient enough to reason, explain, and prove in a way that
attracts them to God's life-changing, heart-transforming message.

*Jesus, I want to use Your words to eliminate barriers to new life.
The people I talk to will consider You with their mind before
they accept Your rescue by faith. Help me remember that.*

## THANKS BEFORE BLESSING

*Save us, O LORD our God! Gather us back from among the nations,
so we can thank your holy name and rejoice and praise you.*
PSALM 106:47 NLT

. . . . . . . . . . . . . . . . . . . . . . .

Lost people need to be rescued, and the beauty of this predicament is when grateful people ask God for help, *He helps.* It means they have spent time considering their situation and have discovered that no matter how hard they've tried, they can't rescue themselves.

The writer of Psalm 106 understood this place of mental paralysis. He could have hated the place where he was but refused to ask God for help. But the exact opposite was the reality. The psalmist admitted his nation's role in becoming lost but recognized God as the Rescuer. He had taken the time to consider what life would be like after rescue, and that brought about a heart of gratitude and a God cheer. Maybe this was also partly because he could also remember how hard it was without rescue.

You can thank God today for blessings you have yet to receive. It's an aspect of faith when you believe God will supply before He actually supplies. Offer thanks before blessings—and again when God blesses.

*Father, I will need everyday rescues. I cannot rescue myself,
but knowing that You can and will help me is a relief
and a cause for a heart of gratitude. Thank You.*

# AN INVITATION TO THINK

*David wouldn't take no for an answer.*
1 CHRONICLES 21:4 MSG

. . . . . . . . . . . . . . . . . . . . . . .

Bad ideas are just that—bad ideas. Sometimes the one who has the idea can't see any reason to deviate from their bad decision. Teens can hear their parents say no, and they still want to accomplish their bad idea. You probably have had those moments.

You can read about a bad decision King David made in today's scripture reading in 1 Chronicles. But you may not need to know what that decision was to be able to identify with the king's lapse in thinking.

David had made poor choices before and would do so again, but each of those moments was a reminder to think before acting, to ask God to help him with the decision, and to invite Him to change his mind.

God can use other people to ask you to think, and He can use His Word to instruct you, but it's hard to *make* you do the right thing when you have a tendency to say no.

You can even be temporarily convinced that you don't need to make good choices, but that always ends in regret. Some of the consequences for this lapse in judgment can last a lifetime.

Think. God wants you to. Really. He does. Think.

*You gave me a mind for a reason, God. Help me use it
to think, reason, and make decisions that show that
I understand that Your plan is always best.*

## THE MAN FROM ELOQUENT

*Now a Jew named Apollos, a native of Alexandria, came
to Ephesus. He was an eloquent man, competent in the
Scriptures. He had been instructed in the way of the Lord.*

ACTS 18:24–25 ESV

· · · · · · · · · · · · · · · · · · · · · ·

God never asked people to think He's cool and then make things up about Him, but some people do that very thing, often basing their conclusions on experiences and feelings that don't match up with what His Word actually says.

The Bible doesn't say much about a Jewish man named Apollos, but we do know he was a thinking man. He could string words together in a way that's described using the word *eloquent*. He was knowledgeable enough to speak accurately about the Bible. He had been instructed, which means he had learned about the faith he spoke about.

Apollos's life can be an encouragement for us to do as he did. We should talk about Jesus, but we should make sure we're sharing heart-changing truth and not guesses. We should use our minds to read and learn and refuse to share what we're unsure of. God's truth will always have a greater impact on people's hearts than our best guesses.

*Father, I need to learn to share what I know. But before
I can do that, I need to take the time to really get to
know You and what You want me to tell others.*

# THE WAY OF PERSONAL PAIN

*Some became fools through their rebellious ways and*
*suffered affliction because of their iniquities.*

PSALM 107:17 NIV

. . . . . . . . . . . . . . . . . . . . . . . .

Foolishness and trouble are cause-and-effect companions. The cause is foolishness, and the effect is trouble. No one wants trouble to show up, but foolishness opens the door to its entry.

A fool isn't interested in the truth. He is prone to rebellion and likes to wander a path of his own choosing. That path often has spiritual thistles, unseen drop-offs, and multiple tripping hazards. Yet time and again a fool will smile and choose the way of personal pain, thinking it will be different this time. But it never is. It isn't now. It never will be. *Ever.*

The good news is that you do not have to choose the path fools take. That path is an option worth rejection for no other reason than it has proved a failed option.

Let's turn that around. A wise person refuses rebellion —and, while he may suffer as much as anyone else, the suffering he experiences will not be due to his own rebellious choices.

Set aside personal rebellion, and things will begin to improve. It will mean a change of heart, thinking, and the way to respond to God.

*God, I don't need to have a testimony of foolishness to tell others*
*about You. I don't need to keep being foolish because You've always*
*been right. Help me believe that and use it to make wise decisions.*

# THE PRIMARY GOAL

*And you, Solomon my son, know the God of your father [have personal knowledge of Him, be acquainted with, and understand Him; appreciate, heed, and cherish Him] and serve Him with a blameless heart and a willing mind. For the Lord searches all hearts and minds and understands all the wanderings of the thoughts. If you seek Him [inquiring for and of Him and requiring Him as your first and vital necessity] you will find Him.*

1 CHRONICLES 28:9 AMPC

· · · · · · · · · · · · · · · · · · · · · · ·

It was time for King David to pass the kingdom to his son, Solomon. His wisdom for the incoming king is good wisdom for you. Are you ready to take a closer look? Know, understand, appreciate, obey, and cherish God. Serve Him with a heart that refuses rebellion and a mind that is ready for a God adventure. God can and will search the core of who you are, and He is fully aware of the tendency to wander. Seek God, pray to Him, learn from Him. Make that your primary goal, and you will find God.

That's an amazing bit of advice. It encourages every part of you to enlist in a lifetime of learning, a heart of wisdom, and a spirit that recognizes the goodness of God.

*Father, help me take David's advice and gain wisdom. Help me take that wisdom and let it change my heart. I can't do that alone.*

# THE SERMON

*Paul was preaching to them, and since he was leaving
the next day, he kept talking until midnight.*
ACTS 20:7 NLT

. . . . . . . . . . . . . . . . . . . . . . .

If you ever thought that a sermon dragged on a little long, then consider this story from Acts. Paul started preaching when the sun was shining, but he had a lot to say and he would be leaving in the morning. His sermon went until midnight. That wasn't the end of the sermon, but something happened that caused an unexpected intermission. A man sitting on the windowsill fell asleep, fell backward, and died. No one expected that.

Paul went downstairs to check on the young man, Eutychus. He was miraculously brought back to life. They both went back upstairs and had communion, and then Paul continued preaching until dawn.

Maybe you've read this story before, but if there is a takeaway for you today, it's that there are things worth pursuing in the Bible, even if it takes time. God can bring dead things to life, and the people who heard Paul preach stayed to learn.

Take the time, embrace new life, linger, and learn.

*Lord, there are times when I want to read Your Word. I start and my mind wanders. But when I stick with it, You teach me just what I need to know.*

## THE LEARNING CENTER

*[Solomon said,] God said he would dwell*
*in a cloud, but I've built a temple.*
2 Chronicles 6:2 msg

. . . . . . . . . . . . . . . . . . . . . . .

Some have called church a hospital because people who are sick spiritually can expect to get well there. Some think of it as a place where disciples grow. King Solomon seemed to think something similar. He didn't call the temple a *learning center*, but that's what happened there.

This was something God allowed the wisest king in history to build. There hadn't been a permanent place to learn about God before. This learning center taught people the value of community, enhanced the idea of spending time with God, and was a place to get answers.

Teaching would occur there. Learning was the choice of those who came expecting to learn. God doesn't disappoint His students.

So think of a church as a place where spiritually hurting people can have their hearts healed *and then* learn how to live a new and revitalized life. It really can—and should—be both.

Is it any wonder that God says staying away from His learning center is a very bad idea?

---

*You teach, and I can learn, Father. Help me understand what seems*
*like a mystery and then believe what You tell me is truth. May the*
*people I worship with be both those who need healing and those*
*who continue to be healed because they stay close to You.*

# THE APPEAL COURT

*[Solomon said,] "If your people Israel are defeated before the enemy because they have sinned against you, and they turn again and acknowledge your name and pray and plead with you in this house, then hear from heaven and forgive the sin of your people."*

2 CHRONICLES 6:24–25 ESV

. . . . . . . . . . . . . . . . . . . . . . .

King Solomon—the wise king—spoke to God in prayer. He recognized that God could withhold His blessing when rebellion beat wildly in the heart of humanity. He prayed for God's favor. Solomon had to know that God didn't have to agree to his request, but the earthly king appealed to the goodness of the heavenly King. Solomon wanted to know if God would restore rebellious people when they recognized their rebellion and returned to their place at God's side.

This prayer almost reads like a legal argument or an appeal to heaven's highest court. It was a mix of plea bargain and promises of better choices. God would never excuse sin, but He will forgive. The thinking man will advance this appeal. You have no standing if you ask God to look away while you rebel. You do have the privilege to say from your heart, "You were right. I was wrong. I rebelled. Please forgive me."

*God, I can't ask You to act as if my sin didn't happen. But I can turn around, come back, and seek Your forgiveness. May I always come back when I find myself walking away.*

# HELP THEM SEE YOU

*Help me, O Lord my God; O save me according to Your*
*mercy and loving-kindness!—That they may know that*
*this is Your hand, that You, Lord, have done it.*
PSALM 109:26–27 AMPC

· · · · · · · · · · · · · · · · · · · · · · ·

Like son, like father. King Solomon was seeking God's restorative care on behalf of a sinning public in yesterday's reading. His father, King David, prayed a different prayer in Psalm 109—and it was incredibly personal.

David knew enough about God to recognize that He wanted people to know Him. The king was asking for protection because God is merciful (exactly what Solomon brought up in his appeal for the people). David wanted enemies of his country to recognize—to think about—God. He didn't want those advancing against him to have any doubt that they were encountering the one and only God. David wanted them to believe any other deity was a non-God. He knew that those who opposed Him had never encountered anything like God.

It is true that David wanted his enemy defeated, but he wanted that defeat to come from the God who could make Himself known in the middle of justice.

---

*Father, You're never limited in how You make Yourself known to*
*people. You can be found in good times and bad, when I'm happy or*
*disappointed, and among the healed and wounded. I want people to*
*recognize You. Make Yourself known wherever people are found.*

# COURT OF PUBLIC OPINION

*[Paul said,] "Brothers and fathers, listen now to my defense."*
ACTS 22:1 NIV

. . . . . . . . . . . . . . . . . . . . . . . .

Paul found himself in the court of public opinion, and it was uncomfortable. He had a testimony to share, and the atmosphere was tense with opposing perspectives. For the third day you get to read about a court case. Solomon appealed to God on behalf of people who sinned, David appealed to God for his enemies to recognize the power of God, and Paul appealed to people to consider the rescuing power of God.

All three instances invited people to think, consider, and ultimately respond to what they learn about God. In two cases, it was an appeal to allow His voice to be heard among all the other noise humans encounter. It was a crowd who had one agenda stopping long enough to hear about a different agenda.

Yes, this was an appeal to the mind, but it had the elements needed to inspire an emotional response. Perhaps the people would remember what Paul said about his past and God's new story for him.

Think about ways three unusual court cases found in God's Word could be used to share Jesus.

*Letting people think whatever they want about You is easy, God. I can avoid arguments that way, but three times in three days I learn that people who loved You wanted others to know You too. Help me be wise enough to want the same thing.*

# ANARCHY AVENUE

*"Look at what you've done—you threw out the priests of*
*GOD, the sons of Aaron, and the Levites, and made priests*
*to suit yourselves, priests just like the pagans have."*
2 CHRONICLES 13:9 MSG

· · · · · · · · · · · · · · · · · · · · · ·

The people were being called out. They were in the grip of sin. It was a condition they had been in for a long time. They had moved from Disinterested Drive to Anarchy Avenue. It was a move that did not benefit any person. God was still God. His power was not weakened in any way by their reaction. He could make them followers, but they had to volunteer their hearts. With their hearts out of reach, they couldn't think straight.

It was like an angry crowd, but they weren't sure why they were angry. They elevated nothing and made it something to worship. They found people who thought like them and made them their preachers. The world had turned upside down, but some thought it was completely normal. This was a time of delusion and spiritual blindness. One thinking voice called to a crowd of those who refused to think. The truth meant they had been living a lie.

You could use the word *ridiculous* and you wouldn't be wrong. Yet this kind of thinking exists to this day.

---

*I don't want to become trapped into believing that You are*
*whatever I want You to be, Father. May everything about*
*me strain, yearn, and long to acknowledge You.*

# LOWER YOUR LEVEL OF FORGETFULNESS

*How amazing are the deeds of the LORD!*
*All who delight in him should ponder them.*
PSALM 111:2 NLT

. . . . . . . . . . . . . . . . . . . . . . . .

He flung the stars more efficiently than anyone who has played disc golf. He orchestrates the changing of seasons while you sigh and change the channel on your television. He has a storehouse for rain, and it's still stocked. God's deeds are wonderful, even when we take them for granted.

King David suggests that pondering the things God does, provides, and promises is a wise use of time. This may not make sense to people who don't know Him, but for the rest, this is a trip down Memory Lane. Mankind has seven wonders they recognize. All are a nod to things humans created. Impressive? Sure, but there are millions of things God created just by speaking—yet those things are often overlooked. You might even enjoy them without ever really thinking about Him.

Today's verse suggests that this level of forgetfulness needs to change. Spend a little more time today considering the beauty, value, and creativity of your impressive God. Then take your worship and pass it His direction.

---

*God, when I'm outside, I can see so many things You created. You say You created these things to help me ponder You. Thank You for each new discovery. May there be many more to come.*

# ALARMED

*As [Paul] reasoned about righteousness and self-control
and the coming judgment, Felix was alarmed.*
ACTS 24:25 ESV

. . . . . . . . . . . . . . . . . . . . . .

Imagine you're a leader. People look to you for guidance, but you've taken advantage of your position. You've been oppressive and overbearing and demanded more from others than you needed to in your position. You've adopted an air of superiority and committed your own share of wrongs. This was Felix, and Paul was in his custody. Perhaps Felix thought he would be entertained by the preacher, so he invited him for a visit.

Paul did not seem amusing. He spoke of the right way to live. *Felix wasn't sure he measured up.* Paul spoke about self-control. *Felix did whatever he wanted.* Paul talked about judgment. *Felix was alarmed.*

The mind of Felix was like that of a child who is discovered stealing a snack when he knows he shouldn't. His mind considered the words Paul spoke, and his heart condemned him. His spirit was unsettled, and he wanted Paul to go away.

Being confronted about personal choices that have led to sin is hard. It's the exposing of a wound that needs to be healed, not covered up. God can and will diagnose rebellion. Only you can accept or reject treatment.

---

*Father, no one likes to hear that they did something wrong. No one wants to hear, "I told you so." You condemn sin but set this sinner free through Jesus the Rescuer when I accepted Your greatest gift.*

# INFECTION EVICTION

*Then Elijah the prophet wrote Jehoram this letter: "This is what the LORD, the God of your ancestor David, says: You have not followed the good example of your father, Jehoshaphat, or your grandfather King Asa of Judah."*

2 CHRONICLES 21:12 NLT

. . . . . . . . . . . . . . . . . . . . . . .

God was not shy in calling sin *sin*. It wasn't a mistake or lapse in judgment. Sin was an act of rebelling against His authority.

That's what was happening in the verse above. The prophet Elijah sent word to King Jehoram that set the record straight. This king witnessed a good example in his father and grandfather but ultimately rejected what he saw. Jehoram was forging a new path that left God out. This king was in rebellion.

You've read the word *rebellion* several times recently. It is often an outward display of an inner wound. Something happens inside the mind, heart, and spirit long before the choice to rebel. Festering wounds stink, they get noticed, and they're unattractive.

Maybe like Jehoram, you need to recognize the wound and then allow God to deal with it. The infection that has permeated every part of your life can be evicted. New life can be delivered. Hope can be restored.

---

*I don't want to live with long-term wounds, God. Help me see You as the only One capable of dealing with my spiritual and emotional wounds. Deal with any rebellion You find in me, and draw me close once more.*

# REFUSING TO BACKPEDAL

*[King] Agrippa said to Paul, "In a short time would you persuade me to be a Christian?" And Paul said, "Whether short or long, I would to God that not only you but also all who hear me this day might become such as I am."*

ACTS 26:28–29 ESV

. . . . . . . . . . . . . . . . . . . . . .

Maybe King Agrippa was amused by the persistent message Paul preached. Maybe he was seriously considering what Paul said. When this king asked Paul, "Would you persuade me to be a Christian?" Paul's response was "I would."

Paul was all about taking the opportunities he met. He'd talked to others who shied away from his message about Jesus, but King Agrippa seemed interested. He was willing to listen.

This opportunity led Paul back to sharing how he met Jesus. It gave him the chance to talk about his new life. What would cause most to close their lips and refuse to speak just made Paul more willing to use what was in his mind, heart, and spirit and cause that information to spill over his lips and out to the public.

There's a lesson in there for you, but it will require a boldness that refuses to backpedal this life-changing news.

*Father, I hate it when my mind thinks about You but my mouth refuses full disclosure. People who need to know You don't hear about You when that happens. Free my mouth to share what You've placed in my heart, mind, and spirit.*

# PERMISSION GRANTED

*Their gods are metal and wood, handmade in a basement shop:*
*carved mouths that can't talk, painted eyes that can't see, tin ears*
*that can't hear, molded noses that can't smell, hands that can't grasp,*
*feet that can't walk or run, throats that never utter a sound.*

PSALM 115:4–7 MSG

. . . . . . . . . . . . . . . . . . . . . . .

The worship of some is relegated to the worship of movie props, carved ducks, and artful clay. But none of those things can do anything because they aren't real. They can't speak because they have no voice. They can't run because they have no feet. They can't hear, smell, or see. They are mere *objects*—perhaps beautiful and appreciated. But there is no power in a painting, statue, or anything else. God called this kind of worship response idolatry.

Today's verses are instructive for people considering the possibility that a deity could claim a thing and give it a power greater than God. A statue stands, paintings hang, and carved ducks sit on shelves. They don't rescue, reward, or redeem.

It's faulty thinking to assume otherwise, and it's another reason why coming to God with every bit of who you are is a sensible option. He can rescue. He rewards those who seek Him with all their hearts.

*You don't need my permission to be awesome, God. You just*
*are. You do want my permission to change me from the inside*
*out—and I give You that permission. Make real change when*
*everything else is a debris field of broken promises.*

# ADVERTISING PERSONAL SUPERIORITY

*When [King Uzziah] had become powerful,*
*he also became proud, which led to his downfall.*
2 CHRONICLES 26:16 NLT

. . . . . . . . . . . . . . . . . . . . . .

There is power in a prideful man. That power is never on the side of the good and wholesome. Prideful men can tear people down, make them feel small, and advertise personal superiority. That may be the allure of pride—the belief that no one is better, bigger, or stronger. But prideful men never really think about comparing themselves to God. Why? They can't measure up. Instead of seeing God as someone to worship, prideful men either resent Him or dismiss Him. Is it any wonder the proud can't stand long?

Think intentionally about all that God has made, done, and keeps doing. He has kept things together since the dawn of creation. He doesn't destroy mankind, even though He could. He gives when people take—even when those same people say they got what they have without His help.

Refuse to be like King Uzziah. Feel free to see your smallness when you compare yourself to God—and in doing so, dismiss pride. Use your mind to accept the truth, your heart to experience truth, and your spirit to listen to the God who defines truth.

---

*You're so much more than I'll ever be, Father. I believe it, but there*
*will be days when You'll need to remind me. Thank You for still*
*loving me when my mouth fails to speak of Your greatness but*
*instead brags about my personal skills and accomplishments.*

# WHAT'S ALL THE TROUBLE?

*Even during this time of trouble, King Ahaz continued to
reject the LORD. He offered sacrifices to the gods of Damascus
who had defeated him, for he said, "Since these gods helped the
kings of Aram, they will help me, too, if I sacrifice to them."
But instead, they led to his ruin and the ruin of all Judah.*

2 CHRONICLES 28:22–23 NLT

. . . . . . . . . . . . . . . . . . . . . . .

King Ahaz had big troubles—all of which he brought on himself. He was
defeated in battle by King Aram and lost thousands of people to captivity;
he was defeated likewise by the king of Israel, who slew 120,000 men,
including the king's son, the officer in charge of the palace, and the king's
second in command. Add to all this, the Edomites and Philistines attacked
outlying areas, took prisoners, and occupied cities. Even bribing the king
of Assyria for help with items from the temple of the Lord backfired.

But despite these troubles—which the Lord brought as a
punishment—King Ahaz did not repent. Instead, he doubled down
on his wickedness, thinking that setting up more altars to false gods "at
every street corner in Jerusalem" (2 Chronicles 28:24 NIV) would help.

There's a saying that if you find yourself in a hole, stop digging!
Troubles are often messages. Whether you choose to humble your heart
and then listen and act—or to harden your heart and ignore them—is
the issue.

*Lord, let me accept "trouble" as a chance to see and think more clearly.*

## THE HEART OF WORSHIP

*The entire assembly then decided to continue the festival another
seven days, so they celebrated joyfully for another week. . . .
The entire assembly of Judah rejoiced, including the priests, the
Levites, all who came from the land of Israel, the foreigners who
came to the festival, and all those who lived in Judah. There was
great joy in the city, for Jerusalem had not seen a celebration
like this one since the days of Solomon, King David's son.
Then the priests and Levites stood and blessed the people, and
God heard their prayer from his holy dwelling in heaven.*

2 CHRONICLES 30:23, 25–27 NLT

. . . . . . . . . . . . . . . . . . . . . . .

With the death of wicked King Ahaz, his twenty-five-year-old son,
Hezekiah, ascended to the throne. Hezekiah was the complete opposite
of his father. "He did what was right in the eyes of the LORD, just as his
father David had done" (2 Chronicles 29:2 NIV), meaning wholeheartedly,
as King David was a man after God's own heart. Hezekiah also shared
David's love of worship, as did another son of David, Solomon, whose
original dedication of the temple some two hundred years earlier was
legendary.

Hezekiah's celebration likewise filled everyone's heart, Jew and
foreigner alike, with wonder and joy. Solomon and Hezekiah foreshadow
yet another "Son of David" who would offer the fullness of worship "in
the Spirit and in truth" (John 4:23 NIV) to the entire world.

*Father, may I be a son of David today, leading others into joyful worship!*

# SEEING THE UNSEEN

*For what can be known about God is plain to them, because God has shown it to them. For his invisible attributes, namely, his eternal power and divine nature, have been clearly perceived, ever since the creation of the world, in the things that have been made. So they are without excuse.*

ROMANS 1:19–20 ESV

. . . . . . . . . . . . . . . . . . . . . . .

To display the invisible Creator, creation by definition must be awesome and overwhelming. God made the universe in such a way as to hold men accountable to "see" at least two of His characteristics. First, His "eternal power," meaning that He is not bound by time, and therefore His strength remains undiminished forever; and second, He is divine, not part of the created order as we are and not subject to its limitations.

Paul's assertion of man's accountability agrees with the psalmist's declaration: "The heavens declare the glory of God, and the sky above proclaims his handiwork. Day to day pours out speech, and night to night reveals knowledge. There is no speech, nor are there words, whose voice is not heard" (Psalm 19:1–3 ESV).

God is declared through all of creation—including man himself, since He made us in His image. But He is only fully revealed in Christ, in whom "all the fullness of the Deity lives in bodily form" (Colossians 2:9 NIV).

*Father, thank You for displaying Your glory in Your creation and more perfectly in Your Son!*

# THE POWER OF REPENTANCE

*Manasseh led Judah and the inhabitants of Jerusalem astray, to do more evil than the nations whom the LORD destroyed before the people of Israel. The LORD spoke to Manasseh and to his people, but they paid no attention. Therefore the LORD brought upon them the commanders of the army of the king of Assyria, who captured Manasseh with hooks and bound him with chains of bronze and brought him to Babylon. And when he was in distress, he entreated the favor of the LORD his God and humbled himself greatly before the God of his fathers. He prayed to him, and God was moved by his entreaty and heard his plea and brought him again to Jerusalem into his kingdom. Then Manasseh knew that the LORD was God.*

2 CHRONICLES 33:9–13 ESV

. . . . . . . . . . . . . . . . . . . . . . .

Manasseh took his grandfather Ahaz's wickedness to a whole new level. He consulted mediums, practiced sorcery, and set up altars in the temple itself to pagan deities—even sacrificing his own sons to false gods!

But Manasseh did what many people never do. He repented. Unlike Ahaz, his heart was softened in his distress and he "humbled himself greatly." And God "was moved by his entreaty." What a testimony to God's amazing mercy and ready grace. He delights in forgiveness! What great news it is for us today still, that "mercy triumphs over judgment" (James 2:13 NIV)!

*Merciful Father, thank You for doing whatever it takes to bring me back into fellowship!*

# THE NARROW GATE

*Open to me the gates of righteousness, that I may enter through them and give thanks to the LORD. This is the gate of the LORD; the righteous shall enter through it. I thank you that you have answered me and have become my salvation.*

PSALM 118:19–21 ESV

. . . . . . . . . . . . . . . . . . . . . . .

When Jesus spoke of finding salvation, He once used the metaphor of a gate: "How narrow is the gate and difficult the road that leads to life, and few find it" (Matthew 7:14 HCSB). That gate is not a lifestyle or a series of decisions on our part, or even what we sometimes call the "Christian walk." Jesus Himself is the Gate to the Father: "I am the way and the truth and the life. No one comes to the Father except through me" (John 14:6 NIV). You will not find a way around the Gate!

The Gate changes everything. We are not righteous and then enter—we *become* righteous when we enter into a new life in Christ. As the psalmist says of the Lord in today's reading: "You have answered me and have become my salvation."

The Lord Himself *is* our Salvation. The "difficult. . .road that leads to life" is humbling our hearts in repentance and asking the one and only Son of God, the one and only Way to the Father, to become our righteousness.

---

*Praise Jesus, our Gate and our Salvation,
our Way and our Righteousness!*

## RIGHTEOUSNESS THAT WORKS

*If, in fact, Abraham was justified by works, he had something to boast about—but not before God. What does Scripture say? "Abraham believed God, and it was credited to him as righteousness." Now to the one who works, wages are not credited as a gift but as an obligation. However, to the one who does not work but trusts God who justifies the ungodly, their faith is credited as righteousness.*

ROMANS 4:2–5 NIV

. . . . . . . . . . . . . . . . . . . . . . .

The word *works* in the scripture can have one of two connotations. It can mean religious duties or actions done in an effort to gain a right standing with the Almighty (i.e., make us righteous). Or it can mean good deeds done *because* we are in a right standing with the Father.

If we believe we can earn favor with God through our works, then our efforts actually do the opposite. If we work to justify ourselves, then "all our righteous acts are like filthy rags" (Isaiah 64:6 NIV).

If, however, we receive righteousness as a gift through faith in Christ, the works that follow are to His glory. From the beginning, his aim was to "purify for himself a people for his own possession who are zealous for good works" (Titus 2:14 ESV). Works have their place, but they must be done out of a heart that has already been made right with God.

*Father, let me glorify Jesus today by works done because He has made me righteous!*

# MOVING BEYOND FEAR

*Despite their fear of the peoples around them, they built the altar on its foundation and sacrificed burnt offerings on it to the LORD, both the morning and evening sacrifices. Then in accordance with what is written, they celebrated the Festival of Tabernacles with the required number of burnt offerings prescribed for each day. After that, they presented the regular burnt offerings, the New Moon sacrifices and the sacrifices for all the appointed sacred festivals of the LORD, as well as those brought as freewill offerings to the LORD. On the first day of the seventh month they began to offer burnt offerings to the LORD, though the foundation of the LORD's temple had not yet been laid.*

EZRA 3:3–6 NIV

. . . . . . . . . . . . . . . . . . . . . . .

You might think that the rebuilding of the temple in Jerusalem after the Babylonian exile, which was prophesied by Jeremiah and supported by no fewer than three Persian kings, would be simple. But it wasn't. The local pagans worked tirelessly to slow the project, bribing officials and sending false information to the king.

But the returning Israelites were not deterred because their heart was in the work. They rebuilt the altar before they rebuilt the temple foundation and walls so they could immediately obey the full Word of God.

If your heart is to follow God, it doesn't mean you won't face opposition, but it does mean you won't allow fear to stop you.

*Great King, fill my heart with resolve to
do all Your will despite opposition.*

# I RECKON SO

*Likewise reckon ye also yourselves to be dead indeed unto sin, but alive unto God through Jesus Christ our Lord. Let not sin therefore reign in your mortal body, that ye should obey it in the lusts thereof. Neither yield ye your members as instruments of unrighteousness unto sin: but yield yourselves unto God, as those that are alive from the dead, and your members as instruments of righteousness unto God.*

ROMANS 6:11–13 KJV

. . . . . . . . . . . . . . . . . . . . . .

The word *reckon* sounds a bit old-fashioned today. If you're a fan of Westerns, you may remember Clint Eastwood's famous "I reckon so" in *The Outlaw Josey Wales* as he reflects on the toll of the Civil War.

To reckon something means to calculate something as fact. In today's passage, we are told to "calculate" that we are dead to the power of sin and alive to God—simply because we are "in Christ."

Once you *reckon* that fact in your heart, your behavior should follow. You won't allow your fleshly desires to have their way but rather "yield yourselves to God." The very members of your body—the eyes, the tongue, the stomach, the sexual organs—will no longer be available to sin but will be submitted to Christ and to bringing Him glory.

Reckoning the facts of your salvation will impact you from head to toe—and in your heart.

---

*Lord of my salvation, I praise You for saving me to the uttermost—body, soul, and spirit!*

## WISDOM, NOT LAW

*Help me understand the meaning of your commandments, and
I will meditate on your wonderful deeds. I weep with sorrow;
encourage me by your word. Keep me from lying to myself; give
me the privilege of knowing your instructions. I have chosen to
be faithful; I have determined to live by your regulations.*

Psalm 119:27–30 NLT

. . . . . . . . . . . . . . . . . . . . . .

The longing to know God can only be fulfilled by starting with His Word.
And not just through some kind of formal study but by living out what
He helps us to grasp. That's why it's so critical that we rely on Him as
we dig into the sacred writings, remembering that it's a privilege to have
His Word. His commandments are life-giving wisdom for those who
commit themselves to following them.

Of course, Christians are not "under" the Law. We don't earn
righteousness from it. The writer of Psalm 119 understood what Paul
said of the scripture: "The law is holy, and the commandment is holy,
righteous and good" (Romans 7:12 NIV). Paul also made it clear that the
Law of God is a "spiritual" thing, while we by definition are "of flesh"
(Romans 7:14 ESV), so that when we combine the two, we will need the
Helper, the Holy Spirit, to understand and apply what we read.

*O Lord, You alone have the words of eternal life.
Help me to embrace Your Word with my whole heart!*

## IT'S A MIND-SET

*Those who live according to the flesh have their minds set on what the flesh desires; but those who live in accordance with the Spirit have their minds set on what the Spirit desires. The mind governed by the flesh is death, but the mind governed by the Spirit is life and peace. The mind governed by the flesh is hostile to God; it does not submit to God's law, nor can it do so. Those who are in the realm of the flesh cannot please God.*

ROMANS 8:5–8 NIV

. . . . . . . . . . . . . . . . . . . . . .

The word *flesh* in the New Testament sometimes refers to our physical bodies, but it also has the connotation of the corrupt part of our nature. Thus, our physical existence is in some way connected to our spiritual poverty as a descendant of Adam.

As God's born-again child, you have the Holy Spirit. The issue is that the flesh and the Spirit "are in conflict with each other" (Galatians 5:17 NIV). As long as you live, you will experience their animosity. Choosing to set your mind on the things of the flesh, even as a believer, is a form of death. How can it not be?

All flesh is headed toward the grave. But the Holy Spirit within us is "life and peace." Setting your mind on the Spirit is your calling and also part of enjoying a portion of your eternal inheritance now.

*Strengthen me, Lord, to set my mind and affections solely on the things of God!*

## WHERE IS THE LOVE?

*Can anything ever separate us from Christ's love? Does it mean he
no longer loves us if we have trouble or calamity, or are persecuted,
or hungry, or destitute, or in danger, or threatened with death?
(As the Scriptures say, "For your sake we are killed every day; we
are being slaughtered like sheep.") No, despite all these things,
overwhelming victory is ours through Christ, who loved us.*

ROMANS 8:35–37 NLT

. . . . . . . . . . . . . . . . . . . . . . . .

No one cries out, "Why me, Lord?" when good things happen. It's only
when people face trials and troubles that they question God's love or even
His goodness. The assumption is: if Christ loves me, then I shouldn't be
suffering. But Paul's list in today's passage was from his own *personal
experience*. He faced enormous trials and hardships—beaten, stoned,
scourged, shipwrecked; in danger from man and beast; hungry, thirsty,
cold, sleepless, poor. And still he proclaimed that "despite all these things"
we have an "overwhelming victory" in Jesus! Paul declared that the victory
was "overwhelming"! In another letter, the apostle went even further: "For
the sake of Christ, then, I am content with weaknesses, insults, hardships,
persecutions, and calamities. For when I am weak, then I am strong" (2
Corinthians 12:10 ESV).

When you face hardship, especially for Jesus' name, remember the
love of Christ has not, and cannot, be lessened—and neither is the victory
He has won on your behalf.

*Strengthen my faith, Father, to trust in Your
great love no matter the circumstances.*

# NO PAIN, NO GAIN

*Teach me good judgment and knowledge: for I have believed thy commandments. Before I was afflicted I went astray: but now have I kept thy word. Thou art good, and doest good; teach me thy statutes.*

PSALM 119:66–68 KJV

. . . . . . . . . . . . . . . . . . . . . .

Affliction in this life is an opportunity to move closer to God.

Sometimes we bring affliction upon ourselves, as did the prodigal son. After squandering his inheritance, he became so hungry that he "longed to fill his stomach with the pods that the pigs were eating" (Luke 15:16 NIV). This young man's own choices had caused his hardship, and yet his difficulties became an opportunity once "he came to his senses" (Luke 15:17 NIV) and repented. Affliction had brought about obedience from the heart.

Other times, affliction comes from the hand of the Father. Jesus Himself experienced this: "Son though he was, he learned obedience from what he suffered" (Hebrews 5:8 NIV). We are God's beloved children too, and so "God disciplines us for our good, in order that we may share in his holiness" (Hebrews 12:10 NIV).

And finally, affliction comes simply from being in this dying world. Jesus reminded His followers, "You will have suffering in this world" but in the same breath added this promise: "Be courageous! I have conquered the world" (John 16:33 HCSB). Be patient in all affliction, and believe in God's goodness through it.

*Father, thank You for anything that draws me closer to You.*

# IF YOU BUILD, YOU FIGHT

*Therefore I stationed some of the people behind the lowest points of the wall at the exposed places, posting them by families, with their swords, spears and bows. After I looked things over, I stood up and said to the nobles, the officials and the rest of the people, "Don't be afraid of them. Remember the Lord, who is great and awesome, and fight for your families, your sons and your daughters, your wives and your homes."*

NEHEMIAH 4:13–14 NIV

. . . . . . . . . . . . . . . . . . . . . . .

Nehemiah's heart was convicted to rebuild the walls of Jerusalem after the temple had been reestablished many years earlier. With the letters from King Artaxerxes, and a cavalry escort, Nehemiah headed out. But the local pagan governors did not want the Jews to prosper, and since the Persian capital was nine hundred miles away, Nehemiah was pretty much on his own.

But threats from his adversaries did not dissuade Nehemiah. His courage was contagious, and work progressed swiftly "for the people worked with all their heart" (Nehemiah 4:6 NIV). But as the walls rose, so did the opposition. To keep the work going, half the men stood guard while the other half worked, and even those wore a sword!

You too have an enemy who will oppose your work for God. So if you want to build something of spiritual value, you will have to do it while dressed for battle.

*Great and awesome God, strengthen me today to stand my ground!*

## THE HEART OF THE MATTER

*If you confess with your mouth that Jesus is Lord and believe
in your heart that God raised him from the dead, you will
be saved. For with the heart one believes and is justified,
and with the mouth one confesses and is saved.*

ROMANS 10:9–10 ESV

. . . . . . . . . . . . . . . . . . . . . . .

Confession means to acknowledge or declare a truth publicly. No one can see into another's heart; the heart must make itself known.

In the Bible, the heart is the core of your being, the place from which all your words and actions come: "Above all else, guard your heart, for everything you do flows from it" (Proverbs 4:23 NIV). Jesus plainly said, "What you say flows from what is in your heart" (Luke 6:45 NLT). Today's passage isn't describing a two-step process but rather the natural progression of faith—if you believe in your heart that Jesus is the risen Savior then your mouth *must* declare His sovereignty. That kind of truth cannot be kept inside!

But the reverse isn't possible. Without the conviction of the heart, no amount of words will matter. God rebuked this type of empty religion: "These people say they are mine. They honor me with their lips, but their hearts are far from me" (Isaiah 29:13 NLT).

Once the heart believes, the mouth overflows, and the hands and feet will follow!

*Risen Savior, I declare today and every day
that You are Lord! Let me walk in Your ways!*

# REJOICE IN THE SACRED

*Then Nehemiah the governor, Ezra the priest and scribe, and the
Levites. . .said to them, "Don't mourn or weep on such a day as
this! For today is a sacred day before the* LORD *your God." For the
people had all been weeping as they listened to the words of the
Law. And Nehemiah continued, "Go and celebrate with a feast of
rich foods and sweet drinks, and share gifts of food with people who
have nothing prepared. This is a sacred day before our Lord. Don't
be dejected and sad, for the joy of the* LORD *is your strength!"*
NEHEMIAH 8:9–10 NLT

. . . . . . . . . . . . . . . . . . . . . . . .

The rebuilding of Jerusalem had begun with the temple and finished with
the fortifications. It was a long and dangerous project, which culminated
in a massive celebration. As the Law was read, many of the people
wept—perhaps from conviction or perhaps for the same reasons as when
the temple was started: "But many of the priests and Levites and heads
of fathers' houses, old men who had seen the first house, wept with a
loud voice when they saw the foundation of this house being laid" (Ezra
3:12 ESV).

While there's a time for tears, Nehemiah reminded the people that
the day God fulfills His Word is a sacred day, one to remember and
rejoice. Let go of the past and be strong in His joy today.

*I rejoice from my heart in God my Savior! Your joy will carry me this day!*

## WE'RE IN THIS TOGETHER

*I give each of you this warning: Don't think you are better*
*than you really are. Be honest in your evaluation of yourselves,*
*measuring yourselves by the faith God has given us.*
ROMANS 12:3 NLT

· · · · · · · · · · · · · · · · · · · · · · ·

Paul spent a lot of time in his letters urging believers toward unity, loving and forgiving each other, and bearing one another's burdens. He wanted the church to fulfill Jesus' command: "A new commandment I give to you, that you love one another: just as I have loved you, you also are to love one another. By this all people will know that you are my disciples, if you have love for one another" (John 13:34–35 ESV). The old standard was only to "love thy neighbor as thyself" (Leviticus 19:18 KJV); the new standard is based on the humble, authentic, and sacrificial love Christ showed for His disciples.

What gets in the way of fulfilling this new commandment today? Often, it's an inflated or inaccurate opinion of oneself. You may be smarter, more talented, more effective than anyone else in your church, but that's only because you've received those things as gifts. As Paul wrote, "What do you have that God hasn't given you?" (1 Corinthians 4:7 NLT). That really changes how you "measure yourself," doesn't it? The more honest you are with yourself, the heathier the body you are a valued part of will function.

*Father, help me to see myself rightly—as gifted by*
*You to serve the other members of Your body.*

# OPPORTUNITY IN CONFLICT

*If possible, so far as it depends on you, live peaceably with all.*
ROMANS 12:18 ESV

. . . . . . . . . . . . . . . . . . . . . . .

What causes conflict in relationships? The first example in the Bible was between Cain and Abel. Cain slew his brother because God regarded Abel's sacrifice and not his own. Six generations later, one of Cain's descendants bragged about killing a man who had injured him. Solomon observed that men toiled for gain from envy of their neighbor. James summed it up this way: "What causes quarrels and what causes fights among you? Is it not this, that your passions are at war within you?" (James 4:1 ESV).

But conflict can also arise for right reasons. Jesus preached the truth and faced opposition throughout His life, growing from public debate to murder: "And they schemed to arrest Jesus secretly and kill him" (Matthew 26:4 NIV). Opposition is part of our calling. Paul said that "everyone who wants to live a godly life in Christ Jesus will be persecuted" (2 Timothy 3:12 NIV).

The challenge for believers is to identify the source of conflict. Does something inside you add to the conflict in your life? God can root that out if you ask Him. Is the conflict because of your stand for Christ? Be encouraged as His servant, not "quarrelsome but kind to everyone, able to teach, patiently enduring evil" (2 Timothy 2:24 ESV).

*Father, forgive me when I cause conflict. Strengthen
me to seek peace where it can be found.*

## CLOSER THAN YESTERDAY

*You know the time, that the hour has come for you to wake from sleep. For salvation is nearer to us now than when we first believed. The night is far gone; the day is at hand. So then let us cast off the works of darkness and put on the armor of light.*
ROMANS 13:11–12 ESV

. . . . . . . . . . . . . . . . . . . . . .

There was a steward who served a nobleman who'd gone to war in distant lands. He oversaw every aspect of the castle and grounds. The lawns and trees were trimmed perfectly, and the table was set daily with sparkling dishes and goblets. Fresh linens covered every bed. One day a traveler stopped in. He was amazed at the condition of the place. "How long has your lord been away?" he inquired. "Four years," replied the steward. "Four years! You keep his household like you expect him back tomorrow!" "Nay, sir," said the steward, "today."

From the day you first believed, you've been called to watchfulness. Watchfulness is faithfulness. The distractions of life often dull our sense of responsibility, perhaps even leading to questionable activities. But facing the Lord is daily growing closer for all of us. But don't be anxious over the prospect! Rejoice in the idea as the psalmist did: "I wait for the Lord more than watchmen wait for the morning, more than watchmen wait for the morning" (Psalm 130:6 NIV).

*Lord, help me to stand watch and to reject distractions as the day of our meeting approaches!*

# THE PURPOSE OF UNITY

*May the God of endurance and encouragement grant you to live in such harmony with one another, in accord with Christ Jesus, that together you may with one voice glorify the God and Father of our Lord Jesus Christ. Therefore welcome one another as Christ has welcomed you, for the glory of God.*

ROMANS 15:5–7 ESV

. . . . . . . . . . . . . . . . . . . . . . .

God's plan has always been to "purify for himself a people for his own possession" (Titus 2:14 ESV). He promised the exiled Israelites a new experience of unity once He effected their return: "They will be my people, and I will be their God. I will give them singleness of heart and action, so that they will always fear me" (Jeremiah 32:38–39 NIV). His people's unity was to be for His glory.

King David, a man well acquainted with strife, declared, "How good and pleasant it is when God's people live together in unity!" (Psalm 133:1 NIV). He experienced firsthand that "if a kingdom is divided against itself, that kingdom cannot stand" (Mark 3:24 NIV). Spiritual harmony allows for eternal purposes to be fulfilled. Jesus prayed for His followers "that they may be brought to complete unity. Then the world will know that you sent me and have loved them even as you have loved me" (John 17:23 NIV). Our unity in Christ is a testimony of God's reality and glory.

*Grant me endurance, Lord, and encourage me toward unity found in Christ.*

## THE DIVINE APPOINTMENT

*Then Mordecai told them to reply to Esther, "Do not think to yourself that in the king's palace you will escape any more than all the other Jews. For if you keep silent at this time, relief and deliverance will rise for the Jews from another place, but you and your father's house will perish. And who knows whether you have not come to the kingdom for such a time as this?"*

ESTHER 4:13–14 ESV

. . . . . . . . . . . . . . . . . . . . . . .

Few stories in the Bible compare to that of Esther for intrigue and excitement. Born during the Babylonian exile, the beautiful cousin of Mordecai is brought into the king Ahasuerus's palace, where she finds favor and is made queen. Later, when Mordecai refuses to bow before the king's top adviser, Haman plots to kill all the Jews in the Persian Empire in retaliation. But neither Haman nor the king is aware that the new queen is a Jew! The moment of truth comes: Will Esther risk her life to save her people? Will Ahasuerus support her once he's discovered her secret?

You may not face a life and death situation like Esther, but you will have opportunities to stand for God in the face of personal risks. He won't force you to step up—He'll work His plan with or without you. But He invites you to be His instrument "for such a time as this"—whenever that time may be.

*Father, open my eyes and strengthen me
to stand ready when the time comes!*

# THE HEART OF PRAYER AND WORSHIP

*May my cry come before you, LORD; give me understanding
according to your word. May my supplication come before you;
deliver me according to your promise. May my lips overflow
with praise, for you teach me your decrees. May my tongue
sing of your word, for all your commands are righteous.*

PSALM 119:169–172 NIV

. . . . . . . . . . . . . . . . . . . . . .

The foundation of our prayers, praise, and thanksgiving is God's unchanging
Word. In the first couplet of today's reading, the psalmist cries out to
the Lord and appeals to Him for understanding; he entreats the Lord
for deliverance based on His own promises. The psalmist has no fear of
asking God to listen, because he knows God has already spoken and will
always act according to His Word. The writer's confidence isn't in his own
sincerity but in what God has made known.

In the second couplet, the writer's heart overflows in praise and song.
Coming to God to be filled always overflows back to God in worship,
"for the mouth speaks what the heart is full of" (Matthew 12:34 NIV).
When you fill your heart with God's Word and experience its truth,
marvel at its insight, and feel its power, you will not be able to contain
the praise that comes.

Cry out to the Lord and ask for understanding; entreat Him according
to His promises; praise God because He has made known His will; sing
to your Father who is wholly righteous and good!

*Father, You are my confidence and joy!*

# NO ROOM FOR RIVALRIES

*And now I make one more appeal, my dear brothers and sisters.*
*Watch out for people who cause divisions and upset people's*
*faith by teaching things contrary to what you have been taught.*
*Stay away from them. Such people are not serving Christ*
*our Lord; they are serving their own personal interests.*
Romans 16:17–18 nlt

. . . . . . . . . . . . . . . . . . . . . .

Paul frequently addressed divisions in the churches, knowing that worldly competition could tear a congregation apart. He included "rivalries, dissensions, divisions" in his list of the "works of the flesh" that should be "evident" to all believers (Galatians 5:19–20 esv). Evident maybe but still common. The Corinthians were rife with factions and received this rebuke: "For while there is jealousy and strife among you, are you not of the flesh and behaving only in a human way? For when one says, 'I follow Paul,' and another, 'I follow Apollos,' are you not being merely human?" (1 Corinthians 3:3–4 esv). We're to be beyond human in Christ's church!

The apostle had no tolerance for self-serving leaders who were "puffed up with conceit. . .imagining that godliness is a means of gain" (1 Timothy 6:4–5 esv). His warning echoes that of Jesus: "Watch and beware of the leaven of the Pharisees and Sadducees," who twisted and added to the scripture (Matthew 16:6 esv).

Stay grounded in God's Word, avoiding worldly factions and protecting your "dear brothers and sisters."

---

*Lord of peace, guard me and my brothers*
*and sisters by Your Word of truth.*

# THE MYSTERY OF SUFFERING

*Then the LORD asked Satan, "Have you noticed my servant Job?*
*He is the finest man in all the earth. He is blameless—a man of*
*complete integrity. He fears God and stays away from evil."*

JOB 1:8 NLT

. . . . . . . . . . . . . . . . . . . . . . .

It's usually a compliment to be noticed. But Job might rather have stayed anonymous! Why would God suggest that Satan take notice of literally the "finest man in all the earth"? Shouldn't God rather cover and protect such a man and keep him out of harm's way?

In suffering, there's always the temptation to oversimplify the purposes of God, whose judgments are "unsearchable" and ways are "mysterious" (Romans 11:33 AMPC). That leads us to the mistake Job's friends made, arguing that Job had sinned in some way and brought punishment upon himself. But Job's sin was not the cause but rather the result of his suffering. He eventually demanded the Almighty justify Himself. That's when God stepped in and corrected Job's presumption, leading Job to withdraw his accusations: "I. . .repent" (Job 42:6 NIV). Job never got answers to his questions, but he did get a deeper relationship with God. Even Jesus, "though He was God's Son, He learned obedience through what He suffered" (Hebrews 5:8 HCSB). No one asks for suffering, but if we cling to God during times of severe testing, He will show Himself faithful, and we will come to know Him better.

*Merciful God, grant me the strength to*
*endure anything to know You more.*

# THINKING BY THE SPIRIT

*And we have received God's Spirit (not the world's spirit), so
we can know the wonderful things God has freely given us.*
1 Corinthians 2:12 NLT

. . . . . . . . . . . . . . . . . . . . . .

When the Creator declared, "Let Us make man in Our image, according
to Our likeness" (Genesis 1:26 HCSB), He gave man an incredible gift:
"The LORD God formed the man out of the dust from the ground and
breathed the breath of life into his nostrils, and the man became a living
being" (Genesis 2:7 HCSB). The "breath of life" allowed man to think,
feel, and fellowship with God. But sin ruined that perfect arrangement,
and the spirit of man became corrupt, separated from the giver. Things
went downhill quickly: "The LORD. . .saw that everything they thought
or imagined was consistently and totally evil" (Genesis 6:5 NLT).

The answer to the problem was a *second* incredible gift: "I will put a
new spirit in you. I will take out your stony, stubborn heart and give you a
tender, responsive heart" (Ezekiel 36:26 NLT). And we have that promise
fulfilled in Christ: "The Helper, the Holy Spirit, whom the Father will send
in my name, he will teach you all things and bring to your remembrance
all that I have said to you" (John 14:26 ESV). God delights in sharing His
thinking and His plans with you through the Spirit!

*Lord, grant that my thinking today will reflect
the presence of the Helper you've given me.*

# A STRONG PARTNERSHIP

*Unless the LORD builds a house, its builders labor over it in vain;
unless the LORD watches over a city, the watchman stays alert in
vain. In vain you get up early and stay up late, working hard
to have enough food—yes, He gives sleep to the one He loves.*
PSALM 127: 1–2 HCSB

. . . . . . . . . . . . . . . . . . . . . . .

Any striving apart from God is useless. The Bible shows time and again
how man's efforts apart from Him come to nothing. Even if your labors
are financially successful, Moses' admonition stands: "You may say to
yourself, 'My power and the strength of my hands have produced this
wealth for me.' But remember the LORD your God, for it is he who gives
you the ability to produce wealth" (Deuteronomy 8:17–18 NIV). God
is the source of earthly success and even more so of spiritual success. Jesus
declared, plainly speaking of spiritual fruit, "Apart from me you can do
nothing" (John 15:5 NIV). Zero!

Yet laboring *with* God is another matter. For the sake of seeing the
fullness of Christ in every believer, Paul said, "To this end I strenuously
contend with all the energy Christ so powerfully works in me" (Colossians
1:29 NIV). Peter urged us to remember, "If anyone serves, they should do
so with the strength God provides" (1 Peter 4:11 NIV). God wants you
to work within His kingdom, and He will supply the strength you need!

---

*God, strengthen me to labor with You for eternal things!*

# DON'T MISS THE RICHES YOU HAVE

*Isn't everything you have and everything you are sheer gifts from
God? So what's the point of all this comparing and competing?
You already have all you need. You already have more access
to God than you can handle. Without bringing either Apollos
or me into it, you're sitting on top of the world—at least God's
world—and we're right there, sitting alongside you!*

1 Corinthians 4:7–8 msg

. . . . . . . . . . . . . . . . . . . . . . .

Published in 1890, *Acres of Diamonds* by Russell Conwell, founder of
Temple University, tells the tale of a prosperous Persian farmer who became
discontent when he heard that diamonds could make him rich beyond
his wildest dreams. Selling everything, he traveled the world only to die
in poverty. The man who bought his farm later found a diamond mine on
that very land! Untold wealth had been right under the old farmer's nose.

Like that ancient farmer, believers can miss the vast wealth they're
already sitting on. Paul says that God "has blessed us in the heavenly
realms with every spiritual blessing in Christ" (Ephesians 1:3 niv) and
prays that "the eyes of your heart may be enlightened in order that you
may know the hope to which he has called you, the riches of his glorious
inheritance in his holy people" (Ephesians 1:18 niv). No need to compare
ourselves with others—we are all already wealthy beyond *our* wildest
dreams in Christ!

*Gracious Father, open the eyes of my heart
that I may see Your riches in Christ!*

# WHO'S KEEPING SCORE?

*If you, LORD, kept a record of sins, Lord, who could stand? But with
you there is forgiveness, so that we can, with reverence, serve you.*

PSALM 130:3–4 NIV

. . . . . . . . . . . . . . . . . . . . . . .

When you understand how much of a problem sin is, you'll begin to
understand how great your Redeemer is. One of the prophets recognized
sin for what it is, and proclaimed, "Will the LORD be pleased with
thousands of rams, with ten thousand rivers of olive oil? Shall I offer my
firstborn for my transgression, the fruit of my body for the sin of my soul?"
(Micah 6:7 NIV). No! Nothing we offer can expunge the record of our sins.

But God made an incredible promise to His people that would later be
fulfilled in Christ: "I will forgive their wickedness and will remember their
sins no more" (Jeremiah 31:34 NIV). The sacrifice of Jesus would allow God
to "forget" the sin of those who accept the free gift of salvation through
faith. When you confessed Christ Jesus as Lord, all your wrongdoings,
shortcomings, and sins were purposely "forgotten." You were removed
from the old system where records were kept to a new system where
they are not: "For he has rescued us from the dominion of darkness and
brought us into the kingdom of the Son he loves" (Colossians 1:13 NIV).
The Father not only wiped your slate clean, He broke that slate into pieces!

*I praise You, Father of my freedom, for remembering my sins no more!*

## A TIME TO BE STILL

*My heart is not proud, LORD, my eyes are not haughty; I do not concern myself with great matters or things too wonderful for me. But I have calmed and quieted myself, I am like a weaned child with its mother; like a weaned child I am content.*

PSALM 131:1–2 NIV

. . . . . . . . . . . . . . . . . . . . . . .

Most of us don't live in a quiet world. Terms like *multitasking*, *stressed out*, and *overworked* are commonly used to describe our day-to-day experience. But in these verses, from a "song of ascents" (a reference to pilgrims coming uphill to Jerusalem to celebrate a festival), we hear a different tone—a purposeful tone describing the humility that leads to a "quieted" soul, a tone that obeys God's command to "be still, and know that I am God" (Psalm 46:10 KJV).

Taking time to pull back from the distractions and demands of life requires intentionality. Jesus Himself had enormous demands on His time once He began His public ministry. Crowds followed Him day and night, looking for healing, bread, or miracles. But to maintain a relationship with His Father, "Jesus often withdrew to lonely places and prayed" (Luke 5:16 NIV). Commit time to quiet your heart and wait for God's "still small voice" (1 Kings 19:12 KJV).

*Lord God, I will quiet my soul to hear You;
I will still my mind to know You are God.*

# A LIVING PROMISE

*The LORD swore an oath to David with a promise he will never take back: "I will place one of your descendants on your throne. If your descendants obey the terms of my covenant and the laws that I teach them, then your royal line will continue forever and ever."*

PSALM 132:11–12 NLT

. . . . . . . . . . . . . . . . . . . . . . .

No man could ever fully keep the Law given to Moses. Even the great psalm writer and shepherd of Israel, David, to whom God swore an oath in today's reading, fell woefully short. David, the one about whom the prophet Samuel said, "The LORD has sought out a man after his own heart" (1 Samuel 13:14 NIV), would later in life commit both adultery and murder. "If your descendants obey," warned the Lord—but if David himself couldn't keep the covenant and laws of God, what hope would any of his descendants have? None. . .except for One.

To the virgin Mary, a descendant of David, the angel Gabriel spoke of the child she would bear, saying, "He will be great and will be called the Son of the Most High. The Lord God will give him the throne of his father David" (Luke 1:32 NIV). Jesus perfectly obeyed the Law, bringing it to an end as a means of gaining righteousness (Romans 10:4), and fulfilled all the terms of God's covenant. Jesus is eternal King, Son of David, and the promise God will never take back!

---

*Thank You, Father, for the promise of Christ, my King!*

# GOD PLANTED YOU
# WHERE HE WANTS YOU

*However, each one must live his life in the situation the Lord assigned when God called him. This is what I command in all the churches.*

1 Corinthians 7:17 hcsb

. . . . . . . . . . . . . . . . . . . . . . .

The plans of God weave their way throughout the history of man, often unnoticed. Paul explained to the Athenian philosophers in the Areopagus that God placed all people where and when it was best for them: "From one man [God] made all the nations, that they should inhabit the whole earth; and he marked out their appointed times in history and the boundaries of their lands. God did this so that they would seek him and perhaps reach out for him and find him, though he is not far from any one of us" (Acts 17:26–27 niv).

More specifically, God has been at work in your life long before you even had a life! His plan for you went back "before the creation of the world" in Christ (Ephesians 1:4 niv). Paul's "command in all the churches" was to assure believers that God was pleased to call them just as they were and where they were. No need to abandon anything but sin! The married should stay married, and the single should stay single. Even slaves could stay in servitude unless the Lord directed otherwise—no one was any better or worse than another, and all were called to one purpose: the glory of God.

---

*Eternal God, open the eyes of my heart to see the purpose for which You've called me.*

# BODY BUILDERS

*But while knowledge makes us feel important, it is love that strengthens the church. Anyone who claims to know all the answers doesn't really know very much. But the person who loves God is the one whom God recognizes.*

1 Corinthians 8:1–3 nlt

. . . . . . . . . . . . . . . . . . . . . . .

Love is the very lifeblood of Christ's body. How we love each other, Jesus told His disciples at the Last Supper, would be a witness to the world of Him. It was so critical that Jesus made it a "new commandment," repeating it twice in the same evening (John 13:34, 15:12 esv). Sometimes we think of Jesus only coming to fulfill God's commandments, not make new ones—but that's exactly what He did, after washing His disciples' feet. The apostle John experienced that moment and echoed it, saying, "If we love one another, God lives in us and his love is made complete in us" (1 John 4:12 niv).

Spiritual knowledge is important, and you should pursue it, but Peter exhorts us to "grow in the grace and knowledge of our Lord and Savior Jesus Christ" (2 Peter 3:18 esv). You can see that the context of knowledge is grace. Knowledge without grace leads to conceit, and God "opposes the proud" (1 Peter 5:5 esv). Strive to love your brothers and sisters from your heart, and be recognized by the Father as a true body builder!

*Father in heaven, help me to love my family in Christ with the sacrificial love of Jesus.*

# GUARDING THE EYES

*"I made a covenant with my eyes not to
look lustfully at a young woman."*

JOB 31:1 NIV

. . . . . . . . . . . . . . . . . . . . . . .

God's seventh commandment—"You shall not commit adultery" (Exodus 20:14 NIV)—is an obvious prohibition against sexual activity with anyone who isn't your spouse. But Jesus offered some tough teaching on the subject of adultery, namely, that it isn't just about where we take our bodies, but (even more importantly) about the impure places our thoughts can so easily go (see Matthew 5:27–28 NIV).

So how do we keep lust-inducing images from entering through our eyes and into our minds? Job, a man who lived thousands of years before Jesus came to earth, offers some practical advice. Job seemed to understood that what a man allows his eyes to focus on can lead his heart and mind to places that dishonor God. The key, he concluded, was to be very, very careful about what we allow our eyes to focus upon.

That's no easy task, especially in today's world, where seemingly every other image that comes across our field of view has the potential to cause us problems. More than anything, though, it's a matter of commitment. . . to your spouse, to your children, and to your Father in heaven.

---

*Father, help me to keep my heart pure from lust and my eyes away
from those things that take my mind and heart to impure places.*

# FIGHTING TEMPTATION

*The temptations in your life are no different from what
others experience. And God is faithful. He will not allow
the temptation to be more than you can stand. When you are
tempted, he will show you a way out so that you can endure.*

1 CORINTHIANS 10:13 NLT

. . . . . . . . . . . . . . . . . . . . . . .

Many young believers come into the faith believing that they will no
longer be tempted to sin in ways they used to before they were saved.
Some quickly become discouraged or disillusioned when they find that
temptation doesn't just "go away."

Temptation will always be a part of our lives here on earth. It was
in the beginning for humanity, and it still is today. But Jesus provided
us the perfect example of how to successfully overcome temptation.
Remember, the devil tempted Jesus three times (see Matthew 4:1–11),
and each time the Lord answered the temptation beginning with the
words "It is written. . . ."

That's Jesus repelling temptation with what the apostle Paul called
the "sword of the Spirit," meaning the written Word of God. The Lord
gave us the Bible to challenge us, to encourage us, and to help us battle
temptation. It is our privilege to follow the example of a psalmist who
wrote, "I have hidden your word in my heart that I might not sin against
you" (Psalm 119:11 NIV).

*Lord, thank You for giving me Your written Word,
which helps keep me from sinning against You.*

# AVOIDING IDOLS

*Therefore, my dear friends, flee from idolatry.*
1 CORINTHIANS 10:14 NIV

. . . . . . . . . . . . . . . . . . . . . . . .

If you're like most Christians today, you probably don't think much about idols or idolatry. To most of us, idols and idolatry were problems God addressed during Old Testament times, when His people so many times turned away from Him and worshipped false deities. Today, we Christians don't worship actual, literal false "gods"—like people in ancient times did.

In reality, though, idolatry is as much of a danger for the man of God today as it was in Old Testament times. We may not worship statues or other inanimate objects, but that doesn't mean we aren't faced with the many temptations toward idolatry today. That is why the apostle John warned, "Dear children, keep yourselves from idols" (1 John 5:21 NIV).

That was sound counsel two thousand years ago, and it's sound counsel today as well.

What kinds of things do you find yourself tempted to "worship"? Money? Position? Social standing? There's a long list of things that, in themselves, aren't sinful. But when we become fixated on them, when we start believing that they can bring us the satisfaction and security we should find in God alone, then they can become idols.

So be careful. Make sure you keep God alone as your object of loving worship.

*Father, help me to avoid even a hint of idolatry in my life.*

# WHOLEHEARTED PRAISE

*I will praise you, LORD, with all my heart; before the "gods" I will sing your praise. I will bow down toward your holy temple and will praise your name for your unfailing love and your faithfulness, for you have so exalted your solemn decree that it surpasses your fame.*

PSALM 138:1–2 NIV

. . . . . . . . . . . . . . . . . . . . . . .

David began Psalm 138 with a strong declaration of devotion to his God, writing that he would praise Him with "all my heart." That's a word picture of a man with an undivided heart, a man who was giving God his all, a man who was holding nothing back from the Lord.

God still wants His people to love Him and praise Him with an undivided heart, soul, and mind (see Matthew 22:37). That, Jesus taught, is God's greatest commandment.

This commandment isn't an easy one to follow on our own. In fact, it's impossible! But when you turned to Jesus for salvation, He put the Holy Spirit inside you, giving you the ability to love God and follow Him with a completely undivided heart.

That's right! Through the work of His Holy Spirit, God gave you a new, undivided heart that can hear Him, respond to what He says to you, and live the kind of life that pleases Him.

---

*Lord, help me to worship You with a completely undivided heart.*

# GOD KNOWS OUR THOUGHTS

*You know when I sit and when I rise;*
*you perceive my thoughts from afar.*
PSALM 139:2 NIV

. . . . . . . . . . . . . . . . . . . . . . . .

Despite what some may believe, it is humanly impossible to know exactly what another person is thinking—to "read people's minds," as the saying goes—and honestly, being able to read others' minds would probably create far more problems than it could possibly solve.

But there is One who knows our every thought, which King David acknowledged when he wrote of his God, "May these words of my mouth and this meditation of my heart be pleasing in your sight, LORD, my Rock and my Redeemer" (Psalm 19:14 NIV).

That's an example of the proverbial two-edged sword, isn't it? On the one hand, we are grateful that God knows everything about us, even our thoughts, and still loves us anyway. On the other hand, we all have those moments when we'd probably prefer that He didn't know about our ugly, angry, lustful, doubting thoughts.

Knowing that God is well aware of every thought we think is at once a cause for gratefulness for His unconditional love for His people and also great motivation to heed the Bible's admonition to "guard your heart, for everything you do flows from it" (Proverbs 4:23 NIV).

*Loving heavenly Father, thank You for loving me, even*
*when my thoughts aren't on what they should be. Please*
*help me to think only on the things that please You.*

# THE MOST EXCELLENT WAY

*And now these three remain: faith, hope
and love. But the greatest of these is love.*

1 Corinthians 13:13 niv

. . . . . . . . . . . . . . . . . . . . . .

In 1 Corinthians 12, the apostle Paul listed for the Christians in Corinth the many spiritual gifts God had given to individuals in the church. He then ends the chapter with these words: "Now eagerly desire the greater gifts. And yet I will show you the most excellent way" (v. 31 niv).

Paul then went on to tell Corinthians that they could put all their spiritual gifts into action, but it wouldn't mean anything if they weren't motivated by love—*agape* love, an unconditional love that is very much like the love God pours out on His people.

Here is what Paul wrote about agape love:

> *Love is patient, love is kind. It does not envy, it does not boast, it is not proud. It does not dishonor others, it is not self-seeking, it is not easily angered, it keeps no record of wrongs. Love does not delight in evil but rejoices with the truth. It always protects, always trusts, always hopes, always perseveres.* (1 Corinthians 13:4–7 niv)

This is an amazing picture of real love, isn't it? It's the kind of love God pours out on you every day, and it's the kind of love He wants you to show to everyone He's placed in your life. That really is the "most excellent way."

*Loving heavenly Father, help me to walk
every day in the most excellent way.*

# INTIMACY WITH GOD

*Search me, God, and know my heart; test me and know*
*my anxious thoughts. See if there is any offensive way*
*in me, and lead me in the way everlasting.*

PSALM 139:23–24 NIV

• • • • • • • • • • • • • • • • • • • • • • •

Many men aren't comfortable sharing their hearts and their most private thoughts with others, even with their closest friends and loved ones—even their spouses. Some of us don't see opening ourselves that way as a "manly" thing to do.

David may have struggled with sharing himself with other people, but in the above verse, he demonstrated a willingness—even a passion—to invite his heavenly Father to search his very heart and mind and reveal to him his anxious thoughts and sinful ways.

This is a picture of a man who wanted true intimacy with God, the kind of intimacy that invites Him to know about everything inside him—the good stuff and the bad stuff alike. That's because David knew that the Lord wanted to lead him in "the way everlasting."

God calls you to that very same level of intimacy with Him today. When you accept that calling, you've taken an important step toward a whole new level of closeness with your loving heavenly Father.

---

*Heavenly Father, thank You for knowing me so intimately and*
*for inviting me to share my heart and my thoughts with You.*
*May I never hesitate to open myself completely to You so that*
*You can forgive my sins and heal and cleanse my heart.*

# THE REAL MESSAGE OF ECCLESIASTES

*Now all has been heard; here is the conclusion of the matter: Fear God and keep his commandments, for this is the duty of all mankind.*

ECCLESIASTES 12:13 NIV

. . . . . . . . . . . . . . . . . . . . . . . .

When you read the first several chapters of Ecclesiastes, you might find yourself wondering what God has to say to you—or anybody—through the book. Most of the book seems to say that life on earth has no real meaning, that the best we can hope for is just to get through it.

But if you stick with and read all twelve chapters of Ecclesiastes, you'll see the point Solomon was trying to make, namely, that life here on earth really is meaningless—*without God, that is.*

A famous mid-seventeenth-century document called the Westminster Shorter Catechism, written in pithy question-answer format, opens with the following:

Q1: "What is the chief end of man?"

A1: "Man's chief end is to glorify God, and to enjoy him forever."

This exact phrase doesn't appear anywhere in the Bible, but the message can be drawn from today's scripture verse. Solomon had written at length about the meaninglessness of life, but in the end (the very last two verses of Ecclesiastes) he states that every man's purpose can be summed up like this: "Fear God and keep his commandments."

*Father, I never have to wonder why You made me or saved me. The overarching theme of the Bible is that You made me to pursue You, love You, and obey You—with all my heart.*

# HE IS RISEN!

*And if Christ has not been raised, our preaching is useless
and so is your faith. . . . And if Christ has not been raised,
your faith is futile; you are still in your sins.*

1 CORINTHIANS 15:14, 17 NIV

. . . . . . . . . . . . . . . . . . . . . .

Jesus' death on the cross is a central event for the Christian faith, for it was at that moment that God took it on Himself to provide the once-and-for-all sacrifice to pay the price for our sin. But in 1 Corinthians 15:14–17, the apostle Paul plainly states that if Jesus' death hadn't been followed three days later by His resurrection, then the Christian faith would be worthless.

Paul wrote much of the importance of Jesus' resurrection from the dead, telling his readers that the resurrection was incontrovertible evidence that Jesus is the Son of God who has conquered sin and death forever. He also wrote that Jesus' resurrection is central to our renewed relationship with God: "He was delivered over to death for our sins and was raised to life for our justification" (Romans 4:25 NIV).

So when you pray and thank God that Jesus died for your sins, don't forget to also thank Him from your heart for raising Jesus from the dead. Because He lives, you will live with Him forever!

---

*Jesus, my heart is filled with joy overflowing when I think
about the wonderful truth that You died for me. . .and that
You were raised from the dead so that I can live forever.*

# YOUR WORDS MATTER

*Set a guard over my mouth, LORD; keep watch over the door of my lips.*
PSALM 141:3 NIV

. . . . . . . . . . . . . . . . . . . . . . .

The apostle James very directly addressed the issue of unwholesome talk when he wrote, "Those who consider themselves religious and yet do not keep a tight rein on their tongues deceive themselves, and their religion is worthless" (James 1:26 NIV).

The Bible is filled with admonitions to speak only words that please God, including David's words in the above verse. David clearly didn't want the same mouth that spoke praises to God to be used to say wicked, foolish things.

Jesus perfectly diagnosed the problem of unholy, unedifying talk when He said, "A good man brings good things out of the good stored up in his heart, and an evil man brings evil things out of the evil stored up in his heart. For the mouth speaks what the heart is full of" (Luke 6:45 NIV).

For you to control your tongue, you'll have to first address the issue of what's in your heart. You can do that by daily surrendering your thoughts and your speech to the control of the Holy Spirit.

*Lord, work in my heart through Your Holy Spirit so that the words
I speak will always glorify You and build others up in their faith.*

# IN TIMES OF STRESS AND FEAR

*I cry aloud to the LORD; I lift up my voice to the LORD for mercy.*
*I pour out before him my complaint; before him I tell my trouble.*
PSALM 142:1–2 NIV

• • • • • • • • • • • • • • • • • • • • • •

David wrote Psalm 142 in a terrible time of stress and fear. King Saul, in a fit of rage and jealousy, had gathered three thousand fighting men and begun a campaign to chase down and kill David. Hiding in a cave in the wilderness of En Gedi, the frightened David poured out his heart to God.

In the remainder of Psalm 142, David cries out to the Lord for help and hope. Though his heart is aching with fear, David acknowledges that God is "my refuge, my portion in the land of the living" (v. 5 NIV) and then pleads with Him for deliverance (v. 6).

Though you'll not likely find yourself needing to hide out in fear for your life, you will go through times when life stresses you, leaving you feeling as though you have nowhere to turn. Like David, though, you're never truly alone during times of stress and fear. The Lord is always there with you, waiting and ready to act on your behalf when you call out to Him for help.

---

*Dear heavenly Father, sometimes life doesn't seem fair. Sometimes it's so hard that I don't know what to do. During those times, help me to remember that I can always turn to You for comfort and help.*

# GOD'S COMPASSION AND COMFORT

*Praise be to the God and Father of our Lord Jesus Christ, the
Father of compassion and the God of all comfort, who comforts
us in all our troubles, so that we can comfort those in any
trouble with the comfort we ourselves receive from God.*

2 CORINTHIANS 1:3–4 NIV

. . . . . . . . . . . . . . . . . . . . . . .

Most of us don't like to think about it, but in this life we will most
certainly suffer pain, loss, regret, and sadness—sometimes all at once
over one particularly difficult life event. In times such as those, it's always
good to have a close friend to lend an ear and helpful words of advice
and encouragement.

As followers of Christ, each of us has the best friend of all in the
person of our heavenly Father. He is with us always and promises to hear
us and comfort us when we face even the worst of troubles in this life.

God freely offers us compassion and comfort whenever we need
them. All we need to do is press in closer to Him, share our hearts with
Him, and then rest in Him as He works to rescue us.

*Loving heavenly Father, thank You for Your heart of compassion
for those You call your own. Thank You for comforting me during
difficult times. Help me to pay that compassion and comfort forward
when You bring me people who are going through difficulties.*

## A HEART FOR MINISTRY

*Then I heard the voice of the Lord saying,*
*"Whom shall I send? And who will go for us?"*
*And I said, "Here am I. Send me!"*
ISAIAH 6:8 NIV

. . . . . . . . . . . . . . . . . . . . . .

Does your heart ever ache over the hurting, needy people in your neighborhood, in our nation, or around the world? Do you ever find yourself grieving over the lostness of humanity, wondering what you can do to reach them with the message of salvation through Jesus Christ? If you answered yes to either of those questions, then it may be that God is preparing you and calling you to some kind of service—just like He did the prophet Isaiah.

God had purified Isaiah and made him fit to serve and to speak the Lord's truth to His people (see Isaiah 6:1–6). Now ready to speak God's message to His hard-hearted people, Isaiah eagerly volunteered when God asked, "Whom shall I send? And who will go for us?" (6:8 NIV).

God has something for you to do for His kingdom. He has given you gifts and can enable you to do what He's calling you to do. Your part in that is spend time in God's presence, like the prophet Isaiah, and then simply ask and listen to what He has to say to you about what He wants you to do. Then, you can eagerly answer, "Here I am! Send me."

*Father, please give a heart to minister to*
*those who need to hear about You.*

# PREPARED FOR BATTLE

*Praise the LORD, who is my rock. He trains my hands for war*
*and gives my fingers skill for battle. He is my loving ally and*
*my fortress, my tower of safety, my rescuer. He is my shield,*
*and I take refuge in him. He makes the nations submit to me.*

PSALM 144:1–2 NLT

. . . . . . . . . . . . . . . . . . . . . . .

Many Christians today believe that the life of faith should be easy and without conflict. But that's not what the Bible teaches. In fact, the apostle Paul enjoined his readers to "put on the full armor of God" as they engaged in spiritual warfare against "the rulers, against the authorities, against the powers of this dark world and against the spiritual forces of evil in the heavenly realms" (Ephesians 6:11–12 NIV).

In the Old Testament and New Testament alike, the writers likened life on this earth for the believer to war. The Bible tells us that we will be at war with our flesh, with the world around us, and with spiritual forces.

Christian man, it really is a war out there! But it's a war we don't have to fight alone—even if we could.

In today's verse, David thanks and praises God for empowering and preparing him for war with his enemies. And our Lord does the same thing today!

---

*God in heaven, train my hands for war and my fingers for battle*
*so that I can reap the victory I would never see on my own.*

# HANDLING FEAR

*"Surely God is my salvation; I will trust and not be afraid. The LORD, the LORD himself, is my strength and my defense; he has become my salvation."*

ISAIAH 12:2 NIV

. . . . . . . . . . . . . . . . . . . . . .

Life has a way of putting us through fearful times. Problems in our marriages, conflicts with our kids, issues at work, and health difficulties can all put any man in a place where he feels afraid, anxious, and stressed out.

Fear is a natural part of life in this fallen world. But we Christian men can live the abundant life Jesus promised when we learn how to handle our fears in a way that honors God.

In today's verse, the prophet Isaiah states that he will choose to trust God and not be afraid—or at least not to surrender to his fears. Centuries later, the apostle Paul gave New Testament voice to this attitude when he wrote, "Do not be anxious about anything, but in every situation, by prayer and petition, with thanksgiving, present your requests to God. And the peace of God, which transcends all understanding, will guard your hearts and your minds in Christ Jesus" (Philippians 4:6–7 NIV).

When life gives you reason to feel afraid, it can be a huge help to remember two things: God is in control. . .and He has promised to comfort you and give you peace when you take your fears to Him.

*Father in heaven, when my heart feels overwhelmed with fear, help me to remember to turn to You.*

# SEEING THE UNSEEN

*So we fix our eyes not on what is seen, but on what is unseen,*
*since what is seen is temporary, but what is unseen is eternal.*
2 CORINTHIANS 4:18 NIV

· · · · · · · · · · · · · · · · · · · · · · ·

In the above verse, the apostle Paul joyfully encourages his readers to keep the eyes of their hearts focused on the unseen and on the eternal rather than on the seen and the temporary.

It's not always easy to focus on what is unseen and eternal. That's why the Old Testament Elisha's servant was so frightened when he woke up one morning and saw a huge army of Arameans surrounding them and the entire city of Dothan (see 2 Kings 6:8–22).

Elisha, though, saw things very differently. "Don't be afraid," he answered. "Those who are with us are more than those who are with them" (2 Kings 6:16 NIV). When Elisha prayed, "Open his eyes, LORD, so that he may see" (2 Kings 6:17 NIV), immediately his servant looked up and saw huge numbers of horses and chariots of fire all around Elisha.

God didn't open the servant's physical eyes at that moment. Those were working just fine. Instead, He opened his spiritual eyes so that he could be comforted and encouraged in knowing that God was in control and that there was nothing to fear.

---

*Lord, when I feel frightened or anxious, do for me what*
*You did for Elisha's servant: open my spiritual eyes that*
*I might focus on the unseen and the eternal.*

# BEYOND HOPE?

*The LORD will strike Egypt, and then he will bring*
*healing. For the Egyptians will turn to the LORD,*
*and he will listen to their pleas and heal them.*
ISAIAH 19:22 NLT

. . . . . . . . . . . . . . . . . . . . . .

Isaiah 19 tells the story of how God sent a series of terrible judgments on the land of Egypt...and about how He would so mercifully and graciously heal many Egyptians when they called out to Him.

Egypt had been an enemy of Israel at different times in the two nations' histories. What's more, the Egyptians had become a proud, rebellious, idolatrous people who seemed to want nothing to do with the one true God of Israel.

But God did not give up on the people of Egypt. One day, He would draw many Egyptians to Himself so that they could be saved. As it turned out, a strong and growing church thrived in Egypt for more than six centuries after Christ returned to heaven.

So, what can we learn from what happened in Egypt many centuries ago? We should never see even the worst of sinners—individuals or people groups—as beyond God's reach. Instead, we should pray that He would do whatever it takes to bring lost people to a point of understanding how desperately they need salvation. When that happens, we need to be ready to speak the message.

---

*Father in heaven, help me to never see anyone as*
*beyond Your ability—and willingness—to save.*

# UNEQUALLY YOKED

*Do not be yoked together with unbelievers. For what do righteousness and wickedness have in common? Or what fellowship can light have with darkness? What harmony is there between Christ and Belial? Or what does a believer have in common with an unbeliever?*

2 CORINTHIANS 6:14–15 NIV

. . . . . . . . . . . . . . . . . . . . . . .

Living as Christians in this fallen world means, among many other things, that each of us will come into various forms of contact with unbelievers. That can be a good thing—as long as we exercise godly wisdom when it comes to relating with the unsaved.

Paul's admonition to "not be yoked together with unbelievers" can be applied to many areas of our lives: who we are close friends with, who we do business with, and many others.

Paul wasn't saying that we Christian men should hide away in a monastery, keeping ourselves completely separated from the "unsaved" world. In fact, he wrote that we are not to separate ourselves from ungodly people but only from professing Christians who are living immoral lives (see 1 Corinthians 5:9–13).

The apostle was getting at the wisdom of keeping ourselves from relationships that could influence our hearts and get us to think, speak, and behave in ways that don't please God and that keep us from growing in our faith.

Remember, "the righteous choose their friends carefully, but the way of the wicked leads them astray" (Proverbs 12:26 NIV).

*Father in heaven, keep my heart from being bound together with those who don't trust or serve You.*

## YOUR ETERNAL EXISTENCE

*He will swallow up death forever. The Sovereign LORD*
*will wipe away the tears from all faces; he will remove his*
*people's disgrace from all the earth. The LORD has spoken.*

ISAIAH 25:8 NIV

. . . . . . . . . . . . . . . . . . . . . .

Life here on earth can be hard, and sometimes well-meaning friends inadvertently make it harder with a platitude like "Just hang in there! Things will get better" when you're enduring difficult times.

You may have politely thanked your friend for his attempt to speak words of encouragement, but you still walked away wondering if your difficulties would ever end. But one of God's most amazing promises is that there will come a day when the kinds of earthly difficulties we face will permanently become things of the past. No more pain, no more death, no more tears. . .only a joyful eternity in our heavenly Father's presence.

The apostle John echoed the amazing promise from today's scripture verse when he wrote, " 'He will wipe every tear from their eyes. There will be no more death' or mourning or crying or pain, for the old order of things has passed away" (Revelation 21:4 NIV).

Living on this earth, it's hard to imagine a time when death, despair, and pain are no longer a part of our existence. But it's God's promise to His people, and it's one that can get us through our most difficult life experiences.

*During difficult times, Lord, calm my heart with*
*reminders of what is ahead for me.*

## CAN I DRINK ALCOHOL?

*Woe to that wreath, the pride of Ephraim's drunkards, to the*
*fading flower, his glorious beauty, set on the head of a fertile*
*valley—to that city, the pride of those laid low by wine!*
ISAIAH 28:1 NIV

. . . . . . . . . . . . . . . . . . . . . . .

It surprises many Christian men to hear this, but nowhere in the Bible
is the consumption of alcoholic beverages forbidden. In fact, our Lord
Jesus drank wine (see Matthew 11:19, Luke 7:34).

God doesn't have a problem with His people drinking in moderation.
Drunkenness, though, is a completely different matter. God repeatedly
condemns drunkenness in His written Word. In today's verse, He addresses
drunkenness among the people of the northern kingdom of Israel (Ephraim).

Here are some other scripture passages that address drunkenness:

- "Wine is a mocker and beer a brawler; whoever is led astray by
  them is not wise" (Proverbs 20:1 NIV).
- "Let us behave decently, as in the daytime, not in carousing and
  drunkenness" (Romans 13:13 NIV).
- "Do not get drunk on wine, which leads to debauchery. Instead,
  be filled with the Spirit" (Ephesians 5:18 NIV).

Drunkenness moves our hearts away from God and can ruin our
professional lives, our families, our health, and our testimony for Jesus.
For those reasons, we would do well to heed the Bible's prohibitions
against drunkenness.

---

*Father in heaven, I know that You don't want me to*
*live a life of drunkenness. Fill my heart with wisdom*
*as I consider whether to consume alcohol at all.*

# GENEROUS, CHEERFUL GIVING

*Remember this: Whoever sows sparingly will also reap sparingly,
and whoever sows generously will also reap generously. Each of
you should give what you have decided in your heart to give, not
reluctantly or under compulsion, for God loves a cheerful giver.*

2 Corinthians 9:6–7 niv

. . . . . . . . . . . . . . . . . . . . . . . .

If many of us were completely honest, we'd have to admit that we find it
hard to give. In the Bible, though, God strongly encourages His followers
to give generously. In the Old Testament, for example, the prophet Malachi
wrote, " 'Bring the whole tithe into the storehouse, that there may be food
in my house. Test me in this,' says the Lord Almighty, 'and see if I will
not throw open the floodgates of heaven and pour out so much blessing
that there will not be room enough to store it' " (Malachi 3:10 niv).

In light of this verse, isn't it possible that our reluctance to give toward
God's work here on this earth has less to do with simple selfishness
and much more to do with our lack of trust in Him to provide what we
need to care for ourselves and our families?

The Bible teaches that that is backward thinking. God promises
that when you give, you put yourself in a position to receive blessings
from above.

*Lord, give me a generous heart, a heart that takes
great joy in giving when I see others in need.*

# COMING JUDGMENT

*The sinners in Zion are terrified; trembling grips the godless: "Who of us can dwell with the consuming fire? Who of us can dwell with everlasting burning?"*

Isaiah 33:14 niv

. . . . . . . . . . . . . . . . . . . . . . .

The sinners and hypocrites in Jerusalem in Isaiah's time were afraid, and they had good reason to be. In Isaiah 33:14–17, the prophet contrasted the sinful people with those who walked righteously before God and did what was right in His eyes. Here is what he wrote about the righteous:

> *Those who walk righteously and speak what is right, who reject gain from extortion and keep their hands from accepting bribes, who stop their ears against plots of murder and shut their eyes against contemplating evil—they are the ones who will dwell on the heights, whose refuge will be the mountain fortress. Their bread will be supplied, and water will not fail them.* (Isaiah 33:15–16 niv)

Those who didn't live godly lives were afraid, but God's loved ones were comforted with the promise of better things ahead. That's how it is today still. Those Jesus has made righteous needn't fear God's wrath. Instead, they can joyfully look forward to everything God has promised them in life to come.

---

*Lord, keep my heart pure before You so that I needn't fear Your wrath but instead look ahead to eternity in Your presence.*

# BE LIKE THE APOSTLE PAUL

*I have worked much harder, been in prison more frequently, been
flogged more severely, and been exposed to death again and again.
Five times I received from the Jews the forty lashes minus one. Three
times I was beaten with rods, once I was pelted with stones, three
times I was shipwrecked, I spent a night and a day in the open sea.*

2 CORINTHIANS 11:23–25 NIV

. . . . . . . . . . . . . . . . . . . . . . . .

In 2 Corinthians 11:23–29, the apostle Paul recounted for the church
in Corinth his terrible suffering for the cause of the message of Jesus
Christ. He had been flogged nearly to death five times, beaten with rods,
pelted with rocks, and shipwrecked. In addition, he had gone without
food, water, and adequate clothing to keep himself warm.

Yet through it all, Paul never complained to God that he was being
treated unfairly. Instead, he kept his heart and mind focused on Jesus
and on the mission He had called Paul to accomplish.

When you're going through difficult times, be like the apostle Paul.
Remember to keep your eyes on Jesus. When you do that, you'll have
peace in your heart and the strength you need to continue on what God
has for you to do.

---

*Father in heaven, when I'm enduring difficulties, keep my heart focused
on You so that I can continue in the work You have for me to do.*

# BE LIKE HEZEKIAH

*Then the angel of the LORD went out and put to death a hundred and eighty-five thousand in the Assyrian camp. When the people got up the next morning—there were all the dead bodies!*
ISAIAH 37:36 NIV

. . . . . . . . . . . . . . . . . . . . . . .

Hezekiah, the godly king of Judah, knew his kingdom was in deep, deep trouble. Sennacherib, the king of Assyria, had invaded Judah and captured forty-six of its fortified cities (Isaiah 36:1). Now, the Assyrians had their eyes on Jerusalem. Hezekiah sent gifts of silver and gold, hoping that would bring peace between Judah and Assyria (2 Kings 18:13–16). But when that didn't work, Hezekiah did all he had left to do: pray (Isaiah 37:14–20).

The soldiers in Jerusalem wouldn't have posed much of a threat for the massive Assyrian army. Fortunately for the people of Jerusalem, they didn't have to be. God had promised King Hezekiah that the Assyrians wouldn't step foot in Jerusalem or shoot a single arrow into the city, and He kept His promise.

What do you do when you're faced with a seemingly impossible situation? If you're like Hezekiah, you turn with your whole heart to the One for whom nothing is impossible. When you do that, you invite your all-powerful, all-living heavenly Father to do the miraculous on your behalf.

*Father, give me a heart to turn to You in all things. Help me to remember always that You are the God who can do anything for me.*

## CALLED TO SERVE

*Behold my servant, whom I uphold; mine elect, in whom
my soul delighteth; I have put my spirit upon him:
he shall bring forth judgment to the Gentiles.*

ISAIAH 42:1 KJV

• • • • • • • • • • • • • • • • • • • • • • •

Jesus spoke often of the importance for His followers of serving others. In Matthew 20:25–28, He told His followers that they were to be different from power-hungry authorities, that they were to lead by first being servants. He concluded this thought by telling them that they should follow His example: "Just as the Son of Man did not come to be served, but to serve, and to give his life as a ransom for many" (Matthew 20:28 NIV).

Centuries before Jesus came to earth, the prophet Isaiah used the term "servant of the Lord" (Isaiah 42:1 NIV) to describe the coming Messiah. Later, the apostle Matthew wrote that Jesus had fulfilled the prophecy in Isaiah 42 (see Matthew 12:17–21). There's no question that Isaiah's Servant was Jesus Christ.

Indeed, Jesus came to earth to serve God and humanity by suffering, dying on a cross, and then rising from the dead. He served us in the most profound way possible, and now He calls us to serve others just as He served us. When we consider what He has done for us, our only response should be to say, "Yes, Lord. I will serve You by serving others."

*Lord, help me to serve others as You have served me.*

# PLEASE GOD FIRST

*Am I now trying to win the approval of human beings, or of God? Or am I trying to please people? If I were still trying to please people, I would not be a servant of Christ.*

GALATIANS 1:10 NIV

. . . . . . . . . . . . . . . . . . . . . . . . .

Some Christian men make the big mistake of being people pleasers ahead of being God pleasers. When we go out of our way to make God's truth more palatable by speaking only "partial truth," or when we fail to answer faulty thinking about the Gospel message because we're afraid of ridicule or rejection, then we've fallen into the trap of trying to please people first.

In today's verse, which the apostle Paul addressed to a Galatian church that had virtually abandoned the message of salvation through faith in Jesus Christ alone, he stated that he was 100 percent committed to pleasing God by speaking the truth of the Gospel, even though it would put him at odds with those who had preached a false message to the Galatian Christians.

Paul set an example we should all follow when he chose to be faithful to God rather than seek the easy way out as he sought to direct people toward the truth of salvation by grace through faith.

---

*Father, You have called me to glorify You by serving people. As I do that, help me to always remember that I am to please You first in everything I do and everything I say.*

# HANDLING GUILT

*I, even I, am he that blotteth out thy transgressions for
mine own sake, and will not remember thy sins.*

Isaiah 43:25 kjv

. . . . . . . . . . . . . . . . . . . . . .

We've all felt guilty over things we've done or failed to do in the past.
Guilt *can* be a useful emotion—when it's due to sin we know we need
to confess to God and then stop doing. But it can also be a heart anchor
that can hold us down and keep us from living that abundant life Jesus
promised those who follow Him.

As a follower of Jesus Christ, you have the privilege of confessing
your sins to God, knowing He will forgive you (see 1 John 1:9). You
needn't dwell on guilt over your past mistakes and sins. And when you
find yourself feeling guilt, you can spend some time dwelling on these
words from today's scripture verse.

God didn't save you, forgive you, and set you on a new path in life
so that you could spend the rest of your days being eaten alive by guilt
over your past sins. So learn from your past mistakes and sins and become
a better man of God through what you've learned, but don't ever let
yourself believe, for even a moment, that God holds that which He has
forgotten against you.

---

*Merciful God, help me to never forget that when You forgive my
sins, You bury them in Your own divine, willful forgetfulness.*

# BECAUSE YOU BELIEVE

*I ask you again, does God give you the Holy Spirit and work
miracles among you because you obey the law? Of course not!
It is because you believe the message you heard about Christ.*

GALATIANS 3:5 NLT

. . . . . . . . . . . . . . . . . . . . . . . .

We men like lists, especially lists of things we need to do to accomplish
something important—be it finding professional success, building a
strong marriage, or raising emotionally and physically healthy children.

But, as the apostle Paul taught the erring Galatian church, receiving
God's Holy Spirit and walking in His power aren't matters of keeping a
list of laws or rules but instead a result of doing one simple thing: believing
from the heart the simple message of Jesus Christ.

No man has ever received God's Spirit or seen His power working in
his life by simply "willing" those things to happen. Those things happen
when we simply believe what God has said in His written Word.

Do you ever find yourself trying to make God act on your behalf by
"doing" things you believe will earn His favor? If so, then stop it. Instead,
simply believe. . .and receive all He has for you.

*Generous heavenly Father, remind me daily that Your gift of
the Holy Spirit—as well as the things He does in and through my
heart—come only because I believe You and Your only Son.*

## ONE IN JESUS!

*There is neither Jew nor Gentile, neither slave nor free, nor is there male and female, for you are all one in Christ Jesus. If you belong to Christ, then you are Abraham's seed, and heirs according to the promise.*

GALATIANS 3:28–29 NIV

· · · · · · · · · · · · · · · · · · · · · ·

Paul wrote the above scripture passage at a time (the first-century church) when divisions within the body of Christ—including between Jewish and non-Jewish believers—threatened the all-important unity within the church.

In the many years since Paul wrote these words, many have interpreted them to mean that God had done away with all differences between people groups. But his message (paraphrased) was simply this: anyone from any people group who comes to faith in Jesus is now bound together as one with every other believer in a wonderful group God calls the body of Christ.

That's a heart bind that will last for all eternity!

God doesn't call us Christians to ignore or discount our individual differences or uniqueness. Instead, He wants us to make sure that we never allow those differences to keep us from focusing on what binds our hearts together forever—that we are truly "one in Christ Jesus."

---

*Thank You, Father, for making us all so different from one another—different in our appearance, in our social and economic standing, different in our gifts. Thank You also that despite all those differences, we can see ourselves the way You do: as one in Jesus Christ.*

# YOU ARE GOD'S OWN CHILD!

*And because we are his children, God has sent the Spirit
of his Son into our hearts, prompting us to call out, "Abba,
Father." Now you are no longer a slave but God's own child.
And since you are his child, God has made you his heir.*

GALATIANS 4:6–7 NLT

. . . . . . . . . . . . . . . . . . . . . . .

In the scripture passage above, Paul called you as a Christian "God's own child" and His "heir." He also wrote that being God's child gives you the privilege of calling out to Him using the highly personal title "Abba, Father."

Jesus gave voice to the depth of a perfect heavenly Father's love for you as His child when He said, "If you, then, though you are evil, know how to give good gifts to your children, how much more will your Father in heaven give good gifts to those who ask him!" (Matthew 7:11 NIV).

Some men grew up without good fathers, and that makes it difficult for them to think of God as a loving heavenly Father. But when God sends His Spirit into our hearts, He gives us the ability to know Him as a God who so loves us that we believe with everything within us that He has given us His kingdom, that He wants to spend time with us, and that He wants to give us all good things.

---

*Thank You, Father, for making me Your own child and
an heir to the good things You have for me.*

# GOD'S PATH TO HOLINESS AND STABILITY

*Keep your heart with all vigilance, for from it flow the springs of life.*
*Put away from you crooked speech, and put devious talk far from you.*
*Let your eyes look directly forward, and your gaze be straight before*
*you. Ponder the path of your feet; then all your ways will be sure.*
PROVERBS 4:23–26 ESV

. . . . . . . . . . . . . . . . . . . . . .

Finding stability and holiness in your life comes from a vigilant outlook that assesses your actions and examines what your heart values. The things you think about will begin to direct your desires and thoughts, and as your desires and thoughts shift, you'll see the impact in how you live. What you say and how you act will be directed by what's stored within your heart.

You can gain a quick and accurate assessment of your life's direction by looking at what you say, how you treat others, and whether your actions are in keeping with God's best for yourself and your neighbors. Taking honest stock of yourself is the first step toward repentance and holiness. Oftentimes guarding your heart and living in obedience to God simply means minding your own business, avoiding quarrels with others, and looking straight ahead at what is in front of you today.

*Lord, help me to live simply and honestly, guarding my heart and keeping*
*a close watch on what I say so that I won't stray from Your paths.*

# ASK GOD TO TRANSFORM
# YOUR THOUGHTS

*Let the wicked forsake their ways and the unrighteous their thoughts.*
*Let them turn to the LORD, and he will have mercy on them, and*
*to our God, for he will freely pardon. "For my thoughts are not your*
*thoughts, neither are your ways my ways," declares the LORD.*
ISAIAH 55:7–8 NIV

. . . . . . . . . . . . . . . . . . . . . . .

Isaiah calls on his readers to seek the Lord while there is an opportunity. Time is limited, and the consequences of sin will come faster than expected. If you feel weighed down by sinful thoughts, desires, or actions, your only hope for deliverance and new life is to turn from your sins and to ask God's forgiveness. Once you've let go of what keeps you from obedience to the Lord, you'll remain clear of sin when you trust in God's power to renew your mind.

On your own, you aren't capable of thinking the way God wants you to. God's thoughts are at a level far above what we humans can reach. God's ways are also higher, so that you can never measure up on your own. Considering God's thoughts and ways beyond your reach isn't a source of discouragement; rather, it's an invitation to rely fully on God's forgiveness and mercy. You can't reach God on your own. That is only possible with God's power at work in your life. Thankfully, God is near, merciful, and more than willing to lift you up.

*Lord, restore my thoughts and renew my actions.*

# DON'T GIVE UP ON THE HOLY SPIRIT

*Don't be misled—you cannot mock the justice of God. You
will always harvest what you plant. Those who live only
to satisfy their own sinful nature will harvest decay and
death from that sinful nature. But those who live to please
the Spirit will harvest everlasting life from the Spirit.*

GALATIANS 6:7–8 NLT

. . . . . . . . . . . . . . . . . . . . . . .

Investing in obedience to God and relying on the Holy Spirit to bring
renewal into your heart may sometimes feel like a long-term investment
that will never pay off. You may feel that there is no guarantee that
obedience will pay off or that you will see blessings from God. Furthermore,
you may become discouraged when you see the wicked and sinful appearing
to prosper. Yet God's justice will one day win out. There is no hiding
your sin and disobedience from God, and that is why Paul insists on
persevering in doing good.

There aren't many examples of making investments where you have to
wait quite so long for a return or benefit as there may be with eternal life.
It's true you may be blessed today by relying on the Lord, and the Holy
Spirit will bring some comfort for the time being. But the full benefit
of investing in pleasing the Holy Spirit is a long-term act of faith that
looks beyond what you can see today.

*Holy Spirit, I invite You into my life to bring renewal and restoration.*

# GOD ROOTS FOR A COMEBACK

*They will rebuild the ancient ruins and restore the places*
*long devastated; they will renew the ruined cities that have*
*been devastated for generations. Strangers will shepherd your*
*flocks; foreigners will work your fields and vineyards.*

ISAIAH 61:4–5 NIV

. . . . . . . . . . . . . . . . . . . . . . . .

Isaiah wrote to people who had suffered calamities beyond imagination—losing their homes, their land, and many of their neighbors to a brutal exile. Even after the people of Israel had resisted the Lord and sinned over and over while ignoring the warnings of prophets, hope remained because of God's mercy and desire to restore them. The things that appeared to be devastated and beyond all hope had a chance for a comeback because God had willed it to be so. Restoration is what God desires more than anything else.

Consider the areas of your life where you may also feel like you're losing hope. The most barren spots are where God will want to bring renewal, new life through the influence of the Holy Spirit. Since your new life is found in Christ, your renewal has more to do with your faith in God's power than in what you can see right now. With the Lord's power at work in your heart, you may see blessings and goodness that not only benefit you but also help many others around you.

*Lord, help me to fully rely on You for my hope and*
*restoration when I feel stuck or hopeless.*

# THE CONSEQUENCES OF INACTION

*Go to the ant, O sluggard; consider her ways, and be wise. Without having any chief, officer, or ruler, she prepares her bread in summer and gathers her food in harvest. How long will you lie there, O sluggard? When will you arise from your sleep? A little sleep, a little slumber, a little folding of the hands to rest, and poverty will come upon you like a robber, and want like an armed man.*
PROVERBS 6:6–11 ESV

· · · · · · · · · · · · · · · · · · · · · · ·

What you don't do may have worse consequences than what you choose to do. Although rest and leisure are important, sloth and inaction will inevitably lead to poverty and struggle. That isn't to say that everyone living in poverty is lazy—calamities beyond our control will happen. Rather, there are real consequences for failing to take initiative in life.

God is merciful and kind, but He will also let you reap what you sow in life. That is true for your spiritual practices and for your work. As you trust God to provide what you need, you remain responsible for taking the initiative and acting on the opportunities you have today. Much like an ant that is motivated to work hard, you shouldn't require accountability or punishments to do what is required to care for yourself.

*Help me, Lord, to work with gratitude for my opportunities.*

# GOD'S LOVE IS YOUR SOURCE OF STRENGTH

*I pray that from his glorious, unlimited resources he will empower
you with inner strength through his Spirit. Then Christ will
make his home in your hearts as you trust in him. Your roots
will grow down into God's love and keep you strong. And may
you have the power to understand, as all God's people should,
how wide, how long, how high, and how deep his love is.*

EPHESIANS 3:16–18 NLT

. . . . . . . . . . . . . . . . . . . . . .

How can you grow in your faith and in spiritual maturity? According to Paul, the key to growing stronger and more resilient in the Lord hinges on your awareness of God's love and whether you rely on it. If you are rooted in God's love, then you will be stable and strong. If not, you may be blown around by every circumstance, distraction, or attractive philosophy.

The nature of God's love is worthy of your attention and meditation. Paul hopes that you will "understand" that God's love is beyond your grasp. God's love is so expansive and beyond grasping in its entirety that you will never fully know how much He loves you. This is why you can begin to live your life rooted in this never-ending, incomprehensibly vast love. You can always go deeper into God's love.

*Jesus, help me to rest fully in You and Your love. May You reside
in my heart, and may my life find its stability in You alone.*

# A NEW NATURE

*Throw off your old sinful nature and your former way of life, which is corrupted by lust and deception. Instead, let the Spirit renew your thoughts and attitudes. Put on your new nature, created to be like God—truly righteous and holy.*

EPHESIANS 4:22–24 NLT

. . . . . . . . . . . . . . . . . . . . . . .

Jesus' message reminds you that He is the Way, the Truth, and the Life. There is no other path to God the Father outside of Jesus, and you will find renewal by trusting in the Holy Spirit to change your life from the inside out. Your own willpower can't bring about the Spirit's power in your life or help you become more like Jesus, but you can choose to trust in Jesus and to receive what the Holy Spirit has given to you.

You have been given a new nature that is tuned in to God's desires and lives in accordance with God's will. But you can only receive the gift of this new nature. Today you have an opportunity to begin again, to trust the Spirit to renew your thoughts and attitudes so that your life will be restored from the inside out with a new nature. This new nature can remain strong in the temptations and trials of life and keep you close to God's present love for you.

*Holy Spirit, bring renewal and true righteousness into my life so that I can fully embody Your goodness and love.*

# WHAT DO YOU TREASURE?

*My son, keep my words and treasure up my commandments
with you; keep my commandments and live; keep my teaching
as the apple of your eye; bind them on your fingers; write
them on the tablet of your heart. Say to wisdom, "You are
my sister," and call insight your intimate friend.*

PROVERBS 7:1–4 ESV

. . . . . . . . . . . . . . . . . . . . . .

The things you treasure and store up in your heart will eventually determine the way you live. There are plenty of things you can think about and treasure rather than the ways of God, and that is often where trouble comes in. What is at the front of your mind right now? Is it God's wisdom and commands, or are your thoughts directed by the worries of life, entertainment, or lofty goals you've set for yourself? The voices on your television, radio, or smartphone can drown out the still, small voice of God's Spirit calling out to you.

Consider how you can treasure God's words for you today. You may need a little more silence to be attentive to Him. You may need a little more time to ponder the words of scripture. Then again, perhaps you need to start with removing the distractions, misplaced priorities, and noise that make it so hard to be aware of God in the first place.

---

*Lord, help me to remove the distractions that keep me from treasuring
Your commandments in my heart. May Your wisdom guide my steps.*

## DO YOUR ACTIONS
## MATCH YOUR BELIEFS?

*"But these people have stubborn and rebellious hearts; they have turned aside and gone away. They do not say to themselves, 'Let us fear the LORD our God, who gives autumn and spring rains in season, who assures us of the regular weeks of harvest.' Your wrongdoings have kept these away; your sins have deprived you of good."*
JEREMIAH 5:23–25 NIV

. . . . . . . . . . . . . . . . . . . . . .

The people of Israel may have shown up at the temple to worship regularly and observe religious feast days, but their hearts remained stubborn and rebellious. Deep down in their hearts, they didn't fear the Lord and didn't expect to face any consequences for their sinful actions. Since they weren't living by faith in God's provision and mercy, they failed to see how their lives could have been better in God's care.

Consider whether your actions match your beliefs today. Are you looking after yourself right now, as if you don't believe God can provide for you? Are you living in such a way that you expect Him to hold you accountable for what you've done? There is no fooling God, and you are likely reaping what you have sown already. God desires to be with you in the highs and lows of life, but if you neglect Him, don't be surprised if your life starts to feel chaotic and overwhelming with no relief in sight.

---

*Help me, Lord, to repent of my rebellion and stubbornness
so that I can live in Your mercy and kindness.*

# GOD CAN ADVANCE WHEN YOU HAVE A SETBACK

*And I want you to know, my dear brothers and sisters, that
everything that has happened to me here has helped to spread
the Good News. For everyone here, including the whole palace
guard, knows that I am in chains because of Christ.*

PHILIPPIANS 1:12–13 NLT

. . . . . . . . . . . . . . . . . . . . . .

When Paul endured difficulties, he looked beyond his own situation. Despite his chains, the Gospel message had been loosed throughout the palace in ways he likely never would have achieved as a free man. While Paul's imprisonment meant the loss of a vitally important witness for the church, others grew in boldness to imitate Paul's reliance on God's power. They saw his sacrifice and faith, and they realized that God would reward them for whatever they might lose here on earth.

If you suffer setback or loss, it's natural to feel discouraged and to mourn the situation. But as you entrust your challenges to God, you can find renewed hope in the rewards He promises, the gifts He can unleash in you, and the ways that others can take steps forward as well. Sharing the new life of God is a team effort where others can step in to help when you have grown weary.

*Lord, help me to trust You with my whole heart in
the midst of discouragement and loss so that I can
faithfully share Your message with others.*

# SLOW DOWN AND REFLECT TO REPENT

*Why then have these people turned away? Why does Jerusalem
always turn away? They cling to deceit; they refuse to return. I
have listened attentively, but they do not say what is right. None
of them repent of their wickedness, saying, "What have I done?"
Each pursues their own course like a horse charging into battle.*

JEREMIAH 8:5–6 NIV

. . . . . . . . . . . . . . . . . . . . . . .

Consider what it could look like to slow down in your life. Moving faster
from one thing to another doesn't leave space for reflection. When the
people of Jerusalem pursued their own way, they charged into it without
reservation. A life that just moves from one thing to another is a life that
is destined to run off course.

How can you slow down your life today? You may not feel like a horse
charging into battle, but everyone surely needs a bit of time to think about
the course of their lives, their priorities, and how God could bring change.

If you can slow down for even a brief moment, you may find that
God is willing to forgive you and that your life could improve significantly
as you pursue a new direction. You may feel a sense of loss as you leave
behind some of your own priorities and desires, but what you receive
back from God will be far greater.

*Help me, Lord, to slow down and to return to You in repentance.*

# THE RIGHT KIND OF BOASTING

*This is what the LORD says: "Let not the wise boast of their wisdom or the strong boast of their strength or the rich boast of their riches, but let the one who boasts boast about this: that they have the understanding to know me, that I am the LORD, who exercises kindness, justice and righteousness on earth, for in these I delight," declares the LORD.*
JEREMIAH 9:23–24 NIV

. . . . . . . . . . . . . . . . . . . . . . . .

If you spend your time and energy boasting about your best qualities and accomplishments, you're missing out on the best parts of life. If you grow in self-absorption, you'll miss out on the people God has placed around you and, most importantly, the Lord's mercy and justice.

God is here right now, reaching out to you and waiting for you to reach out as well. A mysterious and holy God wants you to know Him and His kindness and righteousness today.

When you remain absorbed in your own wisdom, strength, or riches, your joy will be built on a fragile foundation. You can be proved wrong at any time, your strength will surely fail one day, and your riches are hardly guaranteed. There is far more security to be found in the heart pursuit of knowing the Lord and investing in—and boasting about—your relationship with Him.

*Help me, Lord, to seek You above anything else I can gain for myself. When I seek You with my whole heart, I can find lasting peace and rest.*

## JESUS CHANGES WHAT YOU VALUE

*I once thought these things were valuable, but now I consider them worthless because of what Christ has done. Yes, everything else is worthless when compared with the infinite value of knowing Christ Jesus my Lord. For his sake I have discarded everything else, counting it all as garbage, so that I could gain Christ and become one with him.*
PHILIPPIANS 3:7–9 NLT

. . . . . . . . . . . . . . . . . . . . . .

Jesus offers you an opportunity to make a fresh assessment of what you have and what you value. In fact, part of the freedom Jesus offers is freedom *from* the need to acquire and maintain the uncertain, perishing assets of this world. When you can leave behind everything else in this world to pursue a heart union with Christ, you will enjoy a peace and freedom nothing else can touch.

This likely won't be an overnight process. If you have a strong attachment to something or a particular way of thinking, you may need some time to see the goodness of Christ and the inadequacy of everything else. Over time, you will get to see the faithfulness of Jesus, and you will begin to remember how He has stood by your side faithfully.

---

*Jesus, help me to pursue union with You so that I can leave behind everything that pales in comparison.*

# CAN YOU ACCEPT CORRECTION?

*Whoever corrects a scoffer gets himself abuse, and he who reproves a
wicked man incurs injury. Do not reprove a scoffer, or he will hate
you; reprove a wise man, and he will love you. Give instruction to
a wise man, and he will be still wiser; teach a righteous man, and
he will increase in learning. The fear of the LORD is the beginning
of wisdom, and the knowledge of the Holy One is insight.*

PROVERBS 9:7–10 ESV

. . . . . . . . . . . . . . . . . . . . . .

A mark of wisdom is the willingness to accept correction and to admit
wrongdoing. A scoffer, one who mocks others and finds his worth in
degrading someone else, is the least likely person to accept any kind of
constructive criticism or to engage in personal reflection. What's more,
a scoffer is likely to mock even the people trying to offer help.

If you want to guide others in the right direction, look for people
who are interested in growth and improvement, who are willing to do
the hard things today to gain the benefits tomorrow. And when you
receive correction, be careful to consider taking what has been shared
to heart. Even if you disagree with what you've been told, don't scoff.
Consider what you can learn, and remember that God's wisdom and
knowledge are far greater than your own.

*Lord, help me to see myself with humility so that I
accept instruction from You and from others.*

## RECONCILED WITH GOD

*Yet now he has reconciled you to himself through the death of Christ in his physical body. As a result, he has brought you into his own presence, and you are holy and blameless as you stand before him without a single fault. But you must continue to believe this truth and stand firmly in it. Don't drift away from the assurance you received when you heard the Good News.*

Colossians 1:22–23 nlt

. . . . . . . . . . . . . . . . . . . . . . .

How are you approaching God today? Do you have peace and confidence before Him, or are you struggling with guilt, shame, or inadequacy? Paul offers a very encouraging truth that you can claim right now: Jesus offers you the chance to be fully reconciled with God because He fully united Himself with humanity through His incarnation, death, and resurrection. Through the ministry of Jesus on your behalf, you can stand with Him before God the Father as completely holy and blameless. His perfection has become your own.

However, you need to start believing and living in this truth. You have to hold on to it, trust it, and claim it daily, allowing Jesus to guide and direct you. If you rely on your own wisdom and righteousness, you'll soon find yourself struggling to obey and feeling distant from God. But if you remain close to Jesus, you can approach God as a fully accepted and adopted child.

---

*Father, help me to remain close to Jesus
so that I can have peace before You.*

# WHAT IS YOUR LIFE BUILT ON?

*And now, just as you accepted Christ Jesus as your Lord, you must*
*continue to follow him. Let your roots grow down into him, and let*
*your lives be built on him. Then your faith will grow strong in the*
*truth you were taught, and you will overflow with thankfulness.*
COLOSSIANS 2:6–7 NLT

. . . . . . . . . . . . . . . . . . . . . . .

As you consider what your life is built on, or how your roots are growing, it's good to give some thought to what you listen to, who you trust, and how you spend your time. Your roots or foundation are often determined by who offers you guidance and by what you value. If you value time spent in the Lord's presence and meditating on scripture, then you will build on your foundation or send your roots down deeper.

Failing to send your roots deeper in Christ will result in a shaky foundation or roots that aren't stable. When you spend time with the Lord and learn to trust Him with your whole heart, you'll find that your faith can grow regardless of your circumstances. As your awareness of God grows deeper each day, you'll also find more opportunities to offer thanks for His care, peace, and provision. Each life situation becomes a chance to trust God more completely and follow Him more closely.

*Jesus, help me to grow in my trust in You and to replace any unreliable*
*foundations with a deeper commitment to and awareness of You.*

# SPEAK CAREFULLY

*Whoever heeds instruction is on the path to life, but he who rejects reproof leads others astray. The one who conceals hatred has lying lips, and whoever utters slander is a fool. When words are many, transgression is not lacking, but whoever restrains his lips is prudent.*

PROVERBS 10:17–19 ESV

• • • • • • • • • • • • • • • • • • • • • •

You can miss a lot when you are too eager to talk and when you fail to keep a close watch on what you say. For starters, you are likely to ignore the good advice and instruction of others. However, you are also far more likely to speak improperly, even going so far as spreading a lie, slandering, or misspeaking in some way. That's not an inevitable outcome, but it's far more likely if you are quick to speak and slow to consider what you're saying. It's far better to be restrained and deliberate in what you say.

Being quick to speak can have far-reaching consequences for others. You may lead others astray with what you say, or you may discourage or wound someone with a harsh word spoken without care. Careful heart deliberation can give you time to consider what needs to be said and what should be left unsaid, and it can ensure that your words bring the most benefit to others.

*Lord, help me to speak with care and to listen with humility.*

## THE KEY TO A LONG LIFE

*The fear of the LORD prolongs life, but the years of the wicked
will be short. The hope of the righteous brings joy, but the
expectation of the wicked will perish. The way of the LORD is
a stronghold to the blameless, but destruction to evildoers.*

PROVERBS 10:27–29 ESV

. . . . . . . . . . . . . . . . . . . . . . .

What you fear will surely influence the course of your life and your decisions, but the fear of the Lord, which brings about reverence and humility, can lead to a longer life that includes the joy of God's hope.

The self-centered choices you make that reject God's path will surely bring conflict and struggles beyond what you may intend. Indeed, the stress of such choices alone may be enough to cause health problems!

The hope and joy you have from devotion to the Lord will ensure a more peaceful life, and the peace you find with others will bring many benefits in life. With a strong community of God's people around you and a life dedicated to peace and righteousness, you will enjoy a life that is a blessing to others and blessed by God.

*Help me, Lord, to fear You alone and to live at peace with
others as I follow Your path in humble obedience.*

# CONVERSATIONS ABOUT JESUS

*Devote yourselves to prayer with an alert mind and a thankful heart.*
*Pray for us, too, that God will give us many opportunities to speak*
*about his mysterious plan concerning Christ. That is why I am here in*
*chains. Pray that I will proclaim this message as clearly as I should.*

COLOSSIANS 4:2–4 NLT

· · · · · · · · · · · · · · · · · · · · · ·

Paul was hardly a shy missionary, but even he asked his fellow believers to pray for him to have opportunities to share the Gospel boldly. He didn't take his boldness or the opportunities to preach for granted. And since he was so committed to sharing the Gospel, he humbly asked others for their prayer support.

If you aren't sure where to start when talking about Jesus, consider starting with a simple prayer asking God for opportunities and for a bold confidence to speak. Even when Paul was in chains for the Gospel, he believed that God could still give him opportunities to share His love with others. Whatever your limitations are today, you can join Paul in faith and hope, trusting that God can bring opportunities your way to share His plan of salvation.

*Jesus, help me to make the most of every opportunity to*
*share the mystery of Your love and salvation with others.*

# THE GOD WHO RELENTS

*Then Jeremiah said to all the officials and all the people: " The*
*LORD sent me to prophesy against this house and this city all*
*the things you have heard. Now reform your ways and your*
*actions and obey the LORD your God. Then the LORD will relent*
*and not bring the disaster he has pronounced against you."*

JEREMIAH 26:12–13 NIV

. . . . . . . . . . . . . . . . . . . . . . .

Jeremiah surely felt the tension between loving his people while also prophesying against their disobedience. He saw how the people had abandoned God and were on the brink of disaster. God's justice would have its way if they continued on their present course. Yet they were not without hope. If they repented, God would relent and save them from the fate they had chosen.

Even a dire situation like the one God's people faced because of their disobedience wasn't beyond hope, and so your own life can also enjoy renewal and a hopeful future if you take God's justice seriously. If you leave your sinful path behind and begin obeying God, you'll find an opportunity for mercy that can forever shift the direction of your life. God desires to save you and to lead you to hope and restoration beyond what you can imagine. The first step, though, is to admit where you have gone astray and to turn in a new direction.

*Guide me in the way of obedience and peace, Lord,*
*so that I can leave the path of sin behind.*

# BARRIERS TO THE GOSPEL

*Don't you remember, dear brothers and sisters, how hard we worked among you? Night and day we toiled to earn a living so that we would not be a burden to any of you as we preached God's Good News to you. You yourselves are our witnesses—and so is God—that we were devout and honest and faultless toward all of you believers.*

1 Thessalonians 2:9–10 nlt

. . . . . . . . . . . . . . . . . . . . . . .

Paul didn't want to give his listeners any excuses to reject the message of God's love for them. He demonstrated God's saving love by laying down his life for their sake, working doubly hard to both share the Gospel and to pay his own way. He didn't want anyone to accuse him of preaching Jesus for profit.

Consider what kinds of excuses someone could have for not receiving the message of God's love for them. Is it possible that people could very well confuse the messenger with the message? If you share about God's love and sacrifice in a way that undermines the message, you may be doing more harm than good for others. By showing that you recognize the needs of others and that you are acting solely for their benefit, you give greater credibility to the message that God loves them.

*Jesus, help me to see the ways I can serve others and alleviate their reservations about the message of Your love and salvation.*

# HOW YOU LIVE IMPACTS OTHERS

*Whoever trusts in his riches will fall, but the righteous will flourish like a green leaf. Whoever troubles his own household will inherit the wind, and the fool will be servant to the wise of heart. The fruit of the righteous is a tree of life, and whoever captures souls is wise.*

PROVERBS 11:28–30 ESV

. . . . . . . . . . . . . . . . . . . . . . .

The choices you make and the trust that you place in others will have a significant impact on your family and on your long-term security. You may not see the results of some decisions in the short term, but over time you will bear fruit that is in keeping with your choices and with where you place your trust. You can't escape the future that your way of living today is creating.

Consider where you place your trust right now. Do you trust in your bank account, or are you banking on God's presence in your life? Are you working toward reconciliation with others and making peace where there is conflict, or are you stirring up fights and division? The Bible is full of people who assumed they were living the right way, only to find that they were loyal to money or given to combating others. Invest today in the kind of fruit that will be stable and beneficial to others.

*Help me, Lord, to see the ways I've trusted in anything other than You. May I bring peace and unity to others.*

# GOD LONGS TO RESTORE HIS PEOPLE

*"This is the covenant I will make with the people of Israel
after that time," declares the LORD. "I will put my law in
their minds and write it on their hearts. I will be their
God, and they will be my people. . . . For I will forgive their
wickedness and will remember their sins no more."*

JEREMIAH 31:33–34 NIV

. . . . . . . . . . . . . . . . . . . . . . .

After generations of unfaithfulness and disobedience from the people of
Israel, the Lord resolved to restore His people once and for all. This was
an act of pure grace, but it was the only permanent fix to their centuries of
resistance. Even if the Lord had every reason to remember the sins of His
people and to hold their sins against them, He wanted to liberate them,
to no longer remember their sins, and to give them a path to obedience.

God will also treat you with the mercy and grace he showed His
people in Old Testament times. He promises His Holy Spirit to imprint
His law on your heart and teach you through his divine power to remain
rooted in him. You don't have to get your act together first—God will do
it for you. Restoration comes from God's initiative. You have the hope
of intimacy and peace with God because that is the very thing God
desires for you.

*Help me, Jesus, to remain open to and aware of Your Holy Spirit
today so that I may receive Your restoration and mercy.*

# POWER IN WORDS TO HEAL AND TO HARM

*The way of a fool is right in his own eyes, but a wise man listens to advice. The vexation of a fool is known at once, but the prudent ignores an insult. Whoever speaks the truth gives honest evidence, but a false witness utters deceit. There is one whose rash words are like sword thrusts, but the tongue of the wise brings healing.*

PROVERBS 12:15–18 ESV

. . . . . . . . . . . . . . . . . . . . . . .

The words you say and the words you receive can have enormous power in setting the course of your life or bringing healing to others. Consider carefully what you hear, who said it, and how you're receiving it; then think about what you say to others. Everyone thinks they're doing the right thing and making sound choices, but not everyone is humble enough to accept wise advice and to change the course of their lives.

The things that have shaped your life will immediately come to surface when you've been under pressure or when you're insulted. Can you graciously accept criticism or even an insult? Your security in God's love for you may be put to the test when someone speaks harsh words over your life. Regardless of the circumstances, your words will always have a lot of power to either strike someone down or to bring needed healing to a hurting heart.

*Lord, help me to choose my words carefully so they bring life and healing to others.*

# WHERE DO YOU PLACE YOUR CONFIDENCE?

*But the Lord is faithful; he will strengthen you and guard you from the evil one. And we are confident in the Lord that you are doing and will continue to do the things we commanded you. May the Lord lead your hearts into a full understanding and expression of the love of God and the patient endurance that comes from Christ.*

2 Thessalonians 3:3–5 NLT

. . . . . . . . . . . . . . . . . . . . . . .

Whether you are praying for the perseverance in faith of a family member, a friend, or even for yourself, the Lord's faithfulness and strength are where you can find hope. Paul faced both spiritual challenges and persecution, but he didn't look at his own experience, knowledge, or network for security. As he faced uncertainty for his own fate and the churches he planted, he looked only to God's power to help himself and the early church stand strong in a time of suffering and struggle.

Hard times are coming, but God is more than able to sustain you, to encourage you, and to fill you with an understanding of His great love. Patient endurance for the low points of life comes from God alone, not from individual resolve. If you're looking for a way to endure a difficult time, look to the Lord to guide you and to fill you with the endurance and love you need.

*Thank you, Lord, for the promise of Your strength and love in the moments when life becomes most difficult.*

# HOW DO YOU RESPOND TO GOD'S REBUKE?

*The king and all his attendants who heard all these words showed no fear, nor did they tear their clothes. Even though Elnathan, Delaiah and Gemariah urged the king not to burn the scroll, he would not listen to them.*

JEREMIAH 36:24 25 NIV

. . . . . . . . . . . . . . . . . . . . . . .

The king of Judah burned the scroll containing Jeremiah's message of God's judgment and the coming Babylonian invasion. Although the Lord gave the people every chance to repent, they resisted even listening to God's messenger in the first place, showing just how set they were in their ways.

An open and humble heart and a mind that is quick to listen are essential for God's people to live at peace with others and in harmony with Him.

Perhaps you can't imagine what could happen if you resisted God's message for you. Maybe you feel like you are too far gone down your own path to change. Yet the Lord is always willing to forgive those who are willing to respond with repentance and reverence. If you fear the power of God and the consequences that you will one day reap, you have an invitation to begin again today with the help of His mercy and grace.

*Lord, help me to respond to Your Word with a humble, reverent heart, remembering that You are both merciful and just.*

# HOW TO STAY ON TRACK WITH GOD

*The righteous hates falsehood, but the wicked brings*
*shame and disgrace. Righteousness guards him whose*
*way is blameless, but sin overthrows the wicked.*

PROVERBS 13:5–6 ESV

. . . . . . . . . . . . . . . . . . . . . . .

You may not see the impact of sin in your life today or even tomorrow. Yet sin will gradually lead you off course over time. It's very rare that someone stumbles into a large moral failure. Rather, sin grows over time like taking a few wrong turns on the road. Today's reading from Proverbs cuts right to the point that leaving the way of truth and righteousness will result in shame and disgrace one day. Such a fate may not be apparent right now based on your choices, but their negative impact only grows over time.

Clinging to God today is your best action for future security and peace. By fearing God's power over your life and obeying God's laws, you'll become free from the stress and uncertainty that come with leading a double life that ignores God's laws. If you live in obedience to God's teachings, you'll never have to worry about being found out as a fraud or having a secret life exposed. It's best to confess your sins today and to ask for God's help in taking a step forward in living a blameless, holy life.

*Lord, help me to remember that you know my thoughts*
*intimately and forgive me graciously so that I can live*
*without guilt and shame as I obey Your laws.*

# ARE YOU TRAINING TO HOPE IN GOD?

*"Physical training is good, but training for godliness is much better,*
*promising benefits in this life and in the life to come." This is a*
*trustworthy saying, and everyone should accept it. This is why we*
*work hard and continue to struggle, for our hope is in the living God,*
*who is the Savior of all people and particularly of all believers.*
1 Timothy 4:8–10 NLT

. . . . . . . . . . . . . . . . . . . . . . . .

Faith, hope, and love can grow and develop much like the strength of an athlete in training. If you feel that you are lacking in any of these things, there is always hope that you can grow in them—if you devote time to developing them. Each day is an opportunity to engage in the struggle of faith and hope, trusting God to guide you, to provide what you need, and to help you share with others what the Lord has done for you.

The benefits of trusting in God daily will show up in the days to come. Growing in faith and hope will help you endure the challenges that arrive in the future, and you will have the peace that comes from God's Holy Spirit. You can share this strength with others, and over time you will have the peace that comes from a strong faith in God as you pass into the life to come.

*Help me, Lord, to devote my life to training in godliness*
*so that I can one day see You with confidence.*

# HONESTY ABOUT THE PAST YIELDS FUTURE MERCY

*"Have you forgotten the wickedness committed by your ancestors and by the kings and queens of Judah and the wickedness committed by you and your wives in the land of Judah and the streets of Jerusalem? To this day they have not humbled themselves or shown reverence, nor have they followed my law and the decrees I set before you and your ancestors."*

JEREMIAH 44:9–10 NIV

. . . . . . . . . . . . . . . . . . . . . . . .

The people of Judah were in denial about the scale of their sins, which extended back for generations and continued right into the present moment. The pride and resistance to God that characterized their ancestors remained unbroken as they ignored God's teachings, believing they were above accountability for their actions.

Restoring your relationship with God may call for you to look back at your past, even the patterns and practices of generations past. Are you willing to humble your heart before God and to admit the ways you and those before you have failed? Resisting God doesn't have to be your inheritance, but you won't be able to chart a new course until you come clean with both your own sins and the sins of generations past that have influenced where you stand today. God longs to bring you mercy and healing, but the truth of your history needs to come out first.

*Lord, help me to humbly acknowledge both the influence of those who came before me and the ways I have continued in their ways.*

# INVEST IN GOD'S GREAT WEALTH

*Yet true godliness with contentment is itself great wealth. . . . But*
*people who long to be rich fall into temptation and are trapped*
*by many foolish and harmful desires that plunge them into ruin*
*and destruction. For the love of money is the root of all kinds*
*of evil. And some people, craving money, have wandered from*
*the true faith and pierced themselves with many sorrows.*

1 TIMOTHY 6:6, 9–10 NLT

. . . . . . . . . . . . . . . . . . . . . . .

Each day you're surrounded by advertisements and a culture that thrives on creating image and finding fulfillment in what you can buy. This consumer culture is further influenced by the drive to reach financial security and to grow a significant savings and bank account. Yet the pursuit of wealth, image, and security is never ending and quite fragile. These goals can absorb your time and attention, leading you to all sorts of problems that you may not even imagine today.

Jesus calls you to find contentment in what you have and to focus your attention on drawing near to God. By pursuing God rather than wealth or the latest trend, you'll find stability and peace. Your life will be built on a solid foundation, and you will find contentment in God's loving presence rather than waking up each day wondering if you have enough saved up to take care of your needs.

*Help me, Jesus, to find contentment in having You so*
*that I can live by faith in Your provision and care.*

# GOD'S PLANS

*For God saved us and called us to live a holy life. He did this, not because we deserved it, but because that was his plan from before the beginning of time—to show us his grace through Christ Jesus.*

2 TIMOTHY 1:9 NLT

. . . . . . . . . . . . . . . . . . . . . . .

What is your plan for today? According to Paul, God's highest goal for you is to show you grace, to break the power of death, and to lead you toward a holy life. You may have plenty of plans for today, including some time with your family to go trick-or-treating. Yet there is one plan that should be honored above all others. If you can place God's presence before everything else, you'll find that the power of sin and death over you can be broken.

The work of Jesus has already been completed on your behalf. You only need to receive what God has already given you. There is no mystery anymore about how to find God or how to lead a good, holy life. Seek Jesus today, and let His plans shape and direct the choices you make. Along the way, you will find that God's grace and mercy can overcome any doubts you may feel about God or about your own worthiness.

---

*Help me, Jesus, to receive the new life You give and Your power over sin and death.*

## SAY NO TO FALSE GODS

*The word the Lord spoke about Babylon, the land of the Chaldeans,*
*through Jeremiah the prophet: Announce to the nations; proclaim*
*and raise up a signal flag; proclaim, and hide nothing. Say:*
*Babylon is captured; Bel is put to shame; Marduk is devastated;*
*her idols are put to shame; her false gods, devastated.*
Jeremiah 50:1–2 hcsb

. . . . . . . . . . . . . . . . . . . . . . . .

False gods don't stand a chance against the one true God. Yet even we as Christians can be distracted by the "deities" of this world.

Not the Bels or Marduks of Babylon, which Jeremiah prophesied against. Not the Baals or Ashtoreths or Chemoshes or Molechs that pepper the pages of the Old Testament.

But how about those things that grip the hearts of so many men today—wealth, fame, sex, intellect, power? In their proper place, each has value. But if they cause us, as Jesus warned the Christians of Ephesus, to abandon "the love you had at first" (Revelation 2:4 hcsb), we set ourselves up for disappointment and pain. When we consciously and regularly take stock of our attitudes and pursuits, however, we can "keep [ourselves] in the love of God, expecting the mercy of our Lord Jesus Christ for eternal life" (Jude 21 hcsb).

This world is always trying to press you into its mold. Don't let it! By the almighty power of the one true God, say no to every cheap substitute.

---

*Lord, only You are real and true. Keep me in your perfect ways.*

## BE PREPARED

*Indeed, all who desire to live a godly life in Christ Jesus will
be persecuted, while evil people and impostors will go on from
bad to worse, deceiving and being deceived. But as for you,
continue in what you have learned and have firmly believed.*

2 TIMOTHY 3:12–14 ESV

. . . . . . . . . . . . . . . . . . . . . . .

Every generation of humanity has suffered hard, even terrible, times.
Wars, famines, plagues, and spiritual darkness have afflicted people for
millennia. Whatever darkness we face today is nothing new. And yet it
really seems that modern society is crumbling fast.

For those of us in the United States, where the Christian faith
has been generally respected if not universally accepted, opposition is
increasing noticeably. And that's something both Jesus (in John 15:20)
and the apostle Paul (in today's scripture) promised. You can never accuse
God of painting too rosy a picture for those who follow Him.

With this knowledge, we can prepare ourselves for the resistance
of "evil people" who "go on from bad to worse." How? By continuing to
firmly believe what we know about God and Jesus, sin and salvation. We
know these things by our careful study of scripture, which Paul went on to
describe as "breathed out by God and profitable for teaching, for reproof,
for correction, and for training in righteousness" (2 Timothy 3:16 ESV).

Can you commit to an extra ten minutes in the Word today?

*Father, guide me in Your truth so I can
stand against this world's opposition.*

# HEED CORRECTION

*A fool spurns a parent's discipline, but whoever heeds correction shows prudence.*

Proverbs 15:5 niv

. . . . . . . . . . . . . . . . . . . . . .

Maybe *heed* isn't the most common of words. Meaning "to give consideration or attention to," its synonyms include *regard, note,* and *listen to.* However we say it, though, guys should take the idea to heart.

Proverbs 15:5 says men who heed correction show prudence—other Bible versions say they're "sensible" (hcsb) or "wise" (nlt). Today's verse declares that it's folly to ignore or turn aside "instruction and correction" (ampc), and scripture overall comes down hard on fools. Resentment kills them (Job 5:2); their mouths invite ruin (Proverbs 10:14); honor does not befit them (Proverbs 26:1); they will be servants to the wise (Proverbs 11:29).

We might be tempted to think Proverbs 15:5 is only for teenagers, young bucks who live at home and play tug-of-war over Dad's rules. But many of us older men have a "father in the faith," as Timothy did with the apostle Paul (1 Timothy 1:2). And even if we're old as Methuselah, we still have a Father in heaven. When any of these parent figures speak, it behooves us to listen. . .to heed what they say.

Never let pride prevent you from hearing the loving discipline of someone who cares deeply for you. Heeding their words today can save you a ton of grief tomorrow.

*Father in heaven, may I always heed Your correction—and the discipline of those parent figures You've put in my life.*

# CONTENTMENT IS KEY

*Better to have little, with fear for the LORD, than to have great treasure and inner turmoil. A bowl of vegetables with someone you love is better than steak with someone you hate.*
PROVERBS 15:16–17 NLT

· · · · · · · · · · · · · · · · · · · · · · ·

Everything in this world, it seems, is designed to make you discontent. Phone companies want you to upgrade your device or service, automakers think you need some hotter wheels, pharmaceutical companies imply (even say out loud) that you're too tired, too fat, too bald. What's a guy to do?

Well, a Christian guy should follow the example of the apostle Paul, who "learned how to be content with whatever I have" (Philippians 4:11 NLT). For a man who had enjoyed times of plenty and survived periods of scarcity, Jesus was the key. "I can do everything through Christ, who gives me strength" (Philippians 4:13 NLT).

Paul's words parallel today's scripture. Our "fear for the LORD" makes up any lack we may experience—or any supposed lack the world tries to convince us we're suffering. On the other hand, no earthly treasure could ever make up for the "inner turmoil" of life without God. His love and the love of the friends and family He gives us make whatever we have "better than." But we need to make a decision: Will we be content with what God's given us?

*Father God, You have given me all I need and much that I want. Help me to be content.*

# WHILE THERE IS LIFE, THERE IS HOPE

*The Lord is good to those who wait for Him, to the person who seeks*
*Him. It is good to wait quietly for deliverance from the Lord.*
LAMENTATIONS 3:25–26 HCSB

. . . . . . . . . . . . . . . . . . . . . .

The title above is quoted from old-time Bible commentator Matthew Henry (1662–1714). In his discussion of Lamentations 3, Henry suggested, "Instead of complaining that things are bad, we should encourage ourselves with the hope they will be better." That's what Jeremiah, "the weeping prophet," did in today's scripture.

Lamentations is dreary overall. Describing the destruction of Jerusalem by the Babylonians, it contains graphic accounts of violence and despair, including cannibalism (2:20). In chapter 3, Jeremiah reported his own struggle, the overwhelming feeling that God had turned against him: "He has made me dwell in darkness like those who have been dead for ages" (Lamentations 3:6 HCSB).

But somehow—and we must attribute this to God's goodness—Jeremiah could stop and say, "Yet I call this to mind, and therefore I have hope: Because of the Lord's faithful love we do not perish, for His mercies never end. They are new every morning; great is Your faithfulness! I say: The Lord is my portion, therefore I will put my hope in Him" (Lamentations 3:21–24 HCSB). Jeremiah continued with today's scripture, commending a quiet waiting for God's deliverance.

May we follow his example today and every day.

---

*Lord, You have given me life and therefore hope.*
*May I wait quietly for Your deliverance.*

## HELPFUL, BIGHEARTED, COURTEOUS

*Remind the people to respect the government and be law-abiding,*
*always ready to lend a helping hand. No insults, no fights.*
*God's people should be bighearted and courteous.*

TITUS 3:1–2 MSG

. . . . . . . . . . . . . . . . . . . . . .

Someday, if God delays Jesus' return, historians may call the early twenty-first century "the age of anger." You can't read the news, skim social media, consume entertainment—maybe even step out in public—without being exposed to arguments, name calling, and outright violence. Though none of those things are new, they seem to be metastasizing, putting all of society on edge.

The good news is that this is an excellent time for Christian men to be. . .well, Christian men. When the apostle Paul wrote the words of today's scripture to Titus, the younger man was ministering on the Mediterranean island of Crete, a place filled with "liars, evil brutes, lazy gluttons." In this case, Paul was simply quoting the words of "one of Crete's own prophets" (Titus 1:12 NIV).

How could Titus affect such a culture? By being respectful of government officials, following the law, generously and courteously helping others. Picking fights and insulting his fellow citizens would certainly not help.

As fellow followers of Jesus, we know His command to "love your enemies and pray for those who persecute you" (Matthew 5:44 NIV). The expectation is clear. But how is our commitment to obey it?

*Please, Lord, use me to show Your love to this angry*
*world. I want people to know Your peace.*

## GOD WILL WORK IT OUT

*The LORD works out everything to its proper end—even the
wicked for a day of disaster. The LORD detests all the proud
of heart. Be sure of this: They will not go unpunished.*
PROVERBS 16:4–5 NIV

· · · · · · · · · · · · · · · · · · · · · · ·

For the United States, this first Tuesday that follows a Monday in
November is Election Day. For many people, it's a time of hopeful stress:
"I think my side's going to win!" For a large percentage of the population,
Election Day yields the depressing realization that their candidate lost,
and their opponents' ideas will rule the day for months to come.

Public policy is certainly important. But for us as Christians, it can't
be all-consuming. If the results of an election make us angry, dispirited,
apathetic, or hateful, we're forgetting some very important Bible truths
such as the prophet Daniel's assertion that God "deposes kings and raises
up others" (Daniel 2:21 NIV).

One of those kings God raised up was Solomon, who wrote today's
scripture. And it points out that even wicked people—whether everyday
criminals or powerful rulers—will be appropriately dealt with by God
in His good time. Our all-wise and all-powerful God will work out
everything to His ultimate glory and our ultimate benefit.

No matter who is leading our community or nation, let us humbly
and faithfully honor our God. He has everything under control.

---

*Father in heaven, please guide our political leaders,
and help me to trust in Your ultimate plan.*

# PRIDE GOES BEFORE A FALL

*Pride goeth before destruction, and an haughty spirit before a fall.*
PROVERBS 16:18 KJV

· · · · · · · · · · · · · · · · · · · · · · ·

If you read the title above and thought, *That's not what the Bible says*, give yourself a pat on the back. This is one of those often misquoted verses like "money is the root of all evil" (it's actually "*the love of* money," 1 Timothy 6:10) or "cleanliness is next to godliness" (okay, that's not in the Bible at all).

Proverbs 16:18 clearly states that pride goes before destruction; it's a haughty spirit that precedes a fall. While we should always be careful to quote scripture accurately, in this case a little mixing and matching seems harmless enough. The Proverbs often make their point by restating an idea in parallel terms—"pride" and "a haughty spirit" are essentially the same thing. So are "destruction" and "a fall." Let's be sure we avoid them all!

Pride is the sin that turned Lucifer into the devil. It's the desire that caused Eve to eat the forbidden fruit. It's the ambition that tripped up countless Bible characters and billions of human beings throughout history. And God hates it (Proverbs 8:13).

So how do we avoid pride? With a regular, conscious effort to chip away the crust that's baked onto our hearts. Here's a helpful verse to remember: "God resisteth the proud, but giveth grace unto the humble" (James 4:6 KJV).

---

*Lord God, turn my self-praise into praise of You. Only You are worthy.*

# STAND IN AWE

*But one in a certain place testified, saying, What is man, that thou art mindful of him? or the son of man that thou visitest him?*
HEBREWS 2:6 KJV

. . . . . . . . . . . . . . . . . . . . . .

We don't know exactly who wrote Hebrews, but we know the source he drew upon for today's scripture: David, in Psalm 8:4. In making the argument that Jesus is the supreme example of humankind, Hebrews highlights David's wonder that people are the pinnacle of God's creation: "When I consider thy heavens, the work of thy fingers, the moon and the stars, which thou hast ordained; what is man, that thou art mindful of him? and the son of man, that thou visitest him?" (Psalm 8:3–4 KJV).

It is a mystery that God loves "man"— men and women both—so much that He would send Jesus to die on a cross for our sins. Conversely, only sin can explain mankind's dismissal of the infinite Creator God whose handiwork is so readily apparent (see Romans 1:18–25). Such blatant disrespect of such an awe-inspiring God explains the harshness of His wrath on the unrepentant.

Thankfully, we are not among those who wave a puny fist at Him—as followers of Jesus, we have humbly accepted His incredibly generous offer of salvation. Like David, may we always stand in awe of the vastness of God's universe and the individual attention He lavishes on each one of us.

---

*Lord, You are truly awesome. Thank You for being mindful of me!*

## ROOT OUT THE IDOLS

*"Son of man, do you see what they are doing—the utterly
detestable things the Israelites are doing here, things
that will drive me far from my sanctuary?"*
EZEKIEL 8:6 NIV

. . . . . . . . . . . . . . . . . . . . . .

We modern Christians would never set up an idol at church, right? We'd never be like the Jews of Ezekiel's day, erecting an "idol that provokes to jealousy" in the temple (Ezekiel 8:3 NIV). . .or burning incense before animal images on the temple walls (vv. 9–11). . .or bowing ourselves in worship to the rising sun (v. 16). That stuff was crazy then, and it would be just as crazy now.

But. . .

If idolatry is giving any person or thing more prominence than God in our lives, we should take this account in Ezekiel as a word of warning. We may think we live in more sophisticated times, but Satan is working just as hard to distract us as he did those ancient Jews. And idolatry can creep even into our modern worship experience.

Let's be careful never to view church as a place for social advancement. Let's resist every temptation to envy or judge our fellow congregants. May we never emphasize the style of our church over its substance. May we always enter the sanctuary having prayed for a laser-like focus on God Himself.

Just imagine if every member of your church had that focus. Sound good? It starts with you.

*Father, may my heart and mind be completely Yours.*

# WORK NOW, REST LATER

*Let us, therefore, make every effort to enter that rest.*
HEBREWS 4:11 NIV

．．．．．．．．．．．．．．．．．．．．．．．．

How often have you heard it said, "If it seems too good to be true, it probably is"? That's a great perspective when you're shopping for used cars or considering a "can't miss" investment opportunity. But don't allow that generally accurate statement to color your understanding of the Christian life. Salvation is totally free, a generous gift from a merciful God, an offer of everlasting life that requires nothing but your acceptance.

Why, then, does Hebrews urge us to "make every effort" to enter God's rest?

We must recognize that our salvation is not *by* works but *to* works. We are saved by God's grace, which empowers us to do good things. Sometimes those good things will require "every effort." Growth in grace, the process called *sanctification*, is actually hard work.

According to Hebrews, the work is now, in this life. We must keep our hearts soft before God (Hebrews 4:7). We must allow God's Word to fill and change us (4:12). We must "hold firmly to the faith we profess" (4:14 NIV). We must regularly, confidently, approach God in prayer (4:16).

Having done these things (and many others as taught in scripture), we can be assured of "a Sabbath-rest for the people of God" (Hebrews 4:9 NIV). The rest is coming. Now is the work.

---

*Father in heaven, empower me for the good work You call me to do.*

# BITE YOUR TONGUE

*To start a conflict is to release a flood;*
*stop the dispute before it breaks out.*
PROVERBS 17:14 HCSB

. . . . . . . . . . . . . . . . . . . . . . .

Chapters of the book of Proverbs are like shells in a shotgun. To read them is to pull the trigger. The resulting blast sprays individual pellets, many of which hit a target. Today's scripture likely strikes many of us.

How easy it is to pop off, lashing out with irritation, sarcasm, or insult. Sinful human nature—even the nature blessed by the presence of God's Holy Spirit—is prone to conflict. We want what we want, and everyone else is an obstacle! So, in big ways and small, our common temptation is to seek the advantage, to start the fight.

Proverbs 17:14 provides both a warning and a solution. Warning: Starting fights releases a flood—ever-increasing irritation, sarcasm, and insults, which soon overwhelm our emotional landscape. Solution: *Stop.* Just don't do it. Each of us has the power to bite our tongue and prevent that dispute from ever breaching the dam.

The key is the aforementioned Holy Spirit in our lives. As Christians, we are temples of God's Spirit, who is always present to guide us. When we allow Him free rein, He produces His "fruit" in our lives—love, joy, peace, patience, kindness, and self-control, among them (Galatians 5:22–23).

So let the Spirit lead. Stop that dispute before it starts. Bite your tongue.

*Lord God, give me the wisdom and the will to avoid foolish conflict.*

# WISE WITH WORDS

*Even fools are thought wise when they keep silent;*
*with their mouths shut, they seem intelligent.*
PROVERBS 17:28 NLT

. . . . . . . . . . . . . . . . . . . . . . .

Here's a little grammar lesson: the word *even*, which begins today's scripture, is an adverb. Merriam-Webster's dictionary says it is "used as an intensive to stress an extreme or highly unlikely condition or instance."

The highly unlikely instance here is that a fool is considered wise. A buffoon comes across as intelligent. What causes that unexpected circumstance? Silence. When the fool stops talking, his perceived IQ skyrockets.

Hopefully, you're no fool. But if "even" a fool is considered wise in his silence, how much wiser would a good man seem by simply talking less? Think how often Peter and some of Jesus' other disciples embarrassed themselves by blurting out foolish, impetuous words. Or think about those times *you've* said things you wish you could take back. The wisdom of Proverbs 17:28 becomes crystal clear.

The good news is that this advice can be followed by any man at any time. Silence takes no special knowledge or skill, just an intentional commitment to slow down, listen more, and talk less.

Just think: If others view you as wiser and more intelligent, they may even ask what makes you different. Then you can speak up to tell them about "wisdom itself," Jesus Christ (1 Corinthians 1:30 NLT). What could be smarter than that?

*God of wisdom, may I use my words sparingly—*
*but when I do speak, talk of You.*

# BANISH PRIDE

*"Now this was the iniquity of your sister Sodom: she and her daughters had pride, plenty of food, and comfortable security, but didn't support the poor and needy. They were haughty and did detestable things before Me, so I removed them when I saw this."*

EZEKIEL 16:49–50 HCSB

• • • • • • • • • • • • • • • • • • • • • •

The prophet Ezekiel shows us the other side of Sodom's coin. We know from the story of Abraham that Sodom's men were wicked—they even tried to molest two angels visiting the city (Genesis 19). But in Ezekiel we see the sin of Sodom's *women*: they were prideful and haughty. The tragic ending of Sodom and its twin city, Gomorrah, is well known.

One of the great themes of scripture is God's hatred of human pride. Through the prophet Amos, God said, "I loathe" pride in His people (Amos 6:8 HCSB). Another time, He promised to "remove your proud arrogant people from among you, and you will never again be haughty on My holy mountain" (Zephaniah 3:11 HCSB). God easily humbled powerful leaders like Pharaoh, Haman, Nebuchadnezzar, and Belshazzar. In the psalms, David wrote that God will "humble those with haughty eyes" while He will "rescue an afflicted people" (18:27 HCSB).

We must always guard against creeping feelings of self-satisfaction and self-sufficiency. As Christians, we know that everything we have (and *are*) comes from God. May we consciously direct every bit of praise to Him.

*Lord, help me to banish all pride from my heart. Make Yourself my total focus.*

# WAITING FOR JESUS

*Christ was sacrificed once to take away the sins of many;
and he will appear a second time, not to bear sin, but to
bring salvation to those who are waiting for him.*

HEBREWS 9:28 NIV

. . . . . . . . . . . . . . . . . . . . . . .

This world will never encourage you to "wait for Jesus." To pursue money and possessions? Yep. To drink and party and chase after sex? For sure. To lose yourself in every imaginable form of entertainment? Uh-huh. But to wait for Jesus? Not a chance.

This idea of waiting and watching for Jesus' return, however, appears throughout the New Testament. Besides today's passage, you'll find variations on the theme in Matthew, Mark, Luke, Romans, 1 Corinthians, 1 Thessalonians, Titus, and Jude. Some have said that anything God says is important, but if He repeats Himself, you should really pay attention. Jesus is coming back! And, as Christians, we are instructed to keep that promise front of mind.

So how exactly do we "wait" for Jesus? Well, how would you wait for any loved one returning from a long absence? You'd eagerly anticipate that person's return. You'd prepare yourself, your family, and your home for the big reunion. You'd avoid any distractions that would interfere with the joyful moment you were together again. It's not rocket science—though you will want to keep your eyes on the skies: "Look, he is coming with the clouds" (Revelation 1:7 NIV).

*Lord Jesus, keep me focused and true as I wait for Your return.*

# WHAT YOU SAY

*Words kill, words give life; they're either poison or fruit—you choose.*
PROVERBS 18:21 MSG

• • • • • • • • • • • • • • • • • • • • • •

"You choose." That's the stark summation of the impact of our words. What we say can convey love, joy, peace, hope, courage—in a word, *life*—to another person. Or it can have exactly the opposite effect.

If what Jesus said is true (and of course it is), our speech arises from the depths of our being. "A good man brings good things out of the good stored up in his heart," the Lord told His disciples, "and an evil man brings evil things out of the evil stored up in his heart. For the mouth speaks what the heart is full of" (Luke 6:45 NIV).

So the key to our speech is what's inside us. We have a choice over that too. By filling our hearts and minds with better things, we can neutralize the poison that's already there due to our sinful human nature. God's Word—read, memorized, studied, and applied—is what grows the sweet fruit of good words. Scripture is, in fact, the seed, the fertilizer, and the water.

An old Sunday school song says, "Read your Bible, pray every day, and you'll grow, grow, grow." It sounds almost too simple, but it's true. Everything comes down to the Word God's given us and our response to it. Today, how will you choose?

*Father, I want my words to be fruit. May Your Word be my guide.*

# YOU'LL BE REWARDED

*Remember those earlier days after you had received the light, when you endured in a great conflict full of suffering. Sometimes you were publicly exposed to insult and persecution; at other times you stood side by side with those who were so treated. You suffered along with those in prison and joyfully accepted the confiscation of your property, because you knew that you yourselves had better and lasting possessions. So do not throw away your confidence; it will be richly rewarded.*

HEBREWS 10:32–35 NIV

. . . . . . . . . . . . . . . . . . . . . . .

American Christians have generally been spared the persecution believers in other times and nations have suffered. But those days of ease may be passing. Now, in what some call a "post-Christian culture," committed Jesus followers may soon find themselves like their New Testament forebears. The big question is whether we'll respond with joy and hope.

Nobody wants to be insulted. Or to end up in prison. Or to have his home or livelihood stolen away by haters of Jesus. But the early Christians accepted these things "joyfully."

That's only possible by taking the long view of life. If this world is everything, persecution is a tragedy to be avoided. But if we have "better and lasting possessions" in a world to come (and we do), our losses on earth are so minor as to be almost invisible. Pray with the apostle Paul:

*I consider my present sufferings not worth comparing with the glory that will be revealed in me (Romans 8:18).*

# THIS IS GLORY

*Good sense makes a man restrain his anger, and it is his
glory to overlook a transgression or an offense.*
PROVERBS 19:11 AMPC

In 1985, "the Boss" reached number five on the pop charts with "Glory Days." Bruce Springsteen sang of encountering a high school classmate, and all the guy could talk about were his long-ago exploits on the baseball diamond. Glory days, Springsteen concluded, will "pass you by."

The Proverbs, though, offer a way to keep the glory going: by overlooking the offensive behavior of other people. This kind of "transgression" is never ending, so you'll have plenty of opportunities for glory.

"Good sense"—or, in other translations, "wisdom"—causes men to hold back their angry responses. Not responding to irritations, insults, and imbecility is "glory," a translation of a Hebrew word connoting bravery and honor. Jesus perfectly pictured today's scripture in the final hours of His life: "When He was reviled and insulted, He did not revile or offer insult in return; [when] He was abused and suffered, He made no threats [of vengeance]; but He trusted [Himself and everything] to Him Who judges fairly" (1 Peter 2:23 AMPC).

Nothing could be more lastingly glorious than to imitate our perfect Savior. Let the world do what it does so well; then trust God to do what *He* does so well—provide the good sense to respond like Jesus.

*Lord, when I grow annoyed, speak and act
through me--to Your glory and mine.*

# WHAT MATTERS MOST?

*This message came to me from the LORD: "Son of man, with one blow*
*I will take away your dearest treasure. Yet you must not show any*
*sorrow at her death. Do not weep; let there be no tears. Groan silently,*
*but let there be no wailing at her grave. . . ." So I proclaimed this*
*to the people the next morning, and in the evening my wife died.*
EZEKIEL 24:15–18 NLT

. . . . . . . . . . . . . . . . . . . . . . .

Some absolute shockers dot the pages of scripture. Today's passage is one: as a sign to His sinful people, God took the prophet Ezekiel's "dearest treasure"—his wife.

*How could God be so cruel?* we may ask ourselves.

But consider that this unnamed woman was spared the horrific Babylonian invasion. "What sorrow awaits Jerusalem," God said (Ezekiel 24:6 NLT). If she served Him like Ezekiel did, she would avoid that trauma and receive her reward sooner. Consider too that God was giving sinful people another opportunity to turn and be saved. He would even use dramatic incidents like the death of an innocent woman to get people's attention.

And God has every right to do as He pleases. We may hope that His plans don't fall as heavily on us, but losses of all shapes and sizes can draw us and others closer to Him. Remember: That is what this life is ultimately about.

*Lord, help me to hold very loosely to the things*
*of this earth and very tightly to You.*

# FEAR OF THE LORD

*The fear of the LORD leads to life; then one*
*rests content, untouched by trouble.*

PROVERBS 19:23 NIV

. . . . . . . . . . . . . . . . . . . . . .

An old-time Bible commentator defines "the fear of the LORD" as "a reverence of God's majesty and a dread of His wrath." This two-pronged mind-set, according to Proverbs, "leads to life," and the life it leads to is also two-pronged, experienced in the now and the forever.

In eternity, God will "wipe every tear" from His people's eyes; "there will be no more death or mourning or crying or pain" (Revelation 21:4 NIV). That's when followers of Jesus will rest completely content, untouched by the trouble that our Lord Himself promised *now*: "In this world you will have trouble" (John 16:33 NIV).

Jesus said that, though, so we could have peace. "But take heart!" He continued in the same verse. "I have overcome the world."

And that's how Proverbs 19:23 proves true in the now, even before the forever. When we dread God's wrath, we turn to His offered salvation. Then we can reverence His majesty and find life, contentment, and protection from this world's problems. Even in the worst-case scenario, humanly speaking, death simply ushers us into our Lord's presence (2 Corinthians 5:8).

It's all a matter of mind-set. In a dark, confusing, depressing world, fear the Lord. Remember His awesome power, His searing holiness, and His staggering love. Trouble won't be able to touch you.

*Lord God, help me to fear You. That is the way to life.*

# ROOT OUT BITTERNESS

*Watch out that no poisonous root of bitterness
grows up to trouble you, corrupting many.*
HEBREWS 12:15 NLT

. . . . . . . . . . . . . . . . . . . . . . .

Though salvation is entirely a gift of God, our sanctification—growth in grace—takes effort on our part. The warning above is tucked into a whole paragraph of commands: "Work at living in peace," "work at living a holy life," "look after each other," "make sure that no one is immoral or godless" (Hebrews 12:14–16 NLT).

Most of us, at some time, have wrestled with that "poisonous root of bitterness." Maybe we were cheated in a business deal. Maybe we felt disrespected by our wife or kids or someone at church. Maybe we just expected life to turn out better...and that noxious root begins to stir deep inside, trying to break through the surface of our lives.

The writer of Hebrews would say, "Stop!" Though our life is a soil and circumstances the seed, we don't have to cultivate bitterness. Don't water the seed by consciously replaying offenses. Don't fertilize it with thoughts of getting even. If that bitterness does take root, use the sharp edge of God's Word (Hebrews 4:12) to hack it to pieces.

The responsibility is ours. God will gladly assist, but the duty of obedience falls squarely on each of us. By choosing to do right, we help ourselves and avoid "corrupting many." This is serious!

*Father, I want to grow the fruit of Your Spirit,
not the noxious weeds of bitterness.*

## STABILITY IN A CHANGING WORLD

*Jesus Christ is the same yesterday and today and forever.*
HEBREWS 13:8 ESV

· · · · · · · · · · · · · · · · · · · · · · ·

A seventh-grade social studies teacher wanted to get his students thinking. He asked, "How do you improve upon perfection?" A few students volunteered answers. Mr. A acknowledged their thoughts then declared, "You can't improve on perfection. Perfection is the best there is. Any change makes it less than perfect." (His point has stuck with at least one student in that class for forty years.)

Jesus, as the second person of the Trinity, "very God of very God" in the words of the Nicene Creed, is perfection. He was perfect through eternity past in His relationship with God the Father and the Holy Spirit. He was perfect in His human life and death on earth two millennia ago. He is perfect now in His resurrected life, at the right hand of the Father, praying for all who follow Him by faith. And He will continue in His perfection through all eternity to come. This perfection explains why Hebrews says, "Jesus Christ is the same yesterday and today and forever." Any change would make Him less than perfect, which is an impossibility.

When we begin to grasp this truth, we can live more confidently in a rapidly changing (often worsening) world. We can trust our past, present, and future to the One whose past, present, and future are rock solid.

---

*Lord Jesus, thank You for being my anchor in the raging sea of life.*

# SOMETHING (ELSE) TO BE THANKFUL FOR

*Every good and perfect gift is from above, coming
down from the Father of the heavenly lights,
who does not change like shifting shadows.*

JAMES 1:17 NIV

. . . . . . . . . . . . . . . . . . . . . . .

On this fourth Thursday of November, the United States officially designates a day for gratitude. Biblically speaking, that's great—and President Abraham Lincoln's 1863 proclamation formalizing a national Thanksgiving Day urged "praise to our beneficent Father who dwelleth in the heavens."

Appreciation is implied in today's scripture, where James notes "every good and perfect gift" that comes to us from "the Father of the heavenly lights." Most likely, we're thanking God today for family and friends, our health, and all the physical things we've been given. But the end of James 1:17 points out something else to be thankful for—namely, the unchanging nature of our God.

In a world of constant and often negative change, we have a firm Rock to cling to. "I the LORD do not change," Jehovah proclaimed through Malachi 3:6 (NIV). Jesus Christ, the writer of Hebrews declared, is "the same yesterday and today and forever" (13:8 NIV). We don't need to worry over the aging of our bodies, the twists and turns of the economy, the comings and goings of friends and family. When we are part of God's family through faith in Jesus Christ, the changes of this world simply highlight the perfection of the next.

*Lord, may Your constant, unchanging presence
give me confidence today and every day.*

# THOUGHTS, HEART, ACTIONS

*Every way of a man is right in his own eyes:*
*but the LORD pondereth the hearts.*

PROVERBS 21:2 KJV

• • • • • • • • • • • • • • • • • • • • • • •

The theme of this devotional collection is the correlation between our thoughts, heart, and actions. Today's scripture highlights the challenge: if our thoughts and heart aren't unified under God's authority, poor actions will follow.

Even as Christians, we're human beings and have a strong tendency toward selfishness. That often leads to self-justification. In scriptural terms, "every way of a man is right in his own eyes."

God, however, looks deeper. . .He "pondereth" our hearts. He knows when we're claiming to honor Him but are really just trying to boost ourselves. He knows when we're cutting moral corners while thinking, *Really, it's okay.* That's our human bent, something even the apostle Paul admitted to.

Happily for us, Paul didn't just stop with the diagnosis—he shared the cure. "O wretched man that I am! Who shall deliver me from the body of this death?" he exclaimed (Romans 7:24 KJV). Then he penned verse 25 (KJV): "I thank God through Jesus Christ our Lord."

Yes, God sees and disapproves of our hypocrisies. But He has also provided the perfect solution in Jesus Christ. Accepting Him renews our hearts and brings His Holy Spirit inside us. Like Paul, we'll sometimes wrestle with our ongoing humanity, but we'll also have access to every divine resource to overcome it.

*Lord, You know my heart. Help me to align it with Yours.*

# DON'T LOVE PLEASURE

*Whoever loves pleasure will become poor; whoever loves wine and olive oil will never be rich.*

PROVERBS 21:17 NIV

. . . . . . . . . . . . . . . . . . . . . . .

The entertainment news completely contradicts today's scripture. So many actors, musicians, and athletes, even people just "famous for being famous," love pleasure, and they're doing fine financially. So many who love wine (for their appetites) and oil (for their appearance) are anything but poor. They're laughing all the way to the bank.

Sometimes we have to read scripture overall, and the Proverbs particularly, in ultimate terms. Lovers of pleasure "*will become* poor." We've seen it happen when famous people spend or drink or drug themselves into oblivion. But the poverty may be more like what Asaph described in Psalm 73:18–19 (NIV): "Surely you [God] place them on slippery ground; you cast them down to ruin. How suddenly are they destroyed, completely swept away by terrors!"

Asaph found himself envying the rich, whose lives seemed trouble-free. He had almost lost his faith when he "entered the sanctuary of God; then I understood their final destiny" (Psalm 73:17 NIV).

We should grieve that potentiality and pray even for God haters to know Him. And we must never allow ourselves to envy their lifestyle. Envy leads to foolish pursuits, which bring us right back to our opening verse: "Whoever loves pleasure will become poor; whoever loves wine and olive oil will never be rich."

*Lord, my true riches and pleasure are with You. May I never look elsewhere.*

# HOW TO. . .

*Scripture says: "God opposes the proud but shows favor to the humble."*
*Submit yourselves, then, to God. Resist the devil, and he will flee*
*from you. Come near to God and he will come near to you. Wash your*
*hands, you sinners, and purify your hearts, you double-minded. Grieve,*
*mourn and wail. Change your laughter to mourning and your joy to*
*gloom. Humble yourselves before the Lord, and he will lift you up.*
JAMES 4:6–10 NIV

Many have described James as one of the Bible's most practical books, offering "how-tos" for living as a Christian.

Today's scripture includes a list of mind-sets and actions on the theme of humility. After alluding to Proverbs 3:34, James urged his readers—in the first century and today—to consciously place themselves under God's authority. Knowing we are under God's authority, we can confidently oppose Satan's work in our lives. Having pushed away sin, we can draw even closer to God, enjoying an ever-increasing experience of His presence. We'll adopt a heart attitude that contradicts this world's pattern, choosing the pure, the serious, and the humble. And, in His time and His way, God will show us favor and lift us up.

Every one of these how-tos requires action on our part. *Submit, resist, come, wash, purify, grieve, change,* and *humble* are all commands. If we choose to obey them, we have the promise of God's reward.

*Father, Your commands are simple if not easy. Help me to obey.*

# IN THE DETAILS

*The man measured the gateway entrance, which was 17½ feet*
*wide at the opening and 22¾ feet wide in the gateway passage.*
EZEKIEL 40:11 NLT

. . . . . . . . . . . . . . . . . . . . . . .

If you're an architect (or always wanted to be), you'll love Ezekiel 40. If not, this detailed verbal blueprint of the future temple may be daunting.

God gave Ezekiel a vision of the gateways, outer and inner courtyards, and rooms both for priests and the preparing of sacrifices. There are plenty of measurements and explanations: window placement, numbers of steps, even decorations (carved palm trees appear throughout). The level of detail is reminiscent of the plans for the ark of the covenant that God had given Moses (Exodus 25).

So what does it all mean to us?

One takeaway is simply the immense knowledge of God. The One who flung the farthest stars into the universe has also planned three-inch hooks for the temple's foyer walls (Ezekiel 40:43), a level of detail squaring perfectly with Jesus' teaching: "What is the price of five sparrows—two copper coins? Yet God does not forget a single one of them. And the very hairs on your head are all numbered" (Luke 12:6–7 NLT). And God's not just showing off. Jesus went on to say, "So don't be afraid; you are more valuable than a whole flock of sparrows."

With a God like this, human worry is utterly unnecessary.

---

*Thank You, Lord, for overseeing all the details.*
*Help me to trust You completely.*

# THE REWARD OF FAITH

*You never saw him, yet you love him. You still don't see him, yet you trust him—with laughter and singing. Because you kept on believing, you'll get what you're looking forward to: total salvation.*

1 Peter 1:8–9 MSG

. . . . . . . . . . . . . . . . . . . . . .

Today's scripture illustrates the book of Hebrews' definition of *faith*: "confidence in what we hope for and assurance about what we do not see" (11:1 NIV). Peter, who'd seen, heard, and touched Jesus, commended all who had *not* enjoyed that privilege but still believed. Peter's original audience, Jewish believers scattered by persecution, would receive the ultimate goal of their faith: total salvation. So will we.

We will also, like those first-century Christians, "have to put up with every kind of aggravation in the meantime" (1 Peter 1:6 MSG). Some trials (like cancer, tornadoes, and crabgrass) come just from living in a broken world. But as followers of Jesus, we'll face more specific challenges too—opposition from those who hate our Lord and the exclusivity of His message.

The old Boy Scout motto applies to us: BE PREPARED. Scripture has given us fair warning of the troubles we'll face, so pray and commit yourself to faith in Christ no matter what. You can't lose. As Peter wrote, "God is keeping careful watch over us and the future. The Day is coming when you'll have it all—life healed and whole" (1 Peter 1:4–5 MSG).

---

*Lord, I thank You for Your promise to see me through.*

# NO MYSTERIES HERE

*Have I not written thirty sayings for you, sayings of counsel*
*and knowledge, teaching you to be honest and to speak the truth,*
*so that you bring back truthful reports to those you serve?*
PROVERBS 22:20–21 NIV

. . . . . . . . . . . . . . . . . . . . . . .

Some aspects of scripture are hard to understand. The frightful visions of the book of Revelation come quickly to mind.

But most instructions for living are quite plain. The things God wants us to do, the things that make us holy (set apart to Him), are not mysterious at all. For example, these "thirty sayings" in Proverbs 22–24. "Haven't I told you clearly," Solomon essentially said to his son, "how to be honest and good?"

The sayings address many issues found elsewhere in Proverbs, just in greater detail—rather than a thought-provoking two-liner, these sayings may be two or three or four times as long. All of them, like the moral teaching of the entire Bible, are designed to improve our own lives, bless others around us, and honor our Creator.

God has made His expectations plain. Having seen His rules and requirements in black and white, we now have a choice to make: to obey and be blessed, or to go our own way and reap the consequences. Human as we are, we might struggle to humbly follow God's instructions. But we can never honestly argue that His desires are mysterious.

*Lord, help me to follow scripture's plain instructions*
*while entrusting the truly mysterious to You.*

# THE WAR FOR YOUR SOUL

*Beloved, I urge you as sojourners and exiles to abstain from the*
*passions of the flesh, which wage war against your soul.*
1 PETER 2:11 ESV

. . . . . . . . . . . . . . . . . . . . . . .

If he were writing today, Peter wouldn't win a popularity contest with the exhortation of today's scripture. "What?" many would say. "Go against my feelings? Tell myself no? I can't do that—this is just who I am!"

Before we lob a morality grenade at the unsaved people around us, note exactly who Peter was addressing: "beloved" fellow Christians. He had just described his readers as "a chosen race, a royal priesthood, a holy nation. . .God's people" (1 Peter 2:9–10 ESV). Clearly, the passions of the flesh affect us as Christian men too.

This war for our souls is fierce and ongoing—and even when the battlefield seems quiet, be sure the enemy is preparing another onslaught. Whether your passions run toward sex or alcohol or drugs or overeating or laziness or any of a thousand other temptations, Peter simply says, "Abstain." And what the Bible tells us to do, we can—with the help of God's Holy Spirit inside us.

It will be challenging. Every war is. But "the LORD is a man of war" (Exodus 15:3 ESV), and He'll be in the foxhole with you. When you obey His commands, God guarantees your safety and ultimate victory.

*Lord God, this world is truly a battlefield. Strengthen*
*me to abstain from the passions of my flesh.*

# ENOUGH IS ENOUGH

*Do not wear yourself out to get rich; do not trust your own cleverness. Cast but a glance at riches, and they are gone, for they will surely sprout wings and fly off to the sky like an eagle.*

Proverbs 23:4–5 NIV

· · · · · · · · · · · · · · · · · · · · · · · ·

If it seems like marketing companies are going into overdrive this holiday season, they are. Many retail establishments depend on Christmas to be able to be open the rest of the year. They need us to spend money, promising us that we deserve to get good things, and we can only show others love by buying them things too.

To pay for all these gifts, we work overtime, sacrifice sleep, and end up being grumpy with our family—if we have time to see them!—all in the name of showing them love.

Soon, the holiday season will be over. The money will all be spent. The gifts you give will break or be forgotten, and your family will only remember how you weren't around because you were working so much.

Of course, it doesn't need to be like that. This holiday season, let enough be enough. Learn to be content. Don't buy into the marketing requiring you to buy more, more, more. Spend some time enjoying the gifts of this season together with others. Though the moments may fly by like the proverbial riches, you'll be able to save them in your memory forever.

*Lord, let me be content this holiday season.*

# INFECTED WOUNDS

*Above all, maintain an intense love for each other,*
*since love covers a multitude of sins.*
1 PETER 4:8 HCSB

. . . . . . . . . . . . . . . . . . . . . . .

When we receive a wound, it's important to clean it out right away. Poorly treated wounds can cause abscesses and blood infections. In such cases, medical treatment might involve reopening the wound and introducing powerful antibiotics to overcome the infection. Wounds that aren't properly dealt with can be fatal.

The body of Christ—aka the church—is not immune to wounds. From poor communication to flagrant sinfulness, God's people injure each other all the time. As with a physical wound, we need to deal with these issues quickly lest they prove fatal to our spiritual lives.

Today's verse calls on Jesus' followers to "maintain an intense love for each other." This love is more than a bandage slapped on a wounded relationship. It is a skillful doctor uncovering a wound and carefully cleaning it from infection. This love goes deep and takes time, since old wounds can take months or years to heal.

We don't naturally have the love required to cover a multitude of sins. To love someone (let alone a whole group of people) deeply enough to apply God's healing, we need the Master Physician Himself. Only when God's love flows through us will we foster the community of healing the church is intended to be.

---

*Heavenly Father, give me the skills needed to deal with*
*infected wounds. Heal the body of Christ with Your love.*

# THE FURNACE

*He answered, Behold, I see four men loose, walking*
*in the midst of the fire, and they are not hurt! And*
*the form of the fourth is like a son of the gods!*
DANIEL 3:25 AMPC

. . . . . . . . . . . . . . . . . . . . . . .

Nebuchadnezzar, the greatest leader of the Babylonian Empire, didn't tolerate disobedience. After he built a ninety-foot-tall golden statue and told his subjects to bow down to it, Nebuchadnezzar outlined the consequences for disobedience: "And whoever does not fall down and worship shall that very hour be cast into the midst of a burning fiery furnace" (Daniel 3:6 AMPC).

For Shadrach, Meshach, and Abednego—the trio of Jewish governors who presided over Babylon—the order was problematic. They were subject to a greater authority than Nebuchadnezzar and instructed not to worship anyone else. The question for these three was this: Who were they more afraid of? Nebuchadnezzar or God?

Maybe you know what happened. Shadrach, Meshach, and Abednego refused to worship the idol and went into the fiery furnace, but they didn't burn because they placed their fear and trust in God.

We face the same situation daily. Are we more fearful of God, who controls reality itself, or of what people will think when we refuse to bow down to the idols of pop culture? When we place our fear and trust in God, we needn't fear the furnace either.

*Lord, may I recognize You as in control even*
*when I'm thrown into the furnace.*

# GREAT WHITE SHARKS

*For this very reason, make every effort to supplement your*
*faith with virtue, and virtue with knowledge, and knowledge*
*with self-control, and self-control with steadfastness,*
*and steadfastness with godliness, and godliness with*
*brotherly affection, and brotherly affection with love.*

2 PETER 1:5–7 ESV

· · · · · · · · · · · · · · · · · · · · · · ·

Like most fish, the great white shark "breathes" through gills—respiratory organs like our lungs that extract oxygen from water. Unlike most fish (including most other sharks, actually), the great white shark has to keep swimming for water to continually pass over its gills. If it stops swimming, it runs out of oxygen and dies.

Faith is like a great white shark. It has to keep swimming forward lest we run out of spiritual oxygen. As we swim along, we will naturally add practical expressions of faith to our life. Each expression from today's passage—virtue, knowledge, self-control, steadfastness, godliness, and brotherly affection—starts with faith, and they all move toward love.

Swimming isn't always easy. The currents of culture actively flow against faith, tempting us to abandon love and settle for selfishness, pleasure, and ease. If we give in, our faith may as well be dead.

Are you swimming toward love? Is your faith growing in each virtue? Look for ways to express your faith practically, and ask God to help you overcome the currents of this world.

*Father, swim beside me as I grow in my faith and move toward love.*

# BATTLE STRATEGY

*A wise man is strong; yea, a man of knowledge increaseth*
*strength. For by wise counsel thou shalt make thy war:*
*and in multitude of counsellors there is safety.*
PROVERBS 24:5–6 KJV

. . . . . . . . . . . . . . . . . . . . . .

Although the war's outcome over sin has already been assured, we remain locked in battle here and now. And like it or not, we cannot be pacifists against sin. As warriors, we need a good strategy to survive and bring life to those around us.

Strength and knowledge alone are not enough. To succeed in any military endeavor, one must have strength, knowledge, and the applied wisdom of multiple viewpoints.

We should start each day by listening to our Commander and asking for His assistance. Prayer helps us tap into the strength of God's providence (see 1 John 5:14–15). Reading His Word helps us gain knowledge into His character. Then, when our hearts and minds are aligned with God's, we seek out others who are similarly aligned.

They might be in our families, our churches, our workplaces, or our neighborhoods. It doesn't matter where we find them, as long as we'll listen to their counsel. No matter how strong and smart we think we are, we'll lose when pride leads us to fight sinfulness by ourselves.

If you already belong to a battalion, pray for their safety today. If you don't, pray that God will bring you into one.

*Lord, may I listen to the counsel of others in the battle against sin.*

## LIVING IN THE LIONS' DEN

*So the king gave the order, and they brought Daniel and*
*threw him into the lions' den. The king said to Daniel,*
*"May your God, whom you serve continually, rescue you!"*
DANIEL 6:16 NIV

• • • • • • • • • • • • • • • • • • • • • • •

Daniel was not a young man when he faced the lions' den. He had served Nebuchadnezzar, Nebuchadnezzar's son Belshazzar, and now he served in the court of Darius. His faithful service in the court of Israel's enemies lasted almost seventy years, and in all that time, Daniel's service to God always came first. So when Darius's other advisers plotted the lions' den episode—convincing Darius that the punishment for praying to anyone beside him should be death by lions—to get rid of Daniel, the prophet did as he always had. He trusted God.

The thing Daniel understood, from the moment he was taken from his people as a young man to the moment he was thrown in the pit, was this: Life is a lions' den. There are no safe places. If plotting enemies don't get you, illness and grief and stupidity will. Lions are everywhere, and they're always hungry. The safest plan is to continue serving God, whom even the lions obey.

Whether or not God closes the mouths of the lions, your faithful service will ensure the safety of your soul and your witness to the world will be worth listening to.

*Father, may I always trust You more than I fear the lions.*

# THE FEAST OF DEDICATION

*Those who say they live in God should live their lives as Jesus did.*
1 John 2:6 nlt

. . . . . . . . . . . . . . . . . . . . . . .

Hanukkah was a new celebration, just over a century old, at the time of Jesus' ministry. The holiday—which John 10:22 refers to as the Feast of Dedication—commemorates the rededication of the second temple in Jerusalem by Judas Maccabeus after it had been desecrated by Antiochus Epiphanes.

It was against this background of rededication that Jesus gave the straightest answer yet to the people's question as to whether He was the Messiah, the one they hoped would overthrow their Roman overlords in the fashion of the Maccabean revolt. John 10:25–27 (nlt) says, "Jesus replied, 'I have already told you, and you don't believe me. The proof is the work I do in my Father's name. But you don't believe me because you are not my sheep. My sheep listen to my voice; I know them, and they follow me.'"

Today is the perfect day to rededicate your life to God and recognize Jesus as the Messiah who came not to claim kingship over Israel, but to be Lord and leader of your life. It is time to live as Jesus did, willing to sacrifice everything to show the world that you are His sheep and you recognize His voice.

*Jesus, You are both the Good Shepherd and the sacrificial Lamb. May I follow Your example and show the world who You are because I follow You.*

# HUMILITY VERSUS HUMILIATION

*Don't brag about yourself before the king, and don't stand in the place of the great; for it is better for him to say to you, "Come up here!" than to demote you in plain view of a noble.*
Proverbs 25:6–7 hcsb

. . . . . . . . . . . . . . . . . . . . . .

Humans have an interesting relationship with the earth. Adam's name comes from the Hebrew word for ground: *adamah*. Similarly, the word *human* comes from a Proto-Indo-European (PIE) root—*dhghem*—which means "earth." There is something intrinsically linked with the ground we were created from, the soil we depend on for food, and the dirt to which our bodies will return.

The PIE root for "earth" also shows up in the words *humility* and *humiliation*. Both words mean to be brought low to the ground. The difference between them comes from the circumstances by which we are brought low.

Today's passage encourages readers to stay humble, even when we believe we have achievements worth bragging about, to stay low until those in authority recognize our accomplishments and raise us up. When we brag about ourselves, we are apt to be brought low in front of everyone.

One day, our bodies will return to the dirt and we'll bow down before our Creator. Our highest earthly accomplishments won't matter; only what we've done with God's love will. On that day, will He raise you up or bring you low?

*Lord, keep my heart humble so I might one day be lifted up.*

# TACTFUL COMMUNICATION

*Through patience a ruler can be persuaded,*
*and a gentle tongue can break a bone.*
Proverbs 25:15 NIV

. . . . . . . . . . . . . . . . . . . . . . . .

Today's verse deals with the art of diplomacy—dealing with people in a sensitive and effective way. We typically think of diplomacy in terms of international politics, where diplomats are involved. Perhaps a better word to use is *tact*.

Advertising executive Howard W. Newton once said, "Tact is the knack of making a point without making an enemy." It's a good definition. When we deal with anyone —rulers, bosses, employees, spouses, children, strangers, anyone—the goal of all our communication is to be heard and understood. This requires tact.

The key to communicating tactfully is to maintain respect for people with whom you are speaking. This means listening attentively when they speak, never interrupting them or raising your voice in response to their thoughts. It means thinking through what you say before you say it. It means being patient when you feel like hurrying the conversation along.

When tact is employed in communication, gentle words can create powerful change. People will listen to you because they know you care about them. And that's really where tact begins—in loving others and showing them the respect they deserve as people who bear God's image.

Do you communicate with tact? Ask God to help you listen patiently and speak gently today.

---

*Lord, may my words be Your words and my heart Your own.*

# THE CRAB BUCKET

*Do not be surprised and wonder, brethren,
that the world detests and pursues you with hatred.*

1 JOHN 3:13 AMPC

. . . . . . . . . . . . . . . . . . . . . .

The world is full of people who prioritize themselves over others, which is to say the world is full of people.

From birth, we have wanted the best things for ourselves, and we dislike when others have what we want. In cases where only one person can have something, many would rather see no one have it than someone else have it. This isn't behavior we grow out of, and it isn't unique to humans.

Put crabs in a bucket and although any one crab could easily escape, when one tries, the other crabs pull it down. It's called "crab mentality."

How might a world infected with "crab mentality" look at people adopted into God's family and promised good things for eternity? It would hate us! It would want to pull us back into the bucket, even if it didn't gain anything by doing so.

What do we do about that? We live in love, showing the world a better way, even if it doesn't understand it—even if it hates us for it. First John 3:18 (NLT) says, "Dear children, let's not merely say that we love each other; let us show the truth by our actions."

---

*Jesus, thank You for picking me up out of the crab
bucket. Show me how to bring others out in love.*

# WHO IS GOD?

*"I want you to show love, not offer sacrifices. I want*
*you to know me more than I want burnt offerings."*
Hosea 6:6 nlt

. . . . . . . . . . . . . . . . . . . . . .

What kind of God is God? What does He want from us? Although they are about God, these questions get to the heart of what it means to be human. We want the comfort of knowing that we're on God's good side and that we're doing what He wants. But it is so easy to make bad assumptions about God, even when we immerse ourselves in His Word.

Read the book of Deuteronomy, and you might think God only cares about making us follow rules. The book is filled with rules! Don't boil a young goat in its mother's milk (Deuteronomy 14:21). Celebrate all the feasts properly (Deuteronomy 16). Don't wear cloth of wool and linen mixed together (Deuteronomy 22:11).

It's true that rules and obedience are important to God—He *is* the source of all justice—but when we follow the rules without knowing or caring why, we've lost sight of who He is.

God is love (1 John 4:8). He wants us to show love to others. He wants us to seek His face, to be close enough to feel Him breathe life into our dusty frames. When we seek Him and love others, we'll naturally do the things He wants us to do.

*God, show me more of You. Help me love like You.*

# DOG EARS

*Whoever meddles in a quarrel not his own is
like one who takes a passing dog by the ears.*

PROVERBS 26:17 ESV

. . . . . . . . . . . . . . . . . . . . . . .

Ever wonder why dogs love to have their ears rubbed? Dog ears have a high concentration of nerve endings. When a dog trusts you enough to allow it, a good ear massage can be a euphoric canine experience. But if you're a passing stranger, grabbing a dog by the ears is a great way to get bitten.

No one in their right mind would do something so dumb, right? Well...

Have you ever poked your nose into someone else's problems? We're not talking about when a trusted friend seeks out your advice. We're talking about when you don't have any of the details and dive in anyway. Your intentions may be good. You just want people to get along with each other. But your approach is like grabbing a dog by the ears.

If you really want to help resolve other people's quarrels, pray for them. Get to know them. Show them unconditional, self-sacrificial love. Respect their boundaries. Earn their trust. *Then* offer them some advice.

God wants us involved in the lives of others so we can point them to His peace, but how we get involved matters. Is there someone you'd like to introduce to God's peace? Start by praying for an opportunity to show your trustworthiness.

---

*Lord God, give me wisdom on how to bring
Your peace to the people around me.*

# MODEL CHRISTIANS

*Friend, don't go along with evil. Model the good. The person
who does good does God's work. The person who does evil
falsifies God, doesn't know the first thing about God.*

3 JOHN 11 MSG

. . . . . . . . . . . . . . . . . . . . . . . .

The best thing about Christianity is Jesus. The worst thing about
Christianity is Christians who make Jesus look bad. How?

Christians have had a spotted record when it comes to some major
world issues. Remember the Crusades? The subjugation of Native
Americans? Slavery in the American South? All of these were spearheaded
by Christians and carried out in the name of Jesus.

How is the world supposed to know the peace of God when Christians
keep showing them a face of war? God's children are called, above all else,
to love. We are to model the good. When we act like the world—killing,
stealing, enslaving, and so forth—and call it Christianity, we show that
we don't know the first thing about Jesus or His priorities.

Jesus came to heal the sick, to provide for the powerless, and to
defend the cause of widows and orphans. How can we live like Him?
We do the same.

It's time for Christians to consider the message we're sending when
we fight for the wrong things, when we give power to the already powerful,
and when we wage wars that make more widows and orphans.

Are you living as a model Christian to the world?

---

*Lord, show me the ways my priorities have been giving You a bad name.*

## TONE AND TIMING

*A loud and cheerful greeting early in the*
*morning will be taken as a curse!*
PROVERBS 27:14 NLT

. . . . . . . . . . . . . . . . . . . . . . .

Messages are more than words. Consider the question "Are you serious?"

If spoken loudly while the speaker jumped up and down with wide eyes and a gleeful expression, we'd probably know it expressed excitement over some unbelievable good fortune.

If the same question were uttered with a sneer and a single raised eyebrow, we'd know the speaker was passive-aggressively suggesting that what was being asked of them was unacceptable.

The tone with which we communicate can easily change the meaning of what we say. So can the timing. Poorly timed requests are likely to be refused. Verbal corrections are unhelpful if what is needed is a hug first. And morning people who shout their greetings before the rest of us have had our coffee are likely to be met with cold replies.

As we share the message of God's love with the world, we need to make sure our words are spoken with the correct tone and the proper timing. In fact, the message might not need words at all.

If you notice your neighbor hasn't had time to do their yard work lately, mow their lawn. If a coworker is having car trouble, offer to give them a ride. When your message of love is genuine and fits the needs of the listener, there will be no confusing the message.

---

*Father, help me communicate Your love clearly today.*

# TIMELESS GOD

*"I am the Alpha and the Omega," says the Lord God,*
*"who is, and who was, and who is to come, the Almighty."*
REVELATION 1:8 NIV

• • • • • • • • • • • • • • • • • • • • • • •

Humans like stories. We tell stories to share our understanding of the world, to spend time together, and to be entertained. We like how stories have clearly defined beginnings, middles, and endings. We can relate to the story structure because we have beginnings, middles, and endings too. But God isn't a story. He is *the* story.

While we were made in the image of God, there are aspects of His nature we can't understand. God doesn't *have* a beginning. He *is* the Beginning. He doesn't *have* an end. He *is* the End. God doesn't operate within time like the time-bound beings that we are. He created time for things to happen in, but He exists outside of it in the same way that computer programmers don't live in the computers they program.

Why does this matter? Because God is the Almighty. We don't have to understand His nature or have all our questions answered for Him to be in charge. We are invited to trust that He is for us and that nothing can thwart His plan for us.

God is the timeless One who is, and who was, and who is to come. He loves you, has loved you, and will love you forever.

*Lord, I don't need to fully understand*
*You to trust You with my whole heart.*

# LIONS AND WILDEBEESTS

*The wicked flee when no one is pursuing them,*
*but the righteous are as bold as a lion.*
PROVERBS 28:1 HCSB

. . . . . . . . . . . . . . . . . . . . . . .

Picture a wildebeest. It weighs nearly six hundred pounds, runs almost fifty miles per hour, and has short horns to defend itself. A rampaging wildebeest could do some serious damage to anything in its way, but wildebeests aren't big on confrontation. Their main survival strategy is to run away at the first sign of danger.

Now picture a lion, Africa's apex predator. It weighs as much as a wildebeest and can run about the same speed. Lions have no horns, but they eat wildebeests for breakfast. A lion's main (mane?) survival strategy is to be a lion.

Are you a wildebeest or a lion? Does your guilty conscience have you running from any hint of confrontation, or do you boldly admit your wrongdoing and move on? Do you hide among others who won't try to correct your actions, or do you live in the knowledge that you have nothing to hide?

God has offered His forgiveness and love while we were still sinning against Him, not so we could live like wildebeests, but so we could accept His forgiveness and boldly proclaim His love to the world.

Today, be a lion. Live righteously. If you mess up, fess up and move on.

---

*Lion of Judah, help me live boldly for You. Don't let me dwell on*
*past mistakes, but help me accept Your forgiveness and move on.*

# JESUS KNOCKING

*"Behold, I stand at the door and knock. If anyone*
*hears my voice and opens the door, I will come in*
*to him and eat with him, and he with me."*
REVELATION 3:20 ESV

. . . . . . . . . . . . . . . . . . . . . .

Have you ever read today's verse and pictured Jesus as a homeless beggar standing in the rain, just waiting for someone to open the door of their heart to Him?

Although Jesus *was* homeless during His ministry years (see Matthew 8:20), this is not the image portrayed in this verse. Jesus isn't a sad beggar standing in the rain; He is the Master of the house whose servants are waiting anxiously for His return.

When we give our lives to Christ, He takes His rightful place as the Master of our house. It can be difficult to cede this place to Him. Human nature makes us want to be the masters of our fates. Jesus understands. He isn't banging down the door and asserting His dominance. He's knocking and waiting for us to accept His rightful place. What is especially great is that Jesus doesn't kick us out of the room. He offers us a seat at the table. He desires our companionship and treats us with dignity and respect.

Is Jesus still knocking at the door of your heart? Go let Him in. It'll be okay.

*Jesus, take Your rightful place as Master of my life.*
*Thank you for giving me a seat at Your table.*

# PLUMB LINE

*Then he showed me another vision. I saw the Lord standing
beside a wall that had been built using a plumb line. He
was using a plumb line to see if it was still straight.*

Amos 7:7 nlt

. . . . . . . . . . . . . . . . . . . . . . .

Straight walls need a solid foundation to stay upright, but walls built on solid foundations are not always straight. Plumb lines—a weight tied to a string that uses gravity to make sure walls are structurally sound—can reveal whether the wall has tilted since being built. A wall that leans will eventually fall.

Amos's vision in today's verse shows God checking on the people of Israel. Were they still standing as straight and tall as the foundation on which they were built? What God found with His plumb line was a wall destined to crumble: "The pagan shrines of your ancestors will be ruined, and the temples of Israel will be destroyed; I will bring the dynasty of King Jeroboam to a sudden end" (Amos 7:9 nlt).

When the wall has fallen, God can rebuild it (see Amos 9:11).

Our lives in Christ are built on a solid foundation, but are we living upright for Him? Ask Him to test your life and your heart with His plumb line. If your life leans toward the things of this world, allow God to rebuild it for you lest it crumble when a strong wind comes along.

*Lord, repair my life to be as solid as the foundation You laid on the cross.*

# JONAH'S PRAYER LIFE

*Then Jonah prayed to the LORD his God from the belly of the fish,
saying, "I called out to the LORD, out of my distress, and he answered
me; out of the belly of Sheol I cried, and you heard my voice."*

JONAH 2:1–2 ESV

. . . . . . . . . . . . . . . . . . . . . . .

As a prophet, Jonah wasn't great. He may have occasionally relayed God's words, but his heart was far from God.

When God told Jonah to go to Nineveh—a powerful enemy of Israel—he went in the opposite direction. When the boat he was on encountered a perilous storm, the pagan sailors pleaded with Jonah to pray to His God. Eventually, Jonah was tossed overboard, and the waves subsided.

Jonah did eventually pray not that God would save the sailors whose lives he imperiled with his disobedience but with thanksgiving that his own life was spared.

Our prayer lives can reveal a lot about where our hearts are in relation to God's. Do we see the needs of others and pray for them? Do we recognize how our actions have affected those around us and repent? Or do we go through life not seeing or caring about anyone but ourselves, thanking God for our blessings but not doing what He asks?

We can do better than Jonah. A true man of God prays for others and follows God's call, even (especially) when it means showing love to his enemies.

*Lord, keep me from going the wrong direction
with the message You've entrusted to me.*

# JUSTICE AND LOVE FOR EVERYONE

*The righteous care about justice for the poor,*
*but the wicked have no such concern.*

PROVERBS 29:7 NIV

. . . . . . . . . . . . . . . . . . . . . . .

Waitstaff at dine-in restaurants depend on tips to supplement their income. Salespeople often make a commission on the goods and services they sell. There is often a link between the level of customer service offered and the degree to which the person offering it is compensated. This is normal, everyday wisdom. But what does it suggest about how waitstaff and salespeople approach customers who can't tip or won't buy anything?

The wisdom of God sees a bigger picture than tips and commissions paid out in this life. Righteous people treat *everyone* with love, regardless of whether they have money. They seek justice for those who are overlooked, silenced, or otherwise disregarded because they care about the people more than the payoff.

But there's still a payoff for caring about justice for the poor. When this life is over, we'll stand before God's throne, and He'll either say, *"Well done, good and faithful servant,"* or we'll know we acted no differently than the wicked.

Are you concerned with those who cannot benefit you in this life? Do you offer loving service to everyone, regardless of how they look, smell, or act toward you? Step up today and show the world whether you belong to the righteous camp or the wicked.

---

*Lord, give me a concern for the poor.*

## LOGICAL AND UNPREDICTABLE

*The Lord is slow to anger and great in power and will by no
means clear the guilty. The Lord has His way in the whirlwind
and in the storm, and the clouds are the dust of His feet.*

NAHUM 1:3 AMPC

When man encounters unexplainable phenomena, he tends to make up
his own understanding. Early civilizations regarded destructive forces
and weather patterns to be the work of the gods. The ancient Greeks believed
Zeus threw lightning bolts. The Vikings believed Thor's hammer caused
thunder. Ancient Israel's neighboring countries worshipped storm gods as
well, even sacrificing their children to have favorable weather conditions.

Christianity is different. Yes, we believe that God is responsible for
weather patterns and other natural phenomena, but simply because He is
the Creator of *all* things. His purposes are achieved both in the mundane
patterns of the seasons as well as the individually catastrophic whirlwind.

As you bundle up today—the first official day of winter *and* the
shortest day of the year—thank God for being powerful and good, logical
and unpredictable. Praise Him for creating our weather patterns, for the
tilt of the earth that causes our seasons, and for the snow that reminds
us of His purity. Praise Him for His mercy and grace to intervene on our
behalf in unique and surprising ways. Praise Him that He does what is
right all the time, even when we can't explain it.

*God, You are great in power and greater in love!*

# UNEXPECTED BETHLEHEM

*Bethlehem Ephrathah, you are small among the clans of Judah; One will come from you to be ruler over Israel for Me. His origin is from antiquity, from eternity.*
MICAH 5:2 HCSB

. . . . . . . . . . . . . . . . . . . . . . .

Bethlehem has a significant history in Israel's dalliance with kingship. After the people of Israel chose Saul—tall, handsome, and commanding—to be their king, God lined up Saul's replacement, since He knew that appearances didn't matter. So Samuel, the prophet at the time, was sent to Bethlehem to anoint the next king.

When Samuel came to Jesse's clan, he almost made the same mistake Israel did. "But the LORD said to Samuel, 'Do not look at his appearance or his stature, because I have rejected him. Man does not see what the LORD sees, for man sees what is visible, but the LORD sees the heart' " (1 Samuel 16:7 HCSB).

When Micah prophesied the Messiah's birth as coming from Bethlehem, the suggestion was that He would be a King who didn't fit the image of what people expected to find. He wouldn't be tall or handsome, but God's heart would beat within Him.

As we get closer to Christmas, remember the significance of Jesus' birth in Bethlehem. God doesn't act according to human expectations. He keeps His promises and does what's best according to His heart. We'd be wise to do the same.

*God, make my heart like Yours, and help me to look at what truly matters.*

# SHORTCUTS

*The seventh angel sounded his trumpet, and there were loud voices in heaven, which said: "The kingdom of the world has become the kingdom of our Lord and of his Messiah, and he will reign for ever and ever."*
REVELATION 11:15 NIV

. . . . . . . . . . . . . . . . . . . . . . .

There are no shortcuts to success.

After Adam and Eve ushered sin into the world, God began His rescue plan. The devil would pay for his misdeeds, the sins of man would be righteously punished, and people would one day rejoin Him in the kingdom of heaven. The plan was good, but it took time to accomplish. Thousands of years passed.

Before Jesus began His earthly ministry, the devil tempted Him with a shortcut. If Jesus would only bow down to him, the devil would hand over his earthly kingdom. But Jesus didn't want an earthly kingdom; He was willing to die for the kingdom of heaven. Since then, thousands of years have passed.

At the end of time, when the devil has been cast into the pit, when the sins of man are a thing of the past, the kingdom of the world will become the kingdom of our Lord, of our Messiah.

When faced with a shortcut—to God-like knowledge or an earthly kingdom—wait. Put your success in God's hands, and trust in His timing. Thousands of years may pass, but that's nothing compared to eternally enjoying God's presence in His kingdom.

*Lord, protect me from tempting shortcuts
that lead away from Your kingdom.*

# GOD IN OUR MIDST

*"The LORD your God is in your midst, a mighty one who will save; he will rejoice over you with gladness; he will quiet you by his love; he will exult over you with loud singing."*

ZEPHANIAH 3:17 ESV

. . . . . . . . . . . . . . . . . . . . . . .

Some people imagine God to be a bearded, stoic figure who sits upon His heavenly throne with a look of mild indignation on His holy face. This image shows up in pop culture, but it casts God in entirely the wrong light. Read today's verse again.

God's rescue plan is in motion. He's rejoicing over you with gladness! He is exulting over you with loud singing! This is not a God with His nose turned up at humanity's sin, but a God who takes great joy in saving His people.

Tonight marks the final night before we celebrate how God came physically into the world—how He was literally in the midst of His people. As wonderful as the incarnation is, it is secondary to the fact that He is still in our midst today.

As you sing Christmas carols and celebrate Jesus' birth, know that God is singing over you as well. He is still mighty to save and rejoicing over the fact that you are in His midst through the Holy Spirit. Do you feel His presence? Sing along with the Almighty One!

*Father, may we sing in harmony. Thank You for rescuing me!*

# FEAR AND GLORY

*And I saw another angel flying through the sky, carrying*
*the eternal Good News to proclaim to the people who belong*
*to this world—to every nation, tribe, language, and people.*
*"Fear God," he shouted. "Give glory to him. For the time has*
*come when he will sit as judge. Worship him who made the*
*heavens, the earth, the sea, and all the springs of water."*
REVELATION 14:6–7 NLT

Today, we celebrate how the Creator was born into the world His hands made. We marvel at the holy God who made Himself into the perfect sacrifice for our sins. He will judge the world with righteousness, and everyone will give Him the glory He deserves.

When we think about the joys of Christmas, our minds gravitate toward gifts and family togetherness. We don't think about God's righteous judgment or how we are called to fear Him. But read today's passage again. Notice the "Good News" the angels proclaim at the end of all things.

Christmas is larger and deeper than gifts and family togetherness. It is a call to fear God and give Him glory. He, whose holiness requires complete separation from sin, was born to die for our sins so we can join His family. Jesus, born this day in human frailty, will take His rightful place as judge over all creation.

The Good News has come to pass. Fear God. Give Him glory. Merry Christmas!

*Jesus, You are the true gift who rescues me from what I rightly deserve.*

# VINE AND FIG TREE

*In that day, says the Lord of hosts, you shall invite each man*
*his neighbor under his own vine and his own fig tree.*
ZECHARIAH 3:10 AMPC

. . . . . . . . . . . . . . . . . . . . . . .

Christmas carols often include the phrase *peace on earth*, which comes from Luke 2:14. But what does peace on earth look like?

At the height of Solomon's kingship, Israel had peace in the land (see 1 Kings 4:25). Peace was spending more time in the garden and less time fighting wars.

Since Solomon, the image of vines and figs has come to represent peace and prosperity. Such peace is provided by the strength of God's own army. Micah 4:3–4 (AMPC) says, "And He shall judge between many peoples and shall decide for strong nations afar off, and they shall beat their swords into plowshares and their spears into pruning hooks; nation shall not lift up sword against nation, neither shall they learn war any more. But they shall sit every man under his vine and under his fig tree, and none shall make them afraid, for the mouth of the Lord of hosts has spoken it."

The peace of God has come to earth in the person of Jesus. When we realize that the battle has already been won, that Jesus leads heaven's army, we can beat our swords into plowshares and relax in the shade of our gardens.

*Lord, fill me with the peace that comes from knowing You fight for me.*

# COMPASSION, MERCY, AND JUSTICE

*"This is what the LORD Almighty said: 'Administer true*
*justice; show mercy and compassion to one another. Do*
*not oppress the widow or the fatherless, the foreigner or*
*the poor. Do not plot evil against each other.' "*
ZECHARIAH 7:9–10 NIV

. . . . . . . . . . . . . . . . . . . . . . .

The word *compassion* comes from the Latin word *compassionem* (nominative *compassio*), which is a compound of *com* (meaning "with or together") and *pati* (meaning "to suffer"). The word *mercy* shares linguistic roots with words like *merchant* and *merchandise* and comes from showing kindness to those who cannot repay you.

Setting those words aside, let's consider the concept of justice. Justice is when people get what they deserve. If a person can't work, they don't get money. If they can't afford bread, they don't eat. That's justice, right?

Not really. According to God, true justice shows kindness to those who cannot repay us. It suffers with those who suffer. It provides for people who cannot provide for themselves. True justice accounts for the fact that God has shown kindness to us when we least deserved it and suffered on our behalf when we were suffering.

It is time to stop justifying our lack of compassion and mercy in the name of justice and start looking for opportunities to show kindness to others.

*Father, You are just, merciful, and compassionate.*
*Teach me to suffer with those who suffer and to show*
*kindness to those who cannot repay me.*

## WHY A DONKEY?

*Rejoice greatly, O daughter of Zion! Shout aloud, O
daughter of Jerusalem! Behold, your king is coming to
you; righteous and having salvation is he, humble and
mounted on a donkey, on a colt, the foal of a donkey.*

ZECHARIAH 9:9 ESV

· · · · · · · · · · · · · · · · · · · · · · ·

Jesus' triumphal entry into Jerusalem is among a handful of events mentioned in all four Gospels (Matthew 21:1–11, Mark 11:1–10, Luke 19:28–40, and John 12:12–15). In each account, Jesus sends His disciples to bring back a colt—a young male donkey—for Him to ride into town on.

But why a donkey? Why not a horse?

First, Jesus fulfilled Zechariah's prophecy from today's verse by choosing a donkey to ride into town on. Secondly, the reason Zechariah spoke about a donkey instead of a horse is because of the message it sent.

A king or military leader who conquers a town through force would ride his warhorse into the defeated city to project an image of strength and to enforce compliance through fear. But a king who enters on a donkey does so because he comes in peace. He humbles himself and invites others to follow him of their own free will rather than demanding their compliance.

How do you bring others to Jesus? Get off your warhorse and find yourself a donkey. With a humble heart, lead others to the King of kings who comes in peace.

---

*Jesus, help me follow Your example by leading
with humility over strong-arm tactics.*

# JESUS AND THE DISINHERITED

*Speak up for those who have no voice,*
*for the justice of all who are dispossessed.*
PROVERBS 31:8 HCSB

. . . . . . . . . . . . . . . . . . . . . . . .

The power of the Roman Empire was still growing when Jesus began His earthly ministry. As a poor Jew living in a Roman-controlled Israel, Jesus was a member of the subjugated class. He came in humility and rejected the hopes of His fellow Jews to overthrow the Romans and rule in their place. When Jesus died on a Roman cross, the hopes of the Jews, the poor, and the dispossessed died with Him.

But that wasn't the end of the story.

Jesus rose from the grave, conquering sin and death. The Holy Spirit came in power to live inside His people. The church was established, and a safe haven was created for the poor and defenseless whom Jesus primarily ministered to.

Unfortunately, the church sometimes lost its way. Howard Thurman, civil rights forefather and author of *Jesus and the Disinherited*, wrote, "It cannot be denied that too often the weight of the Christian movement has been on the side of the strong and the powerful and against the weak and oppressed—this, despite the gospel."

Jesus has always advocated for us to speak up for those who have no voice and seek justice for those who society has oppressed. Are you siding with the strong and powerful or with the dispossessed?

*Lord, help me use the power You've entrusted*
*to me to care for those who have no voice.*

# THE FINAL BATTLE

*And I saw them as they went up on the broad plain of the earth and surrounded God's people and the beloved city. But fire from heaven came down on the attacking armies and consumed them.*

REVELATION 20:9 NLT

• • • • • • • • • • • • • • • • • • • • • •

What's the scene that comes to mind when you hear "a fight of biblical proportions"? Godzilla versus King Kong? All the armies of earth pitted against each other? It is probably a fairly equal match between opposing forces, just bigger, right?

The book of Revelation has inspired numerous bestselling books and films that show the final battle between the forces of darkness and God, but the battle itself is anticlimactic. Persuaded by the Antichrist, all the armies of earth show up to attack God's people; then fire comes down from heaven to consume them. That's it.

There is no fight. There's a group of people who want to fight, but they are consumed by fire from heaven. The whole thing is completely one-sided.

When it feels like you are caught up in the battle between good and evil, remember how the story ends. Evil gets burned up. God is the Victor who shares His spoils with those who stay true to Him in their hearts. Your situation may not be comfortable or easy, but the rewards for staying true to God will always outweigh the consequences for siding with the forces of evil.

---

*God, thank You for fighting for me. No force can threaten You.*

# LIGHT FOREVER

*And night will be no more. They will need no light of lamp or sun, for the Lord God will be their light, and they will reign forever and ever.*
REVELATION 22:5 ESV

. . . . . . . . . . . . . . . . . . . . . . . .

Tonight, we will count down the final seconds of the year and celebrate when the new one begins. Humanity is caught up in a pattern of endings and beginnings.

Have you heard the saying "All good things must come to an end"? Actually, that's not exactly the case. According to today's verse, one day all the *bad* things will come to an end, while the good things will go on forever.

As you prepare for a new year, why not let some of the bad things end early? Put away the deeds of darkness. Allow God's light to shine into every dark area of your heart and cleanse them to be used for Him.

Live out 1 John 1:5–7 (ESV) this coming year: "This is the message we have heard from him and proclaim to you, that God is light, and in him is no darkness at all. If we say we have fellowship with him while we walk in darkness, we lie and do not practice the truth. But if we walk in the light, as he is in the light, we have fellowship with one another, and the blood of Jesus his Son cleanses us from all sin."

*Lord, cleanse me, fill my heart with light,
and help me guide others to You.*

# CONTRIBUTORS

**ED CYZEWSKI** is the author of *Reconnect: Spiritual Restoration from Digital Distraction* and *Flee, Be Silent, Pray: Ancient Prayers for Anxious Christians* and is the coauthor of *Unfollowers: Unlikely Lessons on Faith from Those Who Doubted Jesus*. He writes about prayer and imperfectly following Jesus at www.edcyzewski.com. Ed's devotions are found in April and October.

**GLENN A. HASCALL** is an accomplished writer with credits in more than a hundred books. He is a broadcast veteran and voice actor and is actively involved in writing and producing audio drama. Glenn's devotions are found in January and July.

**JESS MACCALLUM** is president of Professional Printers Inc. in Columbia, South Carolina. He has authored three books—two on marriage and one on raising daughters—and has twice been featured on *Family Life Today with Dr. Dennis Rainey*. He also works with two leadership organizations as an executive coach and is a regular contributor to HealthyLeaders.com. Jess has been married over thirty years and has three grown children. Jess's devotions are found in August.

**JOSH MOSEY** is the author of *3-Minute Prayers for Boys* and a contributor to other works. He's a husband, father, and reader. On any given day, Josh can be found in a bookstore, savoring coffee (one sugar, no cream) and the feeling of being surrounded by beautifully arranged words. He also enjoys delving into the truths of scripture and Vikings. On the web: joshmosey.com. Josh's devotions appear in February and December.

**PAUL MUCKLEY** is a longtime editor who, under the pseudonym Paul Kent, has also written several books including *Know Your Bible, Oswald Chambers: A Life in Pictures*, and *Playing with Purpose: Baseball Devotions*.

He and his family live in Ohio's Amish country. Paul's devotions are found in May and November.

**DAVID SANFORD**'s speaking engagements have ranged everywhere from the Billy Graham Center at the Cove (NC) to UC Berkeley (CA). His book and Bible projects have been published by Zondervan, Tyndale House, Thomas Nelson, Doubleday, and Amazon. His professional biography is summarized at www.linkedin.com/in/drsanford. His personal biography features his wife of thirty-eight years, Renée, their five children, and their fourteen grandchildren (including one in heaven). David's devotions are found in June.

**TRACY M. SUMNER** is a freelance author, writer, and editor in Beaverton, Oregon. An avid outdoorsman, he enjoys fly-fishing on world-class Oregon waters. Tracy's devotions are found in March and September.

# SCRIPTURE INDEX

# READ THRU THE BIBLE IN A YEAR PLAN

| | | | |
|---|---|---|---|
| 1-Jan | Gen. 1-2 | Matt. 1 | Ps. 1 |
| 2-Jan | Gen. 3-4 | Matt. 2 | Ps. 2 |
| 3-Jan | Gen. 5-7 | Matt. 3 | Ps. 3 |
| 4-Jan | Gen. 8-10 | Matt. 4 | Ps. 4 |
| 5-Jan | Gen. 11-13 | Matt. 5:1-20 | Ps. 5 |
| 6-Jan | Gen. 14-16 | Matt. 5:21-48 | Ps. 6 |
| 7-Jan | Gen. 17-18 | Matt. 6:1-18 | Ps. 7 |
| 8-Jan | Gen. 19-20 | Matt. 6:19-34 | Ps. 8 |
| 9-Jan | Gen. 21-23 | Matt. 7:1-11 | Ps. 9:1-8 |
| 10-Jan | Gen. 24 | Matt. 7:12-29 | Ps. 9:9-20 |
| 11-Jan | Gen. 25-26 | Matt. 8:1-17 | Ps. 10:1-11 |
| 12-Jan | Gen. 27:1-28:9 | Matt. 8:18-34 | Ps. 10:12-18 |
| 13-Jan | Gen. 28:10-29:35 | Matt. 9 | Ps. 11 |
| 14-Jan | Gen. 30:1-31:21 | Matt. 10:1-15 | Ps. 12 |
| 15-Jan | Gen. 31:22-32:21 | Matt. 10:16-36 | Ps. 13 |
| 16-Jan | Gen. 32:22-34:31 | Matt. 10:37-11:6 | Ps. 14 |
| 17-Jan | Gen. 35-36 | Matt. 11:7-24 | Ps. 15 |
| 18-Jan | Gen. 37-38 | Matt. 11:25-30 | Ps. 16 |
| 19-Jan | Gen. 39-40 | Matt. 12:1-29 | Ps. 17 |
| 20-Jan | Gen. 41 | Matt. 12:30-50 | Ps. 18:1-15 |
| 21-Jan | Gen. 42-43 | Matt. 13:1-9 | Ps. 18:16-29 |
| 22-Jan | Gen. 44-45 | Matt. 13:10-23 | Ps. 18:30-50 |
| 23-Jan | Gen. 46:1-47:26 | Matt. 13:24-43 | Ps. 19 |
| 24-Jan | Gen. 47:27-49:28 | Matt. 13:44-58 | Ps. 20 |
| 25-Jan | Gen. 49:29-Exod. 1:22 | Matt. 14 | Ps. 21 |
| 26-Jan | Exod. 2-3 | Matt. 15:1-28 | Ps. 22:1-21 |
| 27-Jan | Exod. 4:1-5:21 | Matt. 15:29-16:12 | Ps. 22:22-31 |
| 28-Jan | Exod. 5:22-7:24 | Matt. 16:13-28 | Ps. 23 |
| 29-Jan | Exod. 7:25-9:35 | Matt. 17:1-9 | Ps. 24 |
| 30-Jan | Exod. 10-11 | Matt. 17:10-27 | Ps. 25 |
| 31-Jan | Exod. 12 | Matt. 18:1-20 | Ps. 26 |
| 1-Feb | Exod. 13-14 | Matt. 18:21-35 | Ps. 27 |
| 2-Feb | Exod. 15-16 | Matt. 19:1-15 | Ps. 28 |
| 3-Feb | Exod. 17-19 | Matt. 19:16-30 | Ps. 29 |
| 4-Feb | Exod. 20-21 | Matt. 20:1-19 | Ps. 30 |
| 5-Feb | Exod. 22-23 | Matt. 20:20-34 | Ps. 31:1-8 |
| 6-Feb | Exod. 24-25 | Matt. 21:1-27 | Ps. 31:9-18 |
| 7-Feb | Exod. 26-27 | Matt. 21:28-46 | Ps. 31:19-24 |
| 8-Feb | Exod. 28 | Matt. 22 | Ps. 32 |
| 9-Feb | Exod. 29 | Matt. 23:1-36 | Ps. 33:1-12 |
| 10-Feb | Exod. 30-31 | Matt. 23:37-24:28 | Ps. 33:13-22 |
| 11-Feb | Exod. 32-33 | Matt. 24:29-51 | Ps. 34:1-7 |
| 12-Feb | Exod. 34:1-35:29 | Matt. 25:1-13 | Ps. 34:8-22 |
| 13-Feb | Exod. 35:30-37:29 | Matt. 25:14-30 | Ps. 35:1-8 |
| 14-Feb | Exod. 38-39 | Matt. 25:31-46 | Ps. 35:9-17 |
| 15-Feb | Exod. 40 | Matt. 26:1-35 | Ps. 35:18-28 |
| 16-Feb | Lev. 1-3 | Matt. 26:36-68 | Ps. 36:1-6 |
| 17-Feb | Lev. 4:1-5:13 | Matt. 26:69-27:26 | Ps. 36:7-12 |
| 18-Feb | Lev. 5:14-7:21 | Matt. 27:27-50 | Ps. 37:1-6 |
| 19-Feb | Lev. 7:22-8:36 | Matt. 27:51-66 | Ps. 37:7-26 |
| 20-Feb | Lev. 9-10 | Matt. 28 | Ps. 37:27-40 |
| 21-Feb | Lev. 11-12 | Mark 1:1-28 | Ps. 38 |
| 22-Feb | Lev. 13 | Mark 1:29-39 | Ps. 39 |
| 23-Feb | Lev. 14 | Mark 1:40-2:12 | Ps. 40:1-8 |
| 24-Feb | Lev. 15 | Mark 2:13-3:35 | Ps. 40:9-17 |
| 25-Feb | Lev. 16-17 | Mark 4:1-20 | Ps. 41:1-4 |
| 26-Feb | Lev. 18-19 | Mark 4:21-41 | Ps. 41:5-13 |
| 27-Feb | Lev. 20 | Mark 5 | Ps. 42-43 |
| 28-Feb | Lev. 21-22 | Mark 6:1-13 | Ps. 44 |

| | | | |
|---|---|---|---|
| 1-Mar | Lev. 23-24 | Mark 6:14-29 | Ps. 45:1-5 |
| 2-Mar | Lev. 25 | Mark 6:30-56 | Ps. 45:6-12 |
| 3-Mar | Lev. 26 | Mark 7 | Ps. 45:13-17 |
| 4-Mar | Lev. 27 | Mark 8 | Ps. 46 |
| 5-Mar | Num. 1-2 | Mark 9:1-13 | Ps. 47 |
| 6-Mar | Num. 3 | Mark 9:14-50 | Ps. 48:1-8 |
| 7-Mar | Num. 4 | Mark 10:1-34 | Ps. 48:9-14 |
| 8-Mar | Num. 5:1-6:21 | Mark 10:35-52 | Ps. 49:1-9 |
| 9-Mar | Num. 6:22-7:47 | Mark 11 | Ps. 49:10-20 |
| 10-Mar | Num. 7:48-8:4 | Mark 12:1-27 | Ps. 50:1-15 |
| 11-Mar | Num. 8:5-9:23 | Mark 12:28-44 | Ps. 50:16-23 |
| 12-Mar | Num. 10-11 | Mark 13:1-8 | Ps. 51:1-9 |
| 13-Mar | Num. 12-13 | Mark 13:9-37 | Ps. 51:10-19 |
| 14-Mar | Num. 14 | Mark 14:1-31 | Ps. 52 |
| 15-Mar | Num. 15 | Mark 14:32-72 | Ps. 53 |
| 16-Mar | Num. 16 | Mark 15:1-32 | Ps. 54 |
| 17-Mar | Num. 17-18 | Mark 15:33-47 | Ps. 55 |
| 18-Mar | Num. 19-20 | Mark 16 | Ps. 56:1-7 |
| 19-Mar | Num. 21:1-22:20 | Luke 1:1-25 | Ps. 56:8-13 |
| 20-Mar | Num. 22:21-23:30 | Luke 1:26-56 | Ps. 57 |
| 21-Mar | Num. 24-25 | Luke 1:57-2:20 | Ps. 58 |
| 22-Mar | Num. 26:1-27:11 | Luke 2:21-38 | Ps. 59:1-8 |
| 23-Mar | Num. 27:12-29:11 | Luke 2:39-52 | Ps. 59:9-17 |
| 24-Mar | Num. 29:12-30:16 | Luke 3 | Ps. 60:1-5 |
| 25-Mar | Num. 31 | Luke 4 | Ps. 60:6-12 |
| 26-Mar | Num. 32-33 | Luke 5:1-16 | Ps. 61 |
| 27-Mar | Num. 34-36 | Luke 5:17-32 | Ps. 62:1-6 |
| 28-Mar | Deut. 1:1-2:25 | Luke 5:33-6:11 | Ps. 62:7-12 |
| 29-Mar | Deut. 2:26-4:14 | Luke 6:12-35 | Ps. 63:1-5 |
| 30-Mar | Deut. 4:15-5:22 | Luke 6:36-49 | Ps. 63:6-11 |
| 31-Mar | Deut. 5:23-7:26 | Luke 7:1-17 | Ps. 64:1-5 |
| 1-Apr | Deut. 8-9 | Luke 7:18-35 | Ps. 64:6-10 |
| 2-Apr | Deut. 10-11 | Luke 7:36-8:3 | Ps. 65:1-8 |
| 3-Apr | Deut. 12-13 | Luke 8:4-21 | Ps. 65:9-13 |
| 4-Apr | Deut. 14:1-16:8 | Luke 8:22-39 | Ps. 66:1-7 |
| 5-Apr | Deut. 16:9-18:22 | Luke 8:40-56 | Ps. 66:8-15 |
| 6-Apr | Deut. 19:1-21:9 | Luke 9:1-22 | Ps. 66:16-20 |
| 7-Apr | Deut. 21:10-23:8 | Luke 9:23-42 | Ps. 67 |
| 8-Apr | Deut. 23:9-25:19 | Luke 9:43-62 | Ps. 68:1-6 |
| 9-Apr | Deut. 26:1-28:14 | Luke 10:1-20 | Ps. 68:7-14 |
| 10-Apr | Deut. 28:15-68 | Luke 10:21-37 | Ps. 68:15-19 |
| 11-Apr | Deut. 29-30 | Luke 10:38-11:23 | Ps. 68:20-27 |
| 12-Apr | Deut. 31:1-32:22 | Luke 11:24-36 | Ps. 68:28-35 |
| 13-Apr | Deut. 32:23-33:29 | Luke 11:37-54 | Ps. 69:1-9 |
| 14-Apr | Deut. 34-Josh. 2 | Luke 12:1-15 | Ps. 69:10-17 |
| 15-Apr | Josh. 3:1-5:12 | Luke 12:16-40 | Ps. 69:18-28 |
| 16-Apr | Josh. 5:13-7:26 | Luke 12:41-48 | Ps. 69:29-36 |
| 17-Apr | Josh. 8-9 | Luke 12:49-59 | Ps. 70 |
| 18-Apr | Josh. 10:1-11:15 | Luke 13:1-21 | Ps. 71:1-6 |
| 19-Apr | Josh. 11:16-13:33 | Luke 13:22-35 | Ps. 71:7-16 |
| 20-Apr | Josh. 14-16 | Luke 14:1-15 | Ps. 71:17-21 |
| 21-Apr | Josh. 17:1-19:16 | Luke 14:16-35 | Ps. 71:22-24 |
| 22-Apr | Josh. 19:17-21:42 | Luke 15:1-10 | Ps. 72:1-11 |
| 23-Apr | Josh. 21:43-22:34 | Luke 15:11-32 | Ps. 72:12-20 |
| 24-Apr | Josh. 23-24 | Luke 16:1-18 | Ps. 73:1-9 |
| 25-Apr | Judg. 1-2 | Luke 16:19-17:10 | Ps. 73:10-20 |
| 26-Apr | Judg. 3-4 | Luke 17:11-37 | Ps. 73:21-28 |
| 27-Apr | Judg. 5:1-6:24 | Luke 18:1-17 | Ps. 74:1-3 |
| 28-Apr | Judg. 6:25-7:25 | Luke 18:18-43 | Ps. 74:4-11 |
| 29-Apr | Judg. 8:1-9:23 | Luke 19:1-28 | Ps. 74:12-17 |
| 30-Apr | Judg. 9:24-10:18 | Luke 19:29-48 | Ps. 74:18-23 |
| 1-May | Judg. 11:1-12:7 | Luke 20:1-26 | Ps. 75:1-7 |
| 2-May | Judg. 12:8-14:20 | Luke 20:27-47 | Ps. 75:8-10 |
| 3-May | Judg. 15-16 | Luke 21:1-19 | Ps. 76:1-7 |

| | | | |
|---|---|---|---|
| 6-Jul | 2 Kings 24-25 | Acts 12:18-13:13 | Ps. 105:1-7 |
| 7-Jul | 1 Chron. 1-2 | Acts 13:14-43 | Ps. 105:8-15 |
| 8-Jul | 1 Chron. 3:1-5:10 | Acts 13:44-14:10 | Ps. 105:16-28 |
| 9-Jul | 1 Chron. 5:11-6:81 | Acts 14:11-28 | Ps. 105:29-36 |
| 10-Jul | 1 Chron. 7:1-9:9 | Acts 15:1-18 | Ps. 105:37-45 |
| 11-Jul | 1 Chron. 9:10-11:9 | Acts 15:19-41 | Ps. 106:1-12 |
| 12-Jul | 1 Chron. 11:10-12:40 | Acts 16:1-15 | Ps. 106:13-27 |
| 13-Jul | 1 Chron. 13-15 | Acts 16:16-40 | Ps. 106:28-33 |
| 14-Jul | 1 Chron. 16-17 | Acts 17:1-14 | Ps. 106:34-43 |
| 15-Jul | 1 Chron. 18-20 | Acts 17:15-34 | Ps. 106:44-48 |
| 16-Jul | 1 Chron. 21-22 | Acts 18:1-23 | Ps. 107:1-9 |
| 17-Jul | 1 Chron. 23-25 | Acts 18:24-19:10 | Ps. 107:10-16 |
| 18-Jul | 1 Chron. 26-27 | Acts 19:11-22 | Ps. 107:17-32 |
| 19-Jul | 1 Chron. 28-29 | Acts 19:23-41 | Ps. 107:33-38 |
| 20-Jul | 2 Chron. 1-3 | Acts 20:1-16 | Ps. 107:39-43 |
| 21-Jul | 2 Chron. 4:1-6:11 | Acts 20:17-38 | Ps. 108 |
| 22-Jul | 2 Chron. 6:12-7:10 | Acts 21:1-14 | Ps. 109:1-20 |
| 23-Jul | 2 Chron. 7:11-9:28 | Acts 21:15-32 | Ps. 109:21-31 |
| 24-Jul | 2 Chron. 9:29-12:16 | Acts 21:33-22:16 | Ps. 110:1-3 |
| 25-Jul | 2 Chron. 13-15 | Acts 22:17-23:11 | Ps. 110:4-7 |
| 26-Jul | 2 Chron. 16-17 | Acts 23:12-24:21 | Ps. 111 |
| 27-Jul | 2 Chron. 18-19 | Acts 24:22-25:12 | Ps. 112 |
| 28-Jul | 2 Chron. 20-21 | Acts 25:13-27 | Ps. 113 |
| 29-Jul | 2 Chron. 22-23 | Acts 26 | Ps. 114 |
| 30-Jul | 2 Chron. 24:1-25:16 | Acts 27:1-20 | Ps. 115:1-10 |
| 31-Jul | 2 Chron. 25:17-27:9 | Acts 27:21-28:6 | Ps. 115:11-18 |
| 1-Aug | 2 Chron. 28:1-29:19 | Acts 28:7-31 | Ps. 116:1-5 |
| 2-Aug | 2 Chron. 29:20-30:27 | Rom. 1:1-17 | Ps. 116:6-19 |
| 3-Aug | 2 Chron. 31-32 | Rom. 1:18-32 | Ps. 117 |
| 4-Aug | 2 Chron. 33:1-34:7 | Rom. 2 | Ps. 118:1-18 |
| 5-Aug | 2 Chron. 34:8-35:19 | Rom. 3:1-26 | Ps. 118:19-23 |
| 6-Aug | 2 Chron. 35:20-36:23 | Rom. 3:27-4:25 | Ps. 118:24-29 |
| 7-Aug | Ezra 1-3 | Rom. 5 | Ps. 119:1-8 |
| 8-Aug | Ezra 4-5 | Rom. 6:1-7:6 | Ps. 119:9-16 |
| 9-Aug | Ezra 6:1-7:26 | Rom. 7:7-25 | Ps. 119:17-32 |
| 10-Aug | Ezra 7:27-9:4 | Rom. 8:1-27 | Ps. 119:33-40 |
| 11-Aug | Ezra 9:5-10:44 | Rom. 8:28-39 | Ps. 119:41-64 |
| 12-Aug | Neh. 1:1-3:16 | Rom. 9:1-18 | Ps. 119:65-72 |
| 13-Aug | Neh. 3:17-5:13 | Rom. 9:19-33 | Ps. 119:73-80 |
| 14-Aug | Neh. 5:14-7:73 | Rom. 10:1-13 | Ps. 119:81-88 |
| 15-Aug | Neh. 8:1-9:5 | Rom. 10:14-11:24 | Ps. 119:89-104 |
| 16-Aug | Neh. 9:6-10:27 | Rom. 11:25-12:8 | Ps. 119:105-120 |
| 17-Aug | Neh. 10:28-12:26 | Rom. 12:9-13:7 | Ps. 119:121-128 |
| 18-Aug | Neh. 12:27-13:31 | Rom. 13:8-14:12 | Ps. 119:129-136 |
| 19-Aug | Esther 1:1-2:18 | Rom. 14:13-15:13 | Ps. 119:137-152 |
| 20-Aug | Esther 2:19-5:14 | Rom. 15:14-21 | Ps. 119:153-168 |
| 21-Aug | Esther. 6-8 | Rom. 15:22-33 | Ps. 119:169-176 |
| 22-Aug | Esther 9-10 | Rom. 16 | Ps. 120-122 |
| 23-Aug | Job 1-3 | 1 Cor. 1:1-25 | Ps. 123 |
| 24-Aug | Job 4-6 | 1 Cor. 1:26-2:16 | Ps. 124-125 |
| 25-Aug | Job 7-9 | 1 Cor. 3 | Ps. 126-127 |
| 26-Aug | Job 10-13 | 1 Cor. 4:1-13 | Ps. 128-129 |
| 27-Aug | Job 14-16 | 1 Cor. 4:14-5:13 | Ps. 130 |
| 28-Aug | Job 17-20 | 1 Cor. 6 | Ps. 131 |
| 29-Aug | Job 21-23 | 1 Cor. 7:1-16 | Ps. 132 |
| 30-Aug | Job 24-27 | 1 Cor. 7:17-40 | Ps. 133-134 |
| 31-Aug | Job 28-30 | 1 Cor. 8 | Ps. 135 |
| 1-Sep | Job 31-33 | 1 Cor. 9:1-18 | Ps. 136:1-9 |
| 2-Sep | Job 34-36 | 1 Cor. 9:19-10:13 | Ps. 136:10-26 |
| 3-Sep | Job 37-39 | 1 Cor. 10:14-11:1 | Ps. 137 |
| 4-Sep | Job 40-42 | 1 Cor. 11:2-34 | Ps. 138 |
| 5-Sep | Eccles. 1:1-3:15 | 1 Cor. 12:1-26 | Ps. 139:1-6 |
| 6-Sep | Eccles. 3:16-6:12 | 1 Cor. 12:27-13:13 | Ps. 139:7-18 |
| 7-Sep | Eccles. 7:1-9:12 | 1 Cor. 14:1-22 | Ps. 139:19-24 |

| | | |
|---|---|---|
| 11-Nov | Ezek. 11-12 | Heb. 4:4-5:10 | Prov. 17:6-12 |
| 12-Nov | Ezek. 13-14 | Heb. 5:11-6:20 | Prov. 17:13-22 |
| 13-Nov | Ezek. 15:1-16:43 | Heb. 7:1-28 | Prov. 17:23-28 |
| 14-Nov | Ezek. 16:44-17:24 | Heb. 8:1-9:10 | Prov. 18:1-7 |
| 15-Nov | Ezek. 18-19 | Heb. 9:11-28 | Prov. 18:8-17 |
| 16-Nov | Ezek. 20 | Heb. 10:1-25 | Prov. 18:18-24 |
| 17-Nov | Ezek. 21-22 | Heb. 10:26-39 | Prov. 19:1-8 |
| 18-Nov | Ezek. 23 | Heb. 11:1-31 | Prov. 19:9-14 |
| 19-Nov | Ezek. 24-26 | Heb. 11:32-40 | Prov. 19:15-21 |
| 20-Nov | Ezek. 27-28 | Heb. 12:1-13 | Prov. 19:22-29 |
| 21-Nov | Ezek. 29-30 | Heb. 12:14-29 | Prov. 20:1-18 |
| 22-Nov | Ezek. 31-32 | Heb. 13 | Prov. 20:19-24 |
| 23-Nov | Ezek. 33:1-34:10 | Jas. 1 | Prov. 20:25-30 |
| 24-Nov | Ezek. 34:11-36:15 | Jas. 2 | Prov. 21:1-8 |
| 25-Nov | Ezek. 36:16-37:28 | Jas. 3 | Prov. 21:9-18 |
| 26-Nov | Ezek. 38-39 | Jas. 4:1-5:6 | Prov. 21:19-24 |
| 27-Nov | Ezek. 40 | Jas. 5:7-20 | Prov. 21:25-31 |
| 28-Nov | Ezek. 41:1-43:12 | 1 Pet. 1:1-12 | Prov. 22:1-9 |
| 29-Nov | Ezek. 43:13-44:31 | 1 Pet. 1:13-2:3 | Prov. 22:10-23 |
| 30-Nov | Ezek. 45-46 | 1 Pet. 2:4-17 | Prov. 22:24-29 |
| 1-Dec | Ezek. 47-48 | 1 Pet. 2:18-3:7 | Prov. 23:1-9 |
| 2-Dec | Dan. 1:1-2:23 | 1 Pet. 3:8-4:19 | Prov. 23:10-16 |
| 3-Dec | Dan. 2:24-3:30 | 1 Pet. 5 | Prov. 23:17-25 |
| 4-Dec | Dan. 4 | 2 Pet. 1 | Prov. 23:26-35 |
| 5-Dec | Dan. 5 | 2 Pet. 2 | Prov. 24:1-18 |
| 6-Dec | Dan. 6:1-7:14 | 2 Pet. 3 | Prov. 24:19-27 |
| 7-Dec | Dan. 7:15-8:27 | 1 John 1:1-2:17 | Prov. 24:28-34 |
| 8-Dec | Dan. 9-10 | 1 John 2:18-29 | Prov. 25:1-12 |
| 9-Dec | Dan. 11-12 | 1 John 3:1-12 | Prov. 25:13-17 |
| 10-Dec | Hos. 1-3 | 1 John 3:13-4:16 | Prov. 25:18-28 |
| 11-Dec | Hos. 4-6 | 1 John 4:17-5:21 | Prov. 26:1-16 |
| 12-Dec | Hos. 7-10 | 2 John | Prov. 26:17-21 |
| 13-Dec | Hos. 11-14 | 3 John | Prov. 26:22-27:9 |
| 14-Dec | Joel 1:1-2:17 | Jude | Prov. 27:10-17 |
| 15-Dec | Joel 2:18-3:21 | Rev. 1:1-2:11 | Prov. 27:18-27 |
| 16-Dec | Amos 1:1-4:5 | Rev. 2:12-29 | Prov. 28:1-8 |
| 17-Dec | Amos 4:6-6:14 | Rev. 3 | Prov. 28:9-16 |
| 18-Dec | Amos 7-9 | Rev. 4:1-5:5 | Prov. 28:17-24 |
| 19-Dec | Obad.-Jonah | Rev. 5:6-14 | Prov. 28:25-28 |
| 20-Dec | Mic. 1:1-4:5 | Rev. 6:1-7:8 | Prov. 29:1-8 |
| 21-Dec | Mic. 4:6-7:20 | Rev. 7:9-8:13 | Prov. 29:9-14 |
| 22-Dec | Nah. 1-3 | Rev. 9-10 | Prov. 29:15-23 |
| 23-Dec | Hab. 1-3 | Rev. 11 | Prov. 29:24-27 |
| 24-Dec | Zeph. 1-3 | Rev. 12 | Prov. 30:1-6 |
| 25-Dec | Hag. 1-2 | Rev. 13:1-14:13 | Prov. 30:7-16 |
| 26-Dec | Zech. 1-4 | Rev. 14:14-16:3 | Prov. 30:17-20 |
| 27-Dec | Zech. 5-8 | Rev. 16:4-21 | Prov. 30:21-28 |
| 28-Dec | Zech. 9-11 | Rev. 17:1-18:8 | Prov. 30:29-33 |
| 29-Dec | Zech. 12-14 | Rev. 18:9-24 | Prov. 31:1-9 |
| 30-Dec | Mal. 1-2 | Rev. 19-20 | Prov. 31:10-17 |
| 31-Dec | Mal. 3-4 | Rev. 21-22 | Prov. 31:18-31 |